Replenish

Creating Sexual Fulfillment in Marriage

A Guide for LDS Couples

Tammy S. Hill

LMFT, AASECT Member

Artist Bio – Brittney (Cover Illustration)

Brittney has been a professional artist for over 10 years. She earned a degree in graphic arts, but she is highly versatile and is capable of creating anything from jewelry to murals. She draws most of her inspiration from nature, the cosmos and personal growth. Brittney is the creator of Boha Allure, a page she started at the beginning of 2022 to share her illustrations she creates as part of her healing journey. You can find her on Instagram or Facebook under @boha.allure.

Artist Bio – Erica (In-Text Illustrations)

Erica is a graphic designer and illustrator based in Utah Valley. She has always had an artistic eye and found a passion for creating very early in life. She grew up in Southern California and Idaho. Erica attended BYU-Idaho where she received her BFA in graphic design. She currently lives in Utah with her husband and works full-time as a product & packaging designer.

ISBN: 9781611661781

Printed in the United States of America

2nd Printing

Dedication

This book is dedicated to my children. You are my life's greatest contribution to humanity. Mark Mulford and I are eternally blessed to be your parents.

Matthew Jordan Mulford, *my rock*

Our firstborn, I'm certain he was foreordained to be the oldest son. Overtime Jordan has seen me at my worst, yet has never withdrawn his light from guiding and blessing our family. Leaning on his strength, admiring his generous heart, and receiving his wise counsel is a lifelong pattern of mine. His spiritual connection to heaven is a strong influence for me, greatly contributing to my personal growth and development.

Ryan George Mulford, *my gift*

My gift came straight from heaven to Kim's (his birthmother) arms and then into our home. Amazingly enough he has Mark's beautiful blue eyes and sensitive awareness of others' needs. Ryan, even as a young boy has been a protector striving to keep our family safe. Through the years he has observed my needs, listened to my fears, and shared many warm hugs of encouragement, especially on difficult days. His courageous support has helped me keep on keeping on.

Cameran Mark Mulford, *my miracle*

After 13-years of infertility, we miraculously conceived, and welcomed, Cam to our family. As a newborn, we felt to add Mark to his name. This divine inspiration has given him a special connection to his dad, as he lives resolved to honorably bear his name. Though he has no memories of Mark, it's inexplicable how much Cam moves, thinks, and teases just like him! Cam's ability to be direct and "cut to the chase" inspires me to live wholeheartedly aligned.

Madelyn Joye Mulford Curtis, *my joy*

We had to wait fifteen years for our little girl to come. A week after she was born Mark added her middle name Joye, saying, "She's our little joy". Her name fits her personality; she is the embodiment of sunshine, radiance, and light. Even as a toddler her emotional stability, along with her uncanny ability to see things from an eternal perspective, has blessed my life in countless ways. She truly is joy to the world!

Contents

Acknowledgements

I appreciate the expertise of Kent Minson, whose knowledge and skill has been so helpful in moving this project from my computer to this beautiful book.

I'm grateful for my talented daughter-in-law, Erica Olson Hill, who enthusiastically took on the book's graphic illustrations. We joke about our texting chain, where both text and images are incredibly sexually explicit!

I could not have finished this project without the amazing editing abilities of my friend, Heather Kelley. Working with her feels like waking to a good dream: refreshingly inspired and eager for more.

I am eternally thankful for my family's continued encouragement as I've worked on this writing project over the course of seven years. My self-doubt was often short-lived because of these amazing cheerleaders, who are also my dearest friends.

Finally, there is a man who is the champion of my dreams, Jeff Hill. From him I feel the warmest, most passionate friendship. I have the greatest respect for his moral dignity and strength. His willingness to facilitate and support my dreams is deeply and humbly reverenced. Giving and receiving pure charity is at the heart of covenant marriage, and although I don't know how Jeff and I fit in the eternities, I am certain that sharing life with him right now has always been part of the plan.

Introduction

This book is for couples who are searching for a greater understanding of sexuality and who are members of The Church of Jesus Christ of Latter-day Saints. This book provides accurate information and practical application, all within a gospel framework. I have spent years looking for such a book, but the information available is either too vague, too academic, too spiritual, or too pornographic. If you've experienced similar frustrations, then this book is for you! Creating this book has been a 7-year writing journey for me, with decades of deep and often spiritual pondering, personal experiences, graduate school coupled with additional certifications and intensive research, all informing my writing.

I am so excited to be sharing this journey with you!

Throughout my life, I have been blessed with the gift of sexual curiosity. As a young girl I remember thinking about sex with a questioning mind. I had learned through religious teachings that one of the greatest gifts from God is that of procreation. My mother dutifully taught me the facts of life by reading me a book called, A Doctor Talks to 5-to-8 Year Olds. I was shocked to learn that creating new life required only a few brief minutes of time. My young heart could not put together these two facts. They seemed incongruent! My reoccurring question was, "If creating new life is such an important, eternal part of the plan of salvation and a gift from loving Heavenly Parents, shouldn't a couple enjoy it for more than just a few minutes?"

I had been taught that if I had questions, I should seek for further knowledge and prayerfully ask for answers. So, my journey began, both in reading information and prayerfully asking questions. After the conversation with my mother (at age 8), I wanted to learn as much as I could about sexuality. I remember vividly learning about David and Bathsheba in Sunday School and thinking, "Ah! Hah! I can learn more from the Bible!" I went home that day and searched for this story in the Old Testament. When I found the phrase, ". . . he lay with her . . ." you can imagine my disappointment. Upon other scripture study I discovered that "to know someone" also meant to have sex with that person. This wasn't helpful either. My father is a medical doctor. I would frequently look at any of the books in his home library, but again was disappointed. Finally, as a 12-year-old, I found a book in my sister's room that was exciting! As I read about the sexual encounter, I noticed my heart beating faster, my vulva (which I had been taught was my vagina) was feeling warm, moist, and tingly. I wanted to learn more. I liked the way my body felt when I read that book. It wasn't until later in high school that I learned what I was experiencing was sexual arousal. Once in college, I took a Human Sexuality class. My mind was blown. I remember feeling aroused in class, while reading the textbook, while writing papers, while breathing! I was a sponge ready to soak up every bit of knowledge I could find. I will add, this was all in the pre-Internet age. The plethora of information available at our fingertips today would have been difficult for me to navigate in early adolescence.

As I reflect on these experiences, I am grateful that through all of them, I don't remember feeling guilty or ashamed. I was just excited! Perhaps the questioning in my youth had centered me enough in my knowledge that sex was part of our Heavenly Parents' plan, shielding me from some of these other typical responses. Regardless, I do know that my desire to understand the goodness of sex has been unquenchable. In this seeking I have worried that others might think of me as perverse, weird, or twisted, but as for myself, my foundational core belief has been that sex is intended not just for procreation, but for replenishment in marriage as well.

The question in my young heart has played a crucial role in my professional journey. I helped develop the Adult Roles & Responsibilities curriculum for the Utah State Office of Education, and passionately taught this course as a high school Family & Consumer Science teacher. I worked on a Task Force Committee established by Utah Governor Mike Leavitt where I taught parents how to teach their children about sex. I returned to school to become a Licensed Marriage & Family Therapist and over a 3-year span of study, officially became a member of the American Association for Sexual Educators, Counselors and Therapists (AASECT). I own a private therapy practice where I counsel largely with couples. Since 2014, I have been an adjunct faculty member at Brigham Young University, teaching courses in the School of Family Life. I helped create the curriculum for the first sexuality course taught on campus. I teach hundreds of students a semester. My little 8-year-old question has guided my lifetime journey to understand the goodness, pleasure, and exalting capacities of sexual expression in marriage.

As an active member of the Church, throughout the years I have held multiple callings in my wards—all of them in primary. Honestly, for 29 years straight I served in primary! From president (3 times) to music leader (7 times), intermixed with many years as a classroom teacher. I love children, so being in the primary with children was perfectly fine. Why am I telling you this? Because throughout all of these years of teaching children the gospel, children have always known that an essential, central part of our Heavenly Parents' plan is to come to earth and receive a body. From infancy, within the Church, we understand that having a body is very good, a blessing, a way to progress and learn. What we typically don't learn, however, is that sexual pleasure is an important, healthy, and desirable aspect of having a body. Why would we be divinely created in the express image of our Heavenly Parents if this capacity wasn't good?

In my teaching experiences, particularly at Brigham Young University, I frequently have my students ponder this possible future scenario. Imagine you have just returned to heaven. You are welcomed by loved ones and wrapped in the Savior's arms. Finally, you get to have a grand reunion with loving Heavenly Parents. As you relish Their embrace, you are asked, "How well did you enjoy your body?" What is your response? Pause for a moment as you consider this profound question, be honest within your heart, how well are you enjoying your body? Even more specific, how well are you enjoying your sexuality?

My hope and prayer in writing this book, is that couples will read this book together, sharing with each other their thoughts and feelings as they read. I strongly encourage couples to incorporate the sexual experiential homework suggestions I provide with each chapter. Sex is intended to be relational. Sex is also experiential, meaning that it is learned by actually doing it. This means that to gain the full benefit of this book, you will need each other and a willingness to learn about and try new things. More than anything I want you to claim the joy and pleasure that your body was created to experience! I want you to live without the regret that often comes from missed opportunities.

I have regret that plays over in my mind on occasion, especially when I'm trying to recall shared memories with my late husband, Mark Mulford. Almost all my memories of our marriage involve working, living daily life, and serving together. We shared a passionate and fun relationship sexually. We were also really united in things that mattered most: discipleship, parenting, and finances. We were frugal. I can count on one finger the number of times, over our nearly 18-year marriage, that we went away together just the two of us. We would plan for the future (which isn't a bad thing) while neglecting the present. How much I regret this level of frugality. Mark died unexpectedly 5 weeks before our 18th anniversary. Every time I reflect on our marriage, I am filled with regret that Mark and I didn't make more time for us. I don't have memories of romantic getaways or spontaneous dates or vacation trips together. I suspect that Mark regrets this too. I think that both of us wish we would have put more time, money, and energy into creating more playfulness, adventure, and fun in our marriage. Living with regret is not pleasant. This book is intended to help you intentionally build a marriage with more sexual energy, passion, wonder and, ultimately, replenishment so that you won't live with regret of missed opportunities. This book, *Replenish,* is written for you! As a couple, you labor together taking on a multiplicity of life's demands. I hope that you will take the time to build a repertoire of ways to fully replenish as well.

Each chapter will be short, concise, and jam-packed with information. I also include important conversation starters and topics that I encourage you to discuss thoroughly. Listen to understand your spouse. It's okay if you don't agree on everything, but you do need to understand where they're coming from for better connection. If there are differences, I challenge you to pray together for guidance and revelation for your marriage. You will be surprised by how much heart-felt couple prayer can truly bless your sexual relationship. God really cares about your sexual relationship. Each chapter will have some activities for you to do together that focus on creating a stronger, more passionate relationship. Remember, the most important part of all this is the process, not the outcome. The process of sexual exploring and learning will create more depth in your relationship.

I will be speaking in first person throughout the book. This will let you see into my soul and, ultimately, let you know that my greatest desire in this project, is to bless your marriage. I want to provide a means for you to better work through the labors of life, especially family life, as a passionate and dynamic team. Good sex contributes to good marriages. What I hope for your marriage is an erotic friendship and discipleship where you both, as covenant-keeping husband and wife, find passion and joy within the union of your souls.

PART I

Theological Foundations

CHAPTER 1

Why Replenish?

One of my favorite ways to study the gospel is through researching specific words or phrases in the standard works, as well as writings of the prophets. *Replenish* is one word I have spent considerable time pondering and researching. I remember it coming "loud and clear" to my mind when serving in the temple in 2010. During the creation of the world, God commands the animal kingdom to ". . . be fruitful, and multiply, and fill the earth," (Genesis 1:22). After He created, Adam and Eve, male and female. "God blessed them, and God said unto them, Be fruitful, and multiply, and replenish the earth . . ." (Genesis 1:28). For humankind there is a particular difference in the commands given by God. As man and woman, husband and wife, we are told to replenish. Why would God add the word *replenish* to this command if His full objective was merely to reproduce? I believe we are created in the image and function of our Heavenly Parents; we are instructed to have children *and* to replenish ourselves within the marriage relationship.

I believe this aspect of our mortal experience is so important to our Heavenly Parents that we are *appointed* to share a replenishing sexual stewardship within the marriage covenant. The word *appointed* is used in *The Family: A Proclamation to the World* when describing the procreative process. *Appointed* is used throughout the scriptures in reference to callings or church responsibilities. *Appointed* is also used to specify a certain time or place for something to occur. Using these definitions, I like to think of the sexual relationship in marriage as a calling and stewardship.

It is something we designate time and space for, something we nurture and something we choose to honor. Finally, it is a tool to learn from and be refined through on our journey of becoming like God.

Have you ever thought of sex this way? First, as a commandment and second, as a calling and stewardship you devote time and energy to. This fascinates me. Our Heavenly Parents want us to have replenishing sex in marriage. Learning how to have this kind of sex requires making it a priority in your life. I know from personal experience and from the years I've worked with couples as a therapist, that choosing sexual replenishment blesses couples. I believe most couples live far beneath their capacities to enjoy passionate, erotic, and friendly sexual experiences that truly strengthen their connection. Isn't this why you are reading this book? I suspect you want to develop a replenishing sexual relationship. You've taken the first step; you're reading the book! I'm so excited for both of you. This journey isn't always natural or easy, but I believe it is essential in your progression toward Godhood.

Please take your time while you're reading. Go slow! Don't rush past the first chapters to get to "the good part." These chapters provide an essential foundation. Just as you take one step at a time on a ladder, you need to do the deep thinking and have the vulnerable conversations as you step into this journey of prioritizing the sexual relationship and responsibilities you have with one another.

At the end of each chapter, I will provide prompts to help you THINK, PAIR (i.e., connect), and SHARE your thoughts with one another. Some of the prompts throughout the book may feel very vulnerable. The more open and humble you are in approaching these prompts, the more you and your relationship will gain!

THINK. (I encourage you to journal as you ponder the following ideas. I also strongly urge you to search the scriptures for your own revelation.)

- What does your heart and mind tell you about the phrase *multiply and replenish*?

- Why would Adam and Eve be commanded to replenish? Why would *you* be commanded to replenish?
- Study the word "appointed". How does it apply to your life right now? (What are your callings? Responsibilities? Personal talents that need developing?)
- How well are you fulfilling your appointed commitments currently? What needs to change?
- What are your thoughts about the idea of sex, within marriage, being both a commandment and a calling?

PAIR. Take a few minutes to warmly connect. Snuggle, hug, share a bubble bath, pray, or go on a walk. I want you to connect for at least 10 minutes before you start sharing, it doesn't matter how. When both of you feel centered and relaxed, get out your notes from the THINK-ing you've done on this chapter.

SHARE. Now is the time to listen to understand each other. Focus on understanding only! Check-in to make sure you are fully "getting" what is being said by your spouse. Now answer these questions together:

- How much do the two of you align in the ideas and feelings you have each recorded from the questions listed in the THINK portion of this chapter? Are there any big differences between the two of you? What are they? How will you work through these differences?
- Do you need to revisit/study/pray about any of the concepts in this chapter before moving forward?
- Once you're on the same page, it's time to move to the next chapter.

CHAPTER 2

The Gift of our Sexual Theology

In my years studying to better understand sexuality, I have found such comfort and happiness in the sexual theology doctrinally taught within the gospel of Jesus Christ. Notice the phrase "doctrinally taught within the gospel." This is much different than the concepts that have been "culturally taught within the Church." I know that some of what I teach doesn't always line-up with what some of you may consider culturally correct. This will be uncomfortable for some of you and refreshing to others. As a therapist, I am perfectly comfortable with your discomfort! As you move forward in studying this book, there may be ideas you need to deeply think and pray about. I urge you to do so! Don't stop reading simply because you feel uncertain or uncomfortable—facing uncertainty and discomfort is an important part of your development as a person and as a partner. As you move forward through your anxiety, this growth will provide you with deeper personal revelation and understanding.

In my younger years, I thought it was important that my behavior had a "Church Stamp of Approval." As a young bride, I would frequently seek specific guidelines from Church leadership to direct me in sexual decision-making. In January 1982, Spencer W. Kimball issued a statement to general Church leadership stating that loving one another with our mouths was an "unnatural, impure and unholy" practice and that members, even married members, who participated in this practice should be banned from temple worship unless they repented and discontinued the practice. Nine months later, October 1982, another statement was issued from the First Presidency encouraging Church leaders to avoid inquiring about intimate marital relations. Leaders were instructed to ". . .never deviate from the specific questions contained in the temple recommend interview."[1]

This confusing dynamic of conflicting information occurred at its height during my early years of marriage to my late husband, Mark Mulford. Kissing and loving all our body parts was a connecting, passionate, and wonderful part of our marriage. Why would this be considered unnatural and unholy in my marriage? Why would this behavior possibly keep me from being in the temple? Through much study, pondering, and prayerful petitioning, I came to a personal assurance that our sexual relationship was our personal business. Mark and I, together as equal partners, had the authority and responsibility to decide what we created sexually in our marriage. This spiritual assurance brought me much peace.

It wasn't until decades later, in October 2010 General Conference, that this personal revelatory experience was publicly confirmed by Dallin H. Oaks in his address entitled *Two Lines of Communication*. I will never forget the heart-pounding, goosebump producing, mind blowing moment when the Spirit again bore witness to me that my quest for personal sexual revelation was indeed my responsibility! Describing the differences between revelation for the Church and personal revelation, Elder Oaks said,

> The personal line is of paramount importance in personal decisions and in the governance of the family. Unfortunately, some members of our Church underestimate the need for this direct, personal line. Responding to the undoubted importance of prophetic leadership—the priesthood line, which operates principally to govern heavenly communication on Church matters—some seek to have their priesthood leaders make personal decisions for them, decisions that they should make for themselves by inspiration through their personal line. Personal decisions and family governance are principally a matter for the personal line.[2]

Rather than waiting to learn how to behave from Church leaders, our development as mortals is centered in our ability to prayerfully make important decisions for our own personal lives. You are responsible for the personal revelation you receive regarding your sexual relationship. No one else!

You may find it interesting to know that my personal life had drastically changed when I listened to Elder Oaks's powerful message. Mark had died unexpectedly. I had been a widowed, single mother for nearly five years, and was four years into a second marriage to Jeff Hill, a widowed man with eight children. With a new partner, I was again learning how to communicate about sexuality and negotiate sexual decisions within our relationship. Once again, throughout this process, great growth, wisdom, and happiness occurred.

Another thought for you as you seek for guidance and inspiration regarding sex: Remember Who created it! Our Heavenly Parents, as part of Their[3] plan, gave us the opportunity to share sexual pleasure in marriage. When in doubt, seek the greatest Source! Multiple times in my life, I have needed to gain sexual information for both personal and professional situations. I have a sure testimony that, like me, you can seek knowledge, ponder your learning, and ask for revelation on sexual matters.

In my quest for greater knowledge and understanding, I have found true sexual principles within our Church theology. These principles are profoundly beautiful to my soul. As you move through the list below, assess your own comfort with each of these truths. If any of them feel less comfortable to you, that's totally okay. These ideas are great points for beginning your own revelatory processing.

Gospel Principles of Sexual Theology:

- Sexuality is a fundamental aspect of being human, given to us by our Heavenly Parents.
- Embodiment (a spirit coming to earth to get a body) is essential for our spiritual and relational progression.
- We are created in the *image and function* of Heavenly Parents, who are sexual beings.

- One of the purposes of the plan of salvation includes procreation; the necessity of heterosexual relationships is central to this plan.
- We have been given the gift of agency, the opportunity to choose for ourselves. With this agency comes consequences to our sexual choices.
- Moral development is essential for our spiritual progression. This development often occurs within a sexual context.
- Prophetic leaders tell us that sex is to only be shared between a man and a woman united in a marriage relationship.
- Sex is for both procreative opportunities and relational bonding in marital relationships.
- Bodies are created with sexual capacities that provide sensually pleasurable experiences.
- Prophetic leaders advise against the use of pornographic materials.

In summation of these principles, I created what I like to call "The 14th Article of Faith":

> *We believe that sexual intimacy is one of our Heavenly Parents' greatest gifts to both men and women. We have bodies like Theirs. They want us to find joy in our covenant marriage relationships. Giving and receiving pleasure as husband and wife strengthens marital bonds. It is part of God's plan for us to fully love one another. Developing this gift of giving and receiving pleasure is part of our sexual stewardship in a marriage relationship. It is GOOD to want to learn how to pleasure our spouse. It is GOOD to want to learn what pleasures us. It is GOOD to want to develop a sexual relationship that provides pleasure, enhances self-discovery, and strengthens commitment to marriage and family life. In short, we believe in passionate marital sex!*

Ponder this doctrine as you begin to embrace and integrate more fully your own sexuality. This process requires personal integrity as you remember God's command to Adam and Eve, to both multiply and replenish together within the covenant bonds of marriage. Both spouses must get onboard as equal partners in the amazing journey of becoming sexual beings in mortality, and in becoming one another's sexual stewards in marriage.

I don't resonate with the way sexuality is sometimes interpreted in the scriptures. It is often associated with carnal and devilish desires. When someone chooses to be focused on sensuality in sinful ways such as sexual habits, compulsions and addictions, then it is sinful. However, when someone chooses to nurture the sensual part of herself/himself to strengthen a covenant marriage relationship, this is not carnal or devilish. I believe it is constructive and divine.

Although not considered doctrinally essential, a book in the Old Testament, Songs of Solomon (also known as the Song of Songs) is a beautifully poetic sexual source for Christian couples. There are minute and nuanced lovemaking details that couples can read and contemplate together. I have told a few very religious couples, hesitant to read anything filled with too much sexual worldliness, that reading and discussing Songs of Solomon is a simple way to add some steam to their marriages. Indeed, one of the greatest sages in Jewish history, known as Rabbi Akiva, is attributed with the following quote. "God forbid that anyone should say that the Song of Songs renders one's hands impure! The greatest day was the one on which Israel received the Song of Songs. All of the writings in the Bible are holy and the Song of Songs is the holiest of holies."[4]

Truly it is a sacred, holy experience to fully embrace the sexual part of yourself and trustingly share it with your spouse. This completely naked, vulnerable space is a powerful way to both express and receive love, and I believe, it is essential to creating a truly intimate marriage. Sensuality can be divine. Remember, you are created in your Heavenly Parents' image and function. You are like Them. The more you self-develop in becoming like Them, the more fully you give yourself the blissful opportunity of sexual replenishment. Elder Jeffrey R. Holland has said about marital sexuality, "I submit to you that you will never be more like God at any other time in this life than when you are expressing that particular power." Isn't that amazing? An apostle of God has told you that you are never more like your Heavenly Parents than when you are expressing your sexual love as husband and wife.[5]

Take a moment to *really* ponder this statement. Coming to truly understand your sexual divinity is paramount to your endeavors to become like God. To understand your sexual divinity, you need to think about sexuality in a way that embraces both *sexual wisdom* and *sexual creativity.*

Sexual wisdom includes:

- **Sexual knowledge**—an understanding of biological functioning
- **Morality**—sexual conservatism
- **Sexual integration**—acceptance of the sexual part of you that desires passion and sensuality
- **Sexual stewardship**—responsibility for sexual self and responsibility for sexual partner
- **Pro-social behavior**—sexual behavior that builds, enhances and contributes to society, marriage and family life
- **Relational perspective**—sex is only shared in a marriage relationship; it is not an individual activity
- **Sexual sublimation**—projecting sexual energy into fulfilling activities when sexual expression is not a possibility

Sexual creativity includes:

- **Sexual progression**—stretching yourself to become the sexual being you are capable of becoming
- **Playfulness**—viewing sexual activity as a way that you can play and have fun with your spouse
- **Sexual fulfillment**—sexual experiences should lead to feelings of fulfillment, energy, and anticipation

In short, *sexual wisdom* involves learning about body parts and their functioning. It encourages the development of sexual integration, while constructing moral and healthy sexual parameters. In marriage, sexual wisdom is coming to understand sexual stewardship, for yourself and for your spouse. Sexual wisdom also involves sublimation or projecting sexual energy into productive activities that are enjoyable and fulfilling when sexual expression is not a possibility.

Sexual creativity is necessary for your ability to progress and develop sexually within marriage. Eternal marriage is our Heavenly Parent's plan for families. Sexual monotony becomes a struggle in monogamous relationships, making sexual creativity essential for happy and satisfying marriages. There is no better way for couples to energetically and vibrantly live than by wholeheartedly sharing in their sexual creativeness.

In conclusion, fully understanding and accepting both your right and responsibility to receive personal revelation for your sexual relationship is essential. Don't miss out on the growth that can come to you in this process. If there are aspects of the sexual theology presented in this chapter that you feel unsure of, I urge you to think, talk, and pray about them together. This is your sexual journey! You both deserve the freedom that comes from learning, deciding and creating this aspect of your mortal experience together.

THINK. Journal your impressions while reading this chapter. What feels congruent? What doesn't feel quite as comfortable? Ponder your responsibility to sexually develop within your marriage.

PAIR. Find space and time together where you will not be interrupted. Look into one another's eyes and breathe deeply for several minutes. Get comfortable. Begin talking.

SHARE. Share your journal entries. Listen to understand one another. Decide together to work on strengthening your testimonies of a specific aspect of our sexual theology. Consider your shared sexual stewardship. What does that look like right now? What changes would you like to make?

Experiential Activity to Enjoy

Couple Prayer about Sex

Decide together on a point or two of doctrine that you want to better understand. Talk about specific questions you want answered. Decide to pray individually about your questions. Then, come together to pray as a couple. Be still. Ponder. Continue to pray together. As you do so, you will receive subtle impressions of truth. Record these impressions.

CHAPTER 3

Sexual Stewardship

A stewardship is the obligation to carefully and responsibly manage the things entrusted to you by God. Your stewardships include your marriage, family, neighbors, Church callings, and temporal blessings. About a decade ago, my husband, Jeff, and I were given the stewardship of ministering to a new family that had moved into our ward. We learned when given this responsibility that they were both members, not currently active in the Church, with three children. None of the children had been baptized. Faithfully, we dropped by their home month after month, sometimes more than once a month, bringing treats, flowers, garden produce and offerings of friendship. For nearly four years we would visit with them on their front porch. One day they invited us in, and we got to know them even better. Over time we began to exchange recipes, talk about parenting strategies, and share marital experiences. Occasionally, they would come to our house. One time we talked for several hours while we made strawberry jam together. In this conversation we learned that the wife's favorite book was *The Scarlet Pimpernel.* We invited them to a local performance of this musical. Both the performance and the deepening of our friendship through conversation were magical! We continued to invite them to participate in activities, and they invited us over to see household renovations they were making. We connected with each other regularly through texts. I was so surprised when the wife made me a beautifully-pieced lap quilt. I was touched to tears that this dear friend would spend so much time to create this gift for me. Currently, we are planning to take a trip together with this couple. As Jeff and I accepted our stewardship for this family and continued showing genuine respect for their needs, through time, a priceless friendship has been created. I cherish these good people.

This is a metaphor for sexual stewardship in marriage. The sexual aspect of your relationship is a sacred responsibility both of you have as you jointly participate in creating something both of you will grow to cherish. It takes time, small steps, open invitations for exploration and connection, and genuine respect. You may need to try new approaches for deeper connection. To prevent stagnation in the relationship, you will need to proactively seek ways to invest intentionally in the marriage. As you actively take responsibility for your sexual stewardship, it will become increasingly satisfying and sustainable. From your efforts of faith, patience, and diligence, you will truly taste the sweetness of the fruit your marriage produces.

Marriage is a sexual contract, especially in covenant marriages where you pledge complete sexual fidelity. You understand that when you marry, you will share your sexual attraction, affection, and expression with only your spouse. All your romantic energy must be centered in your marriage relationship. This aspect of covenant marriages fosters safety, security, and trust in the relationship. It also brings with it the blessing of sharing an equal partnership in your own and your partner's sexual development.

Appropriate sexual stewardship requires each individual to process his/her sexual conditioning. As a child, you grew up in a home which likely set the patterns for your sexual beliefs and attitudes. I want to make it clear that I believe most parents and church leaders have good intentions as they attempt to teach sexuality. However, in our Church culture, too frequently there is much discomfort when discussing sexual desire, arousal, and pleasure. This silence perpetuates feelings of shame and guilt in children as they experience pleasurable sexual thoughts and feelings as a normal part of their development. The lack of correct, reverent sexual information, mixed with the wide availability of pornography, creates an environment for children to seek information from sources that often portray sex in violent, male centric, irreverent, and immoral patterns. These experiences also create feelings of guilt and shame, especially among religious individuals. Shame thrives in secrecy, so when left unaddressed, shame can lead to a lifetime of self-betrayal. Too little accurate information and too much exposure to worldly views of sex are damaging to our ability to form healthy sexual identities and beliefs. These erroneous beliefs continue into adulthood and are brought to the marriage bedroom where a multitude of sexual problems can occur.

In my teaching, I use the parable of the "Wise Steward" when discussing the development of an individual's sexual capacity. In the New Testament (Matt 25 and Luke 19), the Savior shares the story of a master who puts his servants in charge of his goods while he is away. When he returns, he assesses the stewardship of his servants according to how faithful each was in making wise investments. Financial profits represented growth or faithfulness on the part of the servants. Those servants who had been faithful in investing the goods were rewarded, while the servant who hid his talent or "played it safe" because of fear, did not receive the glory of the Lord or Master. Each son and daughter of God is born with a body that has sexual capacity. I believe that in that great and glorious Final Judgment, with the Savior as our advocate, we may be asked something like, "How did you enjoy your body? Were you able to master your fears? Did you allow yourself to both give and receive sexual pleasure in your marriage?" You have an individual stewardship to understand how your body works sexually. Once married, you also have a stewardship to understand how your spouse's body functions sexually. As a couple, you must learn to labor in righteousness as you create a relationship that not only brings children to the earth, but also replenishes the marriage through healthy, pleasurable sexual expression.

The subliminal understandings, or "rules" you have regarding sex, infiltrate your ability to embrace yourself as a sexual being and limits your comfort in becoming sexual stewards in your marriage. In my work with couples, I find it essential for each spouse to individually process their sexual conditioning. In time, the couple comes together to discuss these rules. They then work together to make necessary adaptations for their marriage by creating their own personal *Marital Sexual Playbook*.

Creating Your Marital Sexual Playbook

Writing your sexual playbook involves reflecting on and writing both the overt (i.e., explicitly stated) and covert (i.e., implicit) rules you developed in your family of origin, in your Church lessons, possibly in your school experiences with teachers or peers, and information from the Internet. To help you understand how this can be done, I have included an example below of what my sexual rulebook looked like when I began my journey to understanding sexual stewardship.

Overt Rules

1. Men are sexually attracted to anything, even a woman's ankle! I have a responsibility to dress appropriately, so that I don't cause this reaction in men.
2. Don't date until 16.
3. Don't have sex until married.
4. Don't "bearhug" dance (or touch bodies while dancing, keep enough space for a Book of Mormon to fit between you).
5. Kisses should be saved for someone really special.
6. French kissing is symbolic of sexual intercourse. This type of kissing creates strong feelings of arousal and should be saved for marriage.
7. Although not officially stated exactly this way, in dating relationships, young women are the "gatekeepers." Meaning that as a woman, I have a responsibility to make sure the physicality in a relationship doesn't cross the line.
8. Somewhere there is a line that I should not cross. I'm not exactly sure what that means, but I know necking (which I envisioned as rubbing necks together) and petting would lead me to cross the line.
9. It is not appropriate to touch my own breasts or genitals, other than when washing.
10. Oral sex is sinful.

Covert Rules

1. Women do their duty by having sex with their husbands.
2. Sex is not really enjoyed by women but is righteously endured.
3. Having babies is the real reason for a woman to have sex.

Once each spouse has written his/her sexual rulebook, the couple processes these rules together. This experience should be done in love with the purpose of better understanding yourself and your spouse. It is the rules, the conditioned thinking, and the things that we believe about sex, or the meanings that we give to sex, that cause most of the psychosocial difficulties in sexual expression.

Editing your sexual rulebooks as you jointly create your own marital playbook is the next step in becoming each other's sexual stewards. This may take some soul searching, and it will definitely require understanding, patience, and teamwork. It will also take time and be an ongoing process. This is your marriage playbook. No one else should be in your bedroom! Not your bishop, your seventh-grade crush, your Young Women or Young Men leader, and especially not your mother! The best questions to ask yourselves as you determine what you want to have in your sexual relationship are "What do I/we really want?", "What type of sexual freedom is important to me/us?", and "What do we want to create together, just the two of us?" I've included an example of my marital sexual playbook below to help you understand more fully what this may look like.

Our Marital Sexual Playbook

1. We will be the only two people invited into our bedroom—physically, emotionally, and mentally!
2. We will not use pornography in our love making.
3. We will not discuss our sexual relationship with anyone! If there is a need for help, we will go together to seek counsel.
4. We commit to helping each other be fully present by helping his/her "head" come to bed. The brain is the largest sex organ; if it doesn't show up, neither will the body. This may include helping each other in household chores, wrapping up business/work,

putting children to bed, putting away electronics, and/or softly talking for emotional connection.

5. We commit to making time each week to explore our sexual capacities.
6. If one of us is "not in the mood," we will hold each other closely, connect emotionally, and touch for 15 minutes. If there is still not the desire for sex, we will make arrangements for when we will sexually connect within 72 hours.
7. We will share our sexual fantasies with each other.
8. If one partner wants to try things that the other partner is not comfortable with, we will both take the necessary time to process why this behavior is important to do or not to do. We will work to discover the source of our ideas regarding the behavior. We will again choose to be the only two people invited into our bedroom, emotionally, physically, and mentally.
9. We will pray for more sexual understanding. We have faith that Heavenly Father will answer our prayers with revelation or peace as we seek His counsel.

As you and your spouse create your own unique sexual playbook, you will develop ideas around how to better become each other's sexual stewards. This is part of your Heavenly Parents' plan for your marriage. They want you to become more like Them. One of the most significant ways to become like Them in mortality is in the development of your sexual capacities as husband and wife. You need to work together to nurture and protect this sacred responsibility.

This process of creating a sexual relationship that provides nourishment for the marriage is more comfortable to some than it is to others. You and your spouse have each been given a variety of unique spiritual gifts. Recognizing this, I encourage couples to approach these differences in their sexual experiences with a "Widow's Mite" mentality. In Luke 21, the Savior teaches His disciples a valuable lesson as they observe a poor widow casting two mites into the treasury. Though the offering had little financial value, it was more substantial than others' offerings because this woman gave all she had. As you and your spouse make sexual offerings in love to one another, you must both recognize the significance of what each of you is doing. It could be that the ever-so-small changes in sexual expression is everything your cherished spouse has to offer. Never forget to hallow the holy spaces where your hearts and bodies meet in faith to offer up everything to one another.

THINK. Begin by pondering your childhood experiences with sexual learning. After you've spent some time reflecting, journal your responses to the following prompts:

- What are your overt and covert rules? The more specific you are, the more helpful this exercise will be for you and your spouse.
- What does sexual stewardship mean to you? How can you become a better sexual steward for your spouse?
- Journal your impressions of the "Wise Steward" and the "Widow's Mite." Apply these ideas to your sexual attitudes.
- Recognizing that sexual development is a lifelong pursuit, what specifically would you like to work on right now? Why?

PAIR. Plan an uninterrupted evening for this activity. Before you begin sharing, connect emotionally through a walk, a bubble bath, or other peaceful activity.

SHARE. Listen to understand one another as you each share your personal sexual rulebooks, along with the experiences behind those rules. After you've both had ample opportunities to share and be heard, begin creating a first draft of your Marital Sexual Playbook. I highly recommend you get a new journal or notebook dedicated solely to your Marital Sexual Playbook, as it will be a living document and an ongoing, ever-changing process. Indeed, each chapter from here on will provide opportunities and prompts for you to add to and modify your sexual playbook.

CHAPTER 4

Choosing Erotic Discipleship

Moral agency is more than random acts of obedience. It is intentionally living your promises to God while diligently relying on the sanctifying goodness of Jesus Christ. Erotic discipleship develops by using our agency to live love through the peaceful connection of our body and spirit as children of Heavenly Parents. This is done by always reverencing the truth that the spirit and the body are the soul of man, and by never minimizing the infinite worth of a soul–your soul or anyone else's. Jeffrey R. Holland discusses this doctrine passionately, as is evident in the following excerpt from a talk he gave at BYU: "In trivializing the soul, *your own or that* of another (please include the word body there), we trivialize the Atonement that saved that soul and guaranteed its continued existence. And when one toys with the Son of Righteousness, the Day Star himself, one toys with white heat and a flame hotter and holier than the noonday sun. You cannot do so and not be burned. You cannot with impunity 'crucify Christ afresh' (see Hebrews 6:6). Exploitation of the body (please include the word soul there) is, in the last analysis, an exploitation of him who is the Light and the Life of the world." Words in parentheses have been added.[6] Becoming an erotic disciple, who is passionate about personal refinement, is at the heart of our mortal existence!

In marriage, this journey of discipleship includes the bringing together of two souls, bodies and spirits, as one flesh. With persistence, and through the infinite goodness of God, the union of these two souls, husband and wife, can eventually claim the greatest blessings of eternity.

Choosing complete fidelity symbolizes the trustworthiness we have in the Atonement of Jesus Christ. Being true to one another requires reverence for self, reverence for spouse, and reverence for sexual covenants with God. Indeed, Jeffrey R. Holland explained that the sexual bonding in marriage "... between a man and a woman is—or certainly was ordained to be—a symbol of total union: union of their hearts, their hopes, their lives, their love, their family, their future, their everything.... We are created as men and women to fit together in such a union. In this ultimate physical expression of one man and one woman they are as nearly and as literally 'one' as two separate physical bodies can ever be. It is in that act of ultimate physical intimacy we most nearly fulfill the commandment of the Lord given to Adam and Eve, living symbols for all married couples, when he invited them to cleave unto one another only, and thus become 'one flesh' (Genesis 2:24)."[7]

Monogamy is the ideal relationship for developing a capacity for lasting love, including erotic love. It doesn't happen automatically; it requires commitment to self-awareness, the ability to avoid panic when desire is lacking, and continual sexual investment within the relationship.[8] Faith is the first principle of the gospel of Jesus Christ. Actively choosing to become erotic disciples includes utilizing faith to nurture a sexual union in marriage.

I believe too many of us don't consider the similarity of passionate, fulfilling sex and true discipleship. Each only comes through personal surrender. One embraces the feelings of embodied pleasure, while the other centers on giving your whole heart or will to God by honoring covenants. Because we believe that sexual relations and religious practices are ultimately about connection, we can have experiences where erotic love and deeply spiritual impressions are intertwined. Jeffrey R. Holland said that "... sexual union is also, in its own profound way, a very real sacrament of the highest order, a union not only of a man and a woman but very much the union of that man and woman with God."[9] Every faithfully erotic couple can share private, personal sacramental experiences that can sanctify the union of their souls with continual replenishment. Truly the gift and purpose of sexual, marital love is to fill us up, inspire us, give us hope, and nourish our faith.

Some of the most heart-wrenching experiences I've had as a therapist have come when marital promises have been broken through sexual deviance. In some of these relationships, couples are incredibly humbled and willing to do the grueling work of repairing their marriages. Unfortunately, many of these couples want help to co-parent children, instead of help to stabilize the marriage. I've found two universal consequences in these counseling experiences. First, a deep and abiding sadness, coupled with painful grieving, for the loss of a relationship that once held such promise. Second, unaddressed or unresolved sexual disillusionment always proceeds the betraying behavior. Generally, this disillusionment is the result of one or both spouses continually focusing on the negative aspects of everyday stress and responsibility, or the avoidance of sexual development and maturity. Both tendencies demonstrate lack of discipline—the root word of *discipleship*.

Several years ago, I met with a lovely woman in her mid-50s. She and her husband had raised their two sons, owned a successful business and, by all accounts, seemed to be living a perfect life. She initially sought my help to process some anxieties regarding her relationship with religion. She was open, direct, and deep-thinking. After several weeks of meeting together, she confided in me that she had a business relationship with a man who lived out of state. They would meet, go to dinner, and enjoy talking at various work-related conferences. He was also married and in his 50s. This friendship had been ongoing for nearly two years and had morphed to communicating emotionally via text, phone, or email on a daily basis. My client was preparing to go on another business trip where this gentleman would also be attending the conference. She was very excited to see him and wanted to discuss the possibility of having an affair. "What would it hurt?" she asked. "I feel alive with this man! My husband and I have been in a rut for years. We've tried to rekindle the spark, but nothing ever really changes. I deserve happiness and fulfillment. Tammy, tell me what to do!" As a therapist, my role is to provide clients with insight, facts, and consequences that will help the client process and make decisions for themselves. Near the end of the session, this woman looked directly into my eyes and said, "Tammy, I just want to know what you would do in this situation?"

I told her that my relationship with myself must align for me to have peace. In that self-alignment, I would obey the commandment to be sexually true to my husband. I believe sex has everything to do with faith and religious convictions. Sex and faith both involve relationships that really matter to me, including my covenant relationship with Heavenly Father and Heavenly Mother. They have asked me to love and cleave unto my spouse and none else (D&C 42:22), and I have promised to obey. This means that my relationship with my spouse is preeminent in my life. My career, my fears, my personal interests and hobbies, my children, or any other person on the planet, does not take precedence over my relationship with my spouse. I also explained that, with intentionality, sex in marriage can become transcendent as it replenishes my courage to live my faith. I believe that real faith in Jesus Christ can develop through the sanctification of ordinary, day-in-day-out marital living. In choosing to labor together, going to bed while holding one another and sharing ourselves sexually together, we are also reassuring one another in faith. In giving and receiving pleasure together, our hearts, minds, and flesh are becoming one. Through sex, we become renewed, recommitted, and replenished.

My client left my office still undecided about the business trip relationship. A few weeks later, she came back to therapy quiet and pensive. I sat with her for several minutes then asked her what she had decided to do. She had chosen to email the gentleman and end the emotional relationship by telling him that she was committed to her husband. She told me that she was feeling both happy and sad about her decision. Happy because she had chosen to be true to her covenants. Sad because she wondered if she'd missed out on something amazing. In the time since her previous session, she had done some soul searching, determining to nobly choose daily investments into her marriage. I observed her courageous choices. Together, we processed the consequences of her decision, one of which was the fact that she wasn't happy sexually in her marriage. She decided to invite her husband to therapy where they could work together to build a more fulfilling sexual relationship.

Why is sexual passion and monogamy part of our Heavenly Parents' plan? How can a long-term relationship sexually complete both spouses? What's the purpose of erotic love in a covenant relationship? I believe the answers to these questions have everything to do with the principle of erotic discipleship. Marriage relationships, created after the divine order of heaven, inherently provide space for each spouse to be refined. With intention, these marriages can also replenish or fill you up, inspire you, and nourish your faith. Choosing to create experiences of novelty, mystery, and playfulness—without judgment of self or spouse—replenishes marriage relationships. Choosing to devote energy, time, and money towards a mutually fulfilling sex life can transform your marriage. When couples thoughtfully touch and mindfully share erotic moments, a feeling or sense that there is something more for them can be experienced. Lovemaking can become transcendent and sacred, life-changingly spiritual, as it connects ordinary people with their divine identities.

Some research conducted on these types of spiritual and sexual experiences suggests that roughly 20% of individuals have experienced a transcendent sexual experience. Reports of these experiences are varied from feeling a sense of timelessness, a mental shifting of space, to a sense of electric light filling the mind and/or the body; most people keep these experiences private.[10] I have had a few transcendent experiences when making love, one in particular that I like to ponder occasionally. Trying to describe it in words does not do justice to the depth of the experience, but as best as I can, I will try to write how it felt to me. It was an overwhelming, abiding feeling of love for myself and for my husband. But it was more; I felt encompassed about with a sense of endless glory and majesty. In this glimpse of divinity, I had never felt more beautiful, powerful, or confident in my identity. It was transcendent and life changing.

I have pondered this soul-touching and intimate experience repeatedly, wanting to understand its meaning more fully. One idea is that I was given the gift of a brief taste of eternal love with my husband just a few months before he died unexpectedly. Perhaps to provide comfort and reassurance of our eternal love and covenants in the months and years ahead. I also wonder if I had this experience to better understand the possibilities of transcendent lovemaking as I teach, write, and coach about the joys of human love. This experience included a realness of being known and loved individually as a daughter of Heavenly Parents. In this glimpse of my identity, my every cell knew that They are real and that mortality is just a slice of eternity! I knew myself, my power, and my potential. I knew me how Heaven knows me. This knowledge has sustained me in my daily walk of life. It is with this pure knowledge that I can unequivocally witness to my children, grandchildren, students, clients, friends and you, dear reader. We are eternal beings on a mortal journey. Perhaps these are a few reasons that I experienced this body/spirit, sexual/spiritual, temporal/eternal moment of time—I'm not fully sure what it all means. I just know that I had this experience, and that through it I have come to understand that erotic discipleship, or transcendent lovemaking, is possible. I know that sexual relations, shared in covenant marriages, can sanctify, fortify, and replenish the souls of men and women.

I believe as a couple sexually commits to one another and sacrifices together, their persistence in living covenants becomes a sanctification process. Through Jesus Christ, our ordinary lives can be refined as we transcend and become extraordinary people. True nobility develops by making daily, consistent, superior choices that are rooted in honorable principles and virtues. Choosing complete fidelity strengthens individuals, marriages, families, and society at large. Intentionality of character is the foundation of divinity.

THINK. Process and journal your thoughts from this chapter. Does anything particularly resonate with you? As you reflect on your experiences, do you feel there have been moments when you felt connected to heaven through sex?

PAIR. Come together in prayer before sharing. Make sure you are expressing your love for one another.

SHARE. There will be some personal sharing in this exchange. Make sure to listen to understand your spouse. What do covenants mean to you? How would you describe your experiences of erotic discipleship?

Adding to your Sexual Playbook: What covenants have you already written about in your sexual playbook? What covenants would you like to add? Based on this chapter and your conversation on the ideas presented here, add specific ways you will honor these covenants.

Experiential Activities to Enjoy

Feelings of Fullness

All long-term relationships have ebbs and flows; sometimes you feel more emotionally connected while other times more distant. It is important to talk together about these experiences, especially without blaming your partner when you feel disconnected. Below are some descriptive words associated with sex. Taking turns, describe experiences you've shared that have made you feel this way or describe what type of touch might help you feel this way. (Remember, manipulation is harmful to relationships. Use this activity to increase your understanding of yourself and your spouse, not to get your way.)

- Cherished
- United
- Ravished
- Appreciated
- Reverenced
- Adored
- Erotic
- Connected (to self, to partner, to God)

Journal Your Experience

If you feel you have experienced a transcendent moment while making love, take time to journal about it now. Record, in as much detail as possible, what you were thinking, feeling, experiencing, and understanding. When/if the time feels right, share your experiences with your spouse.

Pray for Guidance

Is your sexual relationship suffering? Do you want to feel more embodied while making love? Are you hoping to believe more fully that sex is divinely appointed by God? If these, or any other questions you have about sex and spirituality, continually come to your mind, I encourage you to begin praying specifically for answers to these questions. You may even consider fasting together, then ending your fast in prayer. Review *Chapter 2: The Gift of our Sexual Theology* if that is helpful to you on this journey.

The Last Time

I'm sure you think about the first time you made love; we all do! I'm curious, however: do you ever think about the last time you will make love? Due to my life experiences, I have often thought about the last time I made love with my spouse, Mark. I've wondered:

- Was I truly present?
- Did I take the time to communicate my respect, appreciation, and love for him?
- Did we cherish one another?
- Were we able to replenish each other from the demands of everyday life?

When you make love with your sweetheart next, think about these questions. Share your thoughts with one another. Assess if there are ways that you can create a more eternal dimension to your lovemaking.

CHAPTER 5

Sacred Sexual Boundaries

In a covenant marriage, you promise that all your romantic, flirty, sexual energy will be directed toward your spouse. This is a clear, non-permeable boundary that couples need to uphold and *cherish*. Doing so is at the heart of a healthy and replenishing sexual relationship. When the emotional or sexual boundaries of fidelity are violated, the results are heartbreaking. It is so incredibly painful to observe the shame, sorrow, betrayal, and ugliness that enter a relationship when boundaries are not honored. It has been my personal experience, as a therapist, that about half of the couples in this situation end up divorcing and becoming co-parents when children are involved. The other half of couples that I've worked with remained married, though the journey to rebuilding their marriage is often very difficult. This reparative work is some of the most grueling *yet* sacred work that I do as a therapist. When both partners do the work, they claim an eternal prize. These couples often believe that their relationship is even healthier than it was prior to the betrayal after this restoration of trust and healing takes place.

Boundaries are *not* punishments. They are perimeters that reflect what is needed to feel safe, respected, and loved within your marriage. While complete sexual fidelity is a boundary agreed upon by all couples who enter a covenant marriage, many boundaries are unique for each individual and couple. Boundaries should serve as an outward expression of your core values and beliefs. Married couples often establish boundaries in areas such as:

- In-laws and family (e.g., how often we visit extended family members, what personal details they should know about our marriage)
- Personal privacy (e.g., a plan of action for device usage within your relationship)
- Communication (e.g., zero-tolerance for shouting or name-calling, what information about the relationship is shared with others)
- Autonomy (e.g., freedom to make decisions and work toward individual goals or to maintain friendships outside the marriage)
- Physical space (e.g., zero tolerance for violence, agreements on using personal items without asking first)
- Finances (e.g., not hiding money or debt from each other)
- Household care (e.g., expectations on household chores, provisioning, cooking responsibilities)
- Relationship (e.g., the expectation of loyalty and fidelity, shared parenting responsibilities)
- Sexual (e.g., what you do in the bedroom together, how you get help for sexual issues)

Establishing boundaries can sometimes feel like one spouse is limiting the other's power or punishing them. In actuality, boundaries are created for safety and trust, two essential ingredients for a successful marriage. Indeed, through 50 years of research on marriage, Dr. John Gottman found that the most desirable quality in a spouse is trustworthiness. What the movies show and what you might hear in music or see on social media is not the truth—being sexy and attractive is not nearly as important as really being able to trust your partner.[11] Nowhere is trust more important than in establishing a replenishing sexual relationship.

One way we show trust in marriage is by respecting the boundaries that we establish together and by honoring our spouse's boundary requests. It is quite common in therapy to find marriages in a mess when one spouse has betrayed the trust of the other. For instance, if the husband is actively viewing pornography, a wife may set a boundary of safety around her heart to choose not to sleep with him until he gets help or can better control his habit.

Another common problem that negatively impacts trust is the use, or misuse, of money. *Financial infidelity* or *financial deception* are relatively new terms in social science research; however, its practice is not new at all. Financial infidelity, or financial deception, is when one spouse is hiding financial information or financial transactions from the other spouse. An example I've seen several times in my practice is when one spouse has spent or invested a large amount of money without the other's knowledge or consent.

When we establish boundaries in marriage, it is much like installing a fence around your property. It keeps unwanted trespassers out of your space while protecting the family within your space. When we use an equal voice and partnered decision-making skills to unitedly create a boundary, we strengthen partnered trust within the marriage.

Sexual boundaries are two-fold. First, there are the boundaries you establish together within your sexual relationship. Second, there is the sanctity of not disclosing sexual information outside of the relationship without both partners agreeing and being present in this discussion.

Sexual boundaries within the marital relationship look like:

- One partner not wanting to have anal sex.
- One spouse being uncomfortable with the idea of wearing lingerie.
- Both of you agreeing that oral sex is not your thing.

Sexual boundaries outside of the sexual relationship look like:

- Not sharing intimate details of your relationship with your parents, siblings, friends, etc.
- Not seeking sexual help without your partner being present.
- Deciding together what books to read or to visit a therapist for help.

I believe one of the most detrimental trends I see today is the freedom with which individuals share private sexual information. Online, in gyms, at the dinner table, in Sunday School, etc. *Please,* remember that this relationship is most sacred. It is to be kept between the two of you. Should you need help, decide *together* and go *together* to get that help. Please set and keep sexual boundaries. Doing so is essential to claiming the blessing of a replenishing sexual relationship with your spouse. I believe that processing this information is likely to lead to some of the most important sexual conversations you will share in your marriage.

THINK. What sexual boundaries are important to you? Why are they important? As you ponder the sacred responsibility of being a sexual steward in your marriage, in relation to setting and keeping boundaries, what does that mean to you?

PAIR. This time I want you to go to a place that is neutral in power, where both of you feel completely comfortable and safe. Say a little prayer for guidance as you embark on this conversation. Then, get comfortable as you sit in silence for a few minutes.

SHARE. Listen to understand your spouse's perspective on sexual boundaries. Ask questions to make sure you understand your spouse's perspective. Share your perspectives. What, specifically, do you both consider "sexual secrets" just between the two of you? Conversely, what do you both think is appropriate to share and with whom? Give and receive information until you both feel securely heard and understood.

Adding to your Sexual Playbook: Write down the boundaries you've agreed upon. First, journal the boundaries you've created within your sexual relationship. Then, journal the boundaries you've agreed upon for outside your marriage, including when and how you will seek help for your sexual relationship if needed.

Experiential Activities to Enjoy

Helpful steps to creating boundaries (both in and out of the bedroom)[12]

1. Clearly communicate your boundaries once you've decided on them:

    a. "I don't want you to speed when I'm in the car with you."

b. "I am not okay with name calling when things get heated."
c. "I need 30 minutes to decompress when I get home from work before jumping into the needs of the family."
d. "When I'm asleep, please do not wake me unless it is an emergency."
e. "I'm uncomfortable giving you oral sex when you are not clean."

2. When boundaries are violated, establish clear consequences. Not following through shows your partner that you don't respect your own boundaries. If you don't respect your boundaries, he/she won't either.

   a. "I will drive separately next time."
   b. "I will need 30 minutes to be alone if name calling happens."
   c. "You will need to clean the kitchen after dinner if you take more than 30 minutes to decompress after work. I need some time alone too."
   d. "You get to fold the laundry for the week if you wake me up."
   e. "I will take a hard pass on making love if you don't shower before coming to bed."

3. Establishing boundaries is a trial-and-error process, especially if you haven't done this before in your marriage. Understand that you may slip up along the way. Take responsibility when you or your partner make a mistake, offer genuine apologies and always circle back to clear, respectful communication.
4. Be willing to seek help for your struggles. Consulting with a licensed marriage and family therapist or another professional can be extremely beneficial, especially if you are creating "big" boundaries around issues like parenting, sexuality, finances, and extended family relationships. Together, find help. Together, get help.

Role Play Scenarios for Establishing Sexual Boundaries

Think about and discuss with your spouse how you would respond in each of the following scenarios:

1. Your boss wants to hear specifics about your honeymoon.
2. Your buddy starts talking about his sexual experiences, wondering if he's normal.
3. Your sister is getting married; she wants to know all the details.
4. You're at a bridal shower, and everyone is sharing some intimate secrets.
5. You need some sexual help.
6. Your parents come to you for sexual advice.
7. You recognize that you're watching people at the gym who are wearing sexy clothes.
8. You realize that your sexual thoughts are leaning outside of the relationship.
9. You scroll into some pornographic images.
10. You decide that you're not as attracted to your spouse as you once were.

PART II

Sexual Communication and Intentional Lovemaking

CHAPTER 6

Sexual Decision Making as Equal Partners

As you grow into adulthood, you experience an increased amount of responsibility for making your own decisions. When considering a life decision, you gather any relevant information and thoughtfully consider the pros and cons while praying for spiritual guidance. Once you choose among the alternatives, you pray for a confirmation and start acting on your decision. It may sound straightforward, but the process for decisions of substantive consequence is rarely easy. This process can be especially stressful if you haven't had parents or other adult role models exemplify sound judgment in decision-making. As you mature and move forward in life, you recognize patterns of decision-making that contribute to your progression and add goodness to your life, as well as to the lives of others. Your ability to make good decisions empowers you. The way you make decisions about sexuality in your life, and with your spouse as equal partners, is of utmost importance.

Once married, the decision-making process shifts to include your spouse. The process is almost identical to making decisions on your own, only now you get to include your spouse fully and equitably. Equal partnership nourishes a closeness between husband and wife, creating a stronger and happier marriage. Both spouses are more likely to share their thoughts and feelings because the friendship in their marriage enables each spouse to feel better about themselves as well as each other. The enhanced emotional intimacy leads to greater sexual intimacy, a critical part of a thriving marriage. Couples with an equal partnership are more stable in their marriages because they experience less conflict and resentment. Dr. John Gottman has found that all intimate relationships work better when *both* partners have and accept influence. This is particularly true for sexual intimacy. Having and accepting influence is one of the hallmarks of a successful relationship because the pattern of respectful communication includes going back and forth until both partners feel that things are fair.[13]

The enhanced sexual intimacy that comes with equal partnership both improves health and reduces stress. Men in happy marriages are more productive at work. Research shows that for women, having an equal voice in decision-making is the most important contributor to their perceived happiness in marriage. Women typically feel better about themselves and are less depressed and angry when equity and fairness are felt within their marriage relationship.[14] Men and women both feel more hopeful about their marriage relationship and benefit emotionally from equal partnership because there is greater openness between spouses.

Becoming equal partners in marriage includes several aspects that are important for both spouses to consider. First, making decisions as partners requires both spouses to become more self-aware. You do this by first examining your own actions, which include both what you say and what you do. In this self-examination, I encourage you to look at the situation from an aerial view; look at one another with compassion as you unpack your half of the exchange (we'll talk more about self-awareness in *Chapter 11: Sexual Awareness and Sexual Restraint*). Further, have realistic expectations about your partner's ability or willingness to change. As equal partners, you are not trying to change your spouse—you can only change yourself! Second, an important key in becoming equal partners is to choose to listen in order to understand your partner. Listen to *understand* rather than listening to defend your position. Seek out what is really going on underneath your spouse's words; this is where you will find the emotional connection. You don't have to agree with what your spouse is saying, you just need to try to understand what your spouse is saying and feeling. In equal partnership marriages, both spouses need to feel heard and feel understood. John Gottman's *ATTUNEment* format is incredibly helpful as you focus on listening to understand one another.

- **Awareness** refers to knowledge of your spouse's world. Knowing his/her thoughts, feelings, and current circumstances. To have a healthy, positive relationship, you must look for and acknowledge each other's emotions. Getting an emotional temperature reading by asking questions like "What's up?" or "How are you?" fosters awareness.
- **Turning Toward** suggests your willingness to enter your spouse's perspective by reaching out when you sense his/her need for connection. I always encourage spouses to choose to become emotionally available by "turning toward" their spouse with a desire to understand. This is best done by creating intentional space and time, removing distractions, and literally turning towards one another to make eye-contact.
- **Tolerance** refers to the ability to consider different viewpoints and emotions than your own. You must be able to accept your partner's reality and hold off on expressing your reality when attuning. Remember, you do not need to adopt or agree with the other's perspective or feelings, but you do need to be willing to recognize and respect their perspective or feelings, regardless of the discomfort you may experience as you hear this information.
- **Understanding** is the key ingredient in attuning. It refers to your attempt to 'get' your spouse's perspective and emotions. To really understand how he/she is feeling, you need to be willing to momentarily suspend your own beliefs, ideas, and feelings. Useful phrases to use to better understand your spouse are "Help me understand" or "Tell me more about how this makes you feel." Your spouse must know that you care and want to understand him/her.
- **Non-defensive Listening** is the most effective way of responding to the things you may hear while learning to understand your spouse. As the listener, your task is to help the other person clarify his/her feelings and perceptions. In your own words, thoughtfully repeat what you heard. Then, check-in to see if you understood everything by asking, "Did I miss anything?" Responding without judgment encourages open communication and trust.
- **Empathy** includes responding with accurate identification, acknowledgement, and validation of another's feelings. It requires a true

understanding of what it must feel like to be that person within the situation described. Empathy demonstrates tenderness for another's emotions. Your spouse will *feel felt* when you are able to empathize by saying, "It is very reasonable to feel what you're feeling," "Wow, that must be scary, hard, frustrating," or "If I were in your situation, I would feel the same way, etc."

Through *ATTUNEment*, couples can begin to really see one another and impactfully communicate as they become better friends and equal partners. Friendship is at the core of a strong marriage. In marriage, friendship between spouses means they know each other intimately by understanding each other's likes, dislikes, personality quirks, hopes, and dreams. They use this information to bless the relationship, never to manipulate, mock, or belittle one another. In marriage you create sacred space as you come to truly know all the intimate details of one another's lives. I challenge you to communicate openly about every aspect of your relationship, including the sacred sexual part of your marriage.[15] As marriage is a sexual contract, the processes of sexually understanding one another and making decisions, united in equal partnership, is imperative for your sexual relationship to thrive.

In my private practice, couples I work with typically need help sexually attuning in four basic areas of their marriages:

- **Sexual differentiation** is the ability to soothe your own anxieties around sex. It is a maturity that comes through education, self-soothing, and aligning your spirit and body as you work through your own sexual development. It also is the ability to resist being infected by your spouse's sexual anxiety. Personally, I believe this is the work of eternity! It requires us to become our best selves in the most vulnerable of circumstances.
- **Sexual frequency** difficulties arise when couples are not on the same page regarding the amount of sex they are regularly having. Although stereotypically men are portrayed to want more sex than women, in my work as a therapist, roughly 60% of husbands want to have sex more frequently while about 40% of wives are the high-desire partner.
- **Sexual satisfaction** is described as the way you feel about your sex life. It's a relatively subjective idea. Our sexual desires, expectations,

and needs differ from one another and change as we grow and age. Those who experience sexual satisfaction claim to share emotional intimacy, feel free to communicate about sexual wants and needs, and experience sexual desire, arousal, and orgasm. Interestingly, couples high in sexual satisfaction also report taking time to more frequently cuddle, kiss, and talk intimately *after* sex.[16]

- **Sexual unity** is another somewhat subjective idea. I define sexual unity as a profound openness and freedom in the receptivity of pleasure that comes only through individual differentiation and intentional couple sexual processing. It is a wholeness that is mutually felt through sharing erotic passions and dreams, both verbally and physically.

Each equal-partnered sexual decision made as a couple can successfully bring you closer to one another other by deepening your connection and increasing levels of trust. This process takes time as you learn to do your own self-regulatory work and to effectively ATTUNE to one another. What it ultimately says is, "I'm bringing my best self to our relationship. The best in me wants to fully, sexually connect with the best in you." This wholehearted lovemaking means that you are looking out for each other while putting each other's needs equal to (if not above) your own. Real passionate, erotic, and fulfilling lovemaking comes about best when two wholehearted individuals, fully committed to one another, come to play, worship, and pleasure one another.

What do I mean by *wholehearted* individuals? Dr. Brené Brown, a renowned researcher of human behavior, has studied wholeheartedness and vulnerability extensively. Her ideas of wholeheartedness really resonate with me. She claims that a wholehearted person ". . . is willing to show up, to stay engaged and to find the emotional courage to respond in a way that aligns with his/her values."[17] In every aspect of life, becoming increasingly wholehearted is *maturing with hope* as you show up, have courage, and respond in ways that are aligned with who you are and who you want to become. I believe that part of this wholeheartedness comes by cultivating a relationship with your own sexuality. Becoming aware of, accepting, and communicating your sexual interests, desires, thoughts, and arousal patterns are part of one's development; it is also necessary to "bringing your whole self" to bed. The erotic energy that comes through this style of loving, wholehearted connection is the special creative power which allows couples to replenish as they share the responsibilities and labors of family life. I fully believe that these experiences provide earthly glimpses of eternal love.

THINK. As you consider the experiences you have had in making sexual decisions, what have been your typical patterns? Think about the ATTUNEment process. How can you better implement this process into your decision-making?

PAIR. Together, get comfortable. Make and maintain eye-contact for 2 minutes, then hug one another for another 2 minutes in a full-bodied hug with arms softly around one another.

SHARE. Discuss the content in this chapter, comparing it to your impressions of how sexual decisions have been made in the past. Listen to understand without getting defensive. Try to use the information from this chapter to make a sexual decision together.

Adding to your Sexual Playbook: After sharing and discussing approaches to sexual decision-making, write down your agreed-upon process to making sexual decisions.

Experiential Activities to Enjoy

Get ATTUNEd!

Using the *ATTUNEment* principles outlined in this chapter (and Dr. John Gottman's *7 Principles for Making Marriage* workbook), discuss sexual differences experienced in your relationship, including:

- Sexual anxieties
- Sexual desire discrepancies
- Sexual satisfaction discrepancies
- Sexual arousal discrepancies

Sexual Compliments

The husband needs to lie on the bed, either naked or lightly clothed (depending on your mood and comfort level). It's the wife's job to work her way from head to toe, giving compliments to at least five different body parts. Try to go beyond superficial compliments (e.g., "I like your butt") and tell your partner exactly what you love and why. One way to structure this could be: "I love your _____. Thinking about it/them makes me feel _____. And when I see it/them I want to ______."

When your partner is giving you a compliment, do your best to receive it gracefully. So often we don't give credence to the compliments we receive when we reject or downplay them with responses like "Really? But I look so much different now" or "My stretch marks are gross." Practice maintaining eye contact with your partner and simply saying, "Thank you."

After the husband has been sufficiently showered with praise, switch roles. If desired, after giving a compliment, spend some time giving your attention to that body part!

CHAPTER 7

Understanding Your Sexual Soil

Getting married is an adventure! Sometimes it's an exciting adventure full of wonder, and sometimes it's an adventure so hazardous and challenging that you may wonder why you even got married. This is normal! Joining two lives into one is difficult, especially when it comes to sexual expectations and behavior. Research has found that couples who intentionally decide what traditions, beliefs, and attitudes to integrate into their home environment have greater relational satisfaction and stability.[18] This process is described in the following diagram.

Ecology of Marriage Tree

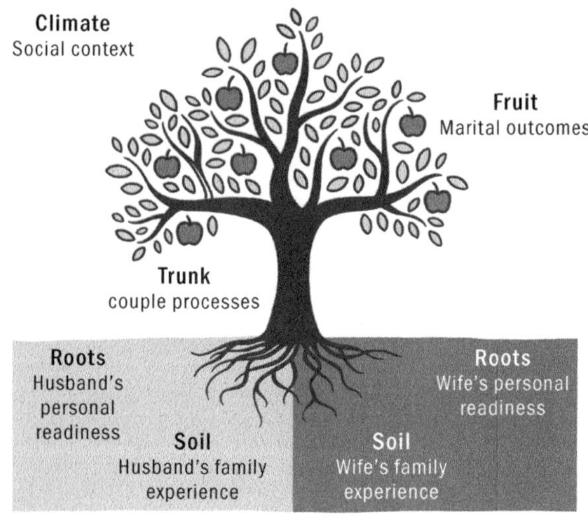

The image shows the different soils in which both husband and wife were nourished as children. Scholars have found that many factors influence the soil, such as the quality of relationships within the family of origin. One's relationship with their own sexuality and their ability to share healthy sexual intimacy in marriage have been found to be particularly influenced by the health of the soil in which the individual was nourished.

The diagram also shows that both husband and wife uproot themselves from their respective families of origin to plant their roots into soil of their own creation. How exciting! The soil the couple creates together is essential to the nourishment of their tender, newly planted roots. The nutrient density of the soil will largely determine the nourishment the relationship receives. In a sexual context, the soil created by the decision-making efforts of the unified couple will nourish the ability for sexual growth and development in marriage. The trunk of the tree indicates the process of the couple's progression. The more harmonious the process of sexual development, the stronger the marriage will be.

Most deliciously, look at the fruit of the tree. This fruit is produced through committed work and from soil that is nutrient rich. Sexually speaking, the fruit grows and ripens with a healthy sexual environment provided by nutrient-rich soil and dedicated labor from both spouses across time. Think of a real fruit tree. If the tree is ignored (e.g., not pruned, watered, or fertilized), there will not be good or delicious fruit to enjoy. If, however, the fruit tree is diligently cared for, the fruit produced is beautiful and delicious. Sexual relationships that are passionate in nature, relationally connecting, and personally rejuvenating require diligent care throughout the life cycle.

As a couple marries, among other factors, they are making a sexual contract with one another. They are promising to be sexually faithful to one another and agreeing upon a sexual stewardship. This stewardship begins with the honeymoon. Thus, it is imperative that couples consider the development of their sexual soil right from the beginning! This is also why the Honeymoon Workshop I offer can be such a helpful step in young couples' sexual fulfillment (you can find more information about this on my website www.tammyhill.com).

Explore Your Personal Sexual Soil

It's important for you to understand that your sexual development began at conception. You have always been a sexual being! Growing sexually, having sexual thoughts and questions, being curious about sexual desire and arousal, and sharing yourself sexually are all part of life's journey. As you learn to accept this truth, you will have more success in understanding your sexual beliefs. This process will also allow you to create your own nutrient-rich soil, which will provide a healthy space for you to grow sexually in your marriage.

At birth, each of us is planted in a unique garden. Your family, community and culture contribute nutrients (ideas/beliefs about sexuality) to the soil you are growing in. As you mature, you discover that many of these ideas/beliefs are nourishing to you. These nutrients allow you to grow and thrive in your sexual understanding and acceptance. You also learn that there are many ideas/beliefs that are not nutrient rich. Because these non-nourishing nutrients create sexual fear and shame, you can often feel confused, overwhelmed, and even angry as you mature and have sexual thoughts and experiences. These ideas/beliefs do not contribute to the development of a healthy space for you to sexually grow in your marriage.

Taking the opportunity to really explore the soil you grew up in will bless your sexual adjustment in marriage. You will discover what messages you want to preserve because they have nourished your soil. You will also have a choice to get rid of the messages that have not been beneficial to your sexual acceptance and understanding. You are responsible for improving the quality of the soil you bring to your marriage. The more you dive into understanding your own soil, the more prepared you will be to determine the quality of the joint soil you and your spouse are creating. It is within this soil that your sexual union is planted and fruitfully nourished. Just like any gardening, this process will take time and environmental adaptations throughout the course of your marriage. Your soil, and the pacing of your soil creation, will be unique to your marriage.

Here are some questions to consider as you explore your personal sexual soil. I encourage you to write your thoughts and impressions as you answer the following questions. This pondering and journaling will prepare you to communicate with your partner as you work to understand each other and together improve your marital soil:

1. The messages I heard or internalized about my body were . . .
2. Growing up, my body made me feel . . .
3. What I learned about pleasure was . . .
4. Exploring my body was . . .
5. I learned that sexual desire was . . .
6. Positive experiences that shaped my sexuality were . . .
7. What I learned about sexuality from church was . . .
8. As I went through puberty, I felt . . .
9. Getting my period was . . .
10. My parents'/caregivers' attitudes about sex were . . .
11. What I learned about pornography was . . .
12. How pornography impacted me was . . .
13. My childhood sexual experiences made me feel . . .
14. The most helpful sexual messages I've received are . . .
15. The most unhelpful sexual messages I've received are . . .
16. The sexual messages I wish I had received are . . .
17. Growing up I learned that being a girl/boy meant . . .
18. Growing up I learned that being LGBTQIA2S+ meant . . .
19. My parents' relationship influenced me by . . .
20. Media, including social media, sexual messages that have influenced me include . . .

Allow yourself time to reflect upon your personal sexual soil. If there are questions that I failed to ask, please add them to your journaling. I strongly encourage you to offer yourself much needed compassion. Remember that you were a child navigating a sexualized world. You did the best that you could with likely limited guidance, support, and education. Going through your soil can often bring up unexpected memories and emotions. These are not necessarily good or bad; they are just part of your journey. Do what you can to provide yourself care and loving acceptance. If there has been unresolved sexual trauma in your life, I urge you to seek help with a trained EMDR therapist.

When you are ready to share your soil with your fiancé(é) or spouse, create ample time and privacy. Make sure you both are well nourished and hydrated. This important and vulnerable conversation can be difficult, but don't shy away from it! An essential skill in marriage is being able to communicate about hard things. This opportunity will give you time to share sexual information with one another. Remember, the space you hold for each other during this process is sacred. Be reverent, reflective, and respectful.

Create Your Marital Sexual Soil

Once both of you have shared your own sexual soil with one another, it is time to decide what beliefs and attitudes you want to keep in your marital sexual soil and what beliefs and attitudes you want to get rid of. Remember that this is a process of making decisions as equal partners. One person should never have a louder/bigger voice than the other.

Start by journaling together the ideas you want to bring into your new soil. You may want to consider these points to guide this conversation:

1. Decide on the aspects of your sexual soils that are most important for you to keep.
2. Decide how you want to show up for each other sexually in your marriage.
3. Specify nutrients/beliefs which could benefit your marital sexual soil.
4. Decide safe ways that you will approach one another to have important sexual conversations.
5. Describe your sexual hopes and expectations.

As sex is intended to be relational, it is important to try and view sex from your partner's perspective. Great sex is about learning to love your spouse in the way he/she wants to be loved. So, as you have this conversation, recognize that together you are creating soil in which both of you will learn and grow.

Now, discuss and journal together the aspects of your individual sexual soil that you want to leave behind. Consider using these questions to guide your conversation:

1. What aspects of our personal sexual soils do we specifically not want to include in our marital sexual soil?
2. What am I willing to discover, evaluate, and change to create soil where both of us can sexually thrive?
3. What aspects of my past am I willing to put away in hopes of creating a more rewarding future?
4. How will I choose to sexually show up differently than I was taught?

In having this conversation, don't agree to things unless you are willing to truly do the work necessary to make the adjustments upon which you both agree. There should be no manipulation or lying as you discuss these adjustments.

This process should create a clear pattern for your journey of creating your marital sexual soil. Remember, you have eternity to grow and develop. It takes years for a fruit tree to produce beautiful fruit! The time, energy, communication, and overall investment you both make in your sexual relationship will determine how delicious this aspect of your life becomes. As you continually create and reevaluate your marital sexual soil together, remember that you are equitable partners with equal voices in the decision-making process. Showing up to understand and to be understood is invaluable.

I believe that as husband and wife, we are commanded to replenish the marriage with both spiritually, and passionately-connecting sex. For this to happen, continual communication and diligent effort are needed. It requires the best in both of you to create soil that nourishes the tree that produces the most delicious fruit. You decide together how much goodness your sexual relationship can offer your marriage.

THINK. Consider the questions listed previously as you reflect on your family of origin influences regarding sexuality. Do the journaling as described.

PAIR. Come together with time and a listening ear to understand your partner. Look into one another's eyes as you consider building a life together.

SHARE. Complete the described activities in this chapter.

Adding to your Sexual Playbook: Integrate what you wrote about your marital sexual soil into your sexual playbook. Review your sexual playbook and make modifications where needed based on your conversations from this chapter.

Experiential Activities to Enjoy

Not Just for Newlyweds

Whether you have been married for one month or 50 years, completing the processing described in this chapter will benefit your life, marriage, and parenting. The questions to ponder and discuss will give insight to yourself as an individual. It will help you better understand your spouse, and it will be a great springboard to teaching sexuality to your children in a style that both of you feel comfortable with and agree upon. Doing this work can really be eye-opening and beneficial to every marriage.

Your Soil and Your Fruit

Go on a date to a local greenhouse. Purchase anything from a small flower to a tree. Let this plant represent your future, shared marriage (moving forward from today). Take the time to research how much sunlight, fertilizer, and water your plant needs. Set reminders in your phone to ensure you water it often enough. As you care for this plant together, make time for conversations about the family system that you are actively creating. What does the sexual soil look like from your perspective? Are there nutrients missing? What changes can be made as you diligently choose to create a healthier sexual environment in your home? Consider the fruit you want in your relationship now, as well as in the future. How is your soil nurturing your marriage so that you can enjoy the delicious fruits that can be harvested?

CHAPTER 8

Understanding Your Sexual Desire Frameworks

Frequently, I counsel with couples who experience a big gap in their sexual desire preferences. If this sounds familiar to your relationship, you're not alone! This is one of the most common reasons my clients reach out for therapy. Discrepancies in sexual desire and frequency are the leading cause of sexual frustration in marriage. Some of the most common reasons couples have these differences include feeling fatigue, experiencing a sense of being underappreciated, not having enough sexual stimulation, using medications that negatively impact libido, feeling emotional distance or distrust in the relationship, and lacking attraction or feeling unattractive. When multiple factors are involved, it can feel especially discouraging, which only adds to increased relational despair. Interestingly, when partners are unhappy in marriage, they attribute bad sex to 50-70 percent of their problems, while happy couples attribute only 15-20 percent of their happiness to a good sex life.[19]

Often in our Western culture, we believe that you either have sexual desire or you don't. The light is either on or off, never in between. When a high-desire partner points a finger at a low-desire partner, two very unhelpful things happen to the relationship. First, by saying that one person (the lower-desire partner) is the problem, a sense of relational teamwork is lost. Second, the person pointing the finger (higher-desire partner) is not owning any responsibility for their contribution to the situation. This dynamic magnifies the great divide from just being a bedroom struggle to becoming a relational issue outside of the bedroom as well. Because differences in sexual desire and frequency create such frustration in marriage, which is then amplified on to other aspects of the relationship, I think it is essential to understand that sexual desire is not an all-or-nothing condition. In her research, sexologist Emily Nagoski describes sexual desire as spontaneous, responsive, or contextual.

Spontaneous sexual desire is exactly what it sounds like. It shows up instantly, with or without stimulation. Dr. Nagoski notes that 75% of men report experiencing spontaneous desire, but only 15% of women report this. As a matter of fact, in early sexual response cycles developed in the 1950s by early sex researchers Masters and Johnson (done primarily on the male brain), sexual desire was not even included on the original continuum of the sexual response cycle experience.

Responsive sexual desire happens when desire shows up in response to stimulation, meaning something sexy happens, and the body responds. Dr. Nagoski found that 5% of men and 30% of women experience responsive desire, meaning these individuals need more than a sexy thought or visualization to want sex.

Contextual sexual desire is when both the environment and the circumstances impact the ability to feel sexual desire. In her exceptional book, *Come as You Are*, Dr. Nagoski's research claims that most people, regardless of gender, fall within a blend of responsive and contextual desire. However, for some, desire can *feel* spontaneous as they simply may not be aware of the other factors at play. This is important for couples to understand because for most of us, context matters. Normalizing how someone feels desire is so important as you remove the burden of feeling flawed, inadequate, or worse yet, 'being the problem.' This adds contextual meaning by acknowledging that when the circumstances are right, a low desire partner is perfectly capable of deep sexual desire, erotic energy, and passionate sex. A high desire partner's ability to understand these differences can also help them recognize that a lack of sexual advancements or attractiveness uncertainty is not a personal attack. Together, a couple can embrace their differences in desire and work on improving how to meet each other's natural sexual response needs. These conversations can be painful, especially if you're not used to talking openly about sex. However, addressing the differences in your relationship will help both of you self-develop as you create a real partnership in your marriage. Don't shortchange your progression! Coming to understand mismatched types of desire can create a framework of creative and unified sexual possibilities.

What Are Your Unified Sexual Possibilities?

I like to think of desire as *possibility*. What could possibly happen if you were to change from an unsatisfied state of sexual living to one that created more energy, happiness, and joy? I like couples to explore this speculation of possibility as they learn more about themselves and each other. Once you have placed your typical sexual desire in a spontaneous, responsive, contextual, or combined framework, ask yourself the following questions. It's imperative to be honest with yourself and with your spouse as you process the answers:

- What are my sexual desires? Be specific.
- What are reasons I do not want to have sex? Be specific.
- What do I desire most from my marital sexual union?
- What sexual possibilities do I envision within myself? Within our marital relationship?
- How can the differences in our sexual desire bring about relational unity?
- How can we use our sexual differences to create a transcendent sexual relationship?

Once a couple comes to understand more fully what they both desire sexually from their marriage, they can really get some great work done—without a therapist! For instance, many couples I work with have the same desire for their sexual relationship—they want to share passion and connect emotionally. With this knowledge, you then can add the psychosexual research which shows that men usually want to have sex *to feel* emotionally connected, while women often want to have sex *once they feel* emotionally connected. Looking at it this way, you can see that both spouses will feel connected on either side of sex. You can visualize this as an Oreo cookie! (I've actually had couples purchase Oreos to have as a visual reminder that, ultimately, they want the same thing—connection!) The hard, crisp "husband and wife" wafers found on either side of the cookie represents emotional closeness. The delicious, soft, sweet center of the cookie is a sexual encounter. The combination of cookie with filling is what makes Oreos so great, just as the emotional closeness and connection that come from good sex make marriage delicious. Processing together your sexual desire framework, along with understanding one another's unifying sexual possibilities, teaches couples to value the intimacy that comes from deeply knowing one another while developing more positive, realistic sexual expectations.

What Are Your Sexual Commonalities?

Through my years of experience, I've come to recognize that an easy way to create unhappiness in marriage is to focus on differences—especially sexual differences. Believe it or not, there are more similarities than differences in male and female sexuality! Both sexes experience sexual desire and arousal, have numerous erogenous zones throughout the body, and experience increased blood flow, heart rate, and other pleasurable sensations with sexual activity. Both sexes also enjoy the pulsating and relaxing release of orgasm.[20]

As you share experiences with different types of touch, your understanding and knowledge of one another will expand. Focus on discovering what touching preferences you have in common. Five types of touch are described by sex therapist, Barry McCarthy, in his book, *Sex Made Simple:*

1. **Affectionate Touch** involves clothes-on touching, or public displays of affection (PDA) such as holding hands, hugging, and kissing.
2. **Sensual Touch** involves non-genital touch. Couples might be clothed, semi-clothed or nude. It includes head, back or foot rubs, cuddling on the couch watching Netflix, being situated in a trust position where partners feel safe and connected, and cradling each other as they go to sleep or wake in the morning.

3. **Playful Touch** intertwines genital and non-genital touch while semi-clothed or nude. It includes touching in the shower or bath, full-body massage, seductive or erotic dancing, and playing games such as strip poker.
4. **Erotic Touch** can include manual, grinding, oral or vibrator stimulation. It can be mutual or one-way, and it can proceed to orgasm or act as a transition to the next stage of touch.
5. **Intercourse** includes important principles to keep in mind for this type of touch. First, intercourse is a natural continuation of a pleasurable and erotic process, not a pass/fail performance test. Second, transition to this touch should only occur when there are high levels of arousal on both sides and when other forms of touch are also being used.

I challenge you to focus on the aspects of sexual touch that you have in common. Write them down. Post them on your fridge or on your bathroom mirror! I hope by now you have come to realize sex isn't about the act of sex. It's not about the number of times you orgasm. Sex is primarily about connection. Both men and women are innately created to pair-bond, to develop a soulmate relationship where sex flourishes. There are seasons of life when capacity and tolerance for sex fluctuates, but the hallmark of a healthy sex life cannot be measured by a number. As you look for sexual commonalities in your relationship, you will discover that differences in desire shrink while your possibilities become limitless.

Sexual Comparisons

In a book titled *The Normal Bar*, authors Chrisanna Northrup, Pepper Schwartz, and James Witte conducted an online study with 70,000 people from 24 countries. They wanted to know what might be different about couples who said they had a great sex life compared to couples who reported having a poor sex life. Recognizing the limitations of self-report data, I still think there are some fascinating findings in their research, as summarized below.

Couples who have a passionate and fulfilling sex life across the planet are doing these things:

1. They say "I love you" every day and really mean it
2. They kiss one another passionately, without expecting anything in return
3. They give spontaneous, thoughtful gifts
4. They know what turns their partner on and off erotically
5. They are physically affectionate, even in public
6. They play and have fun together
7. They cuddle
8. They make sex a priority
9. They are good friends
10. They talk comfortably about their sex life
11. They have weekly dates
12. They take romantic vacations
13. They are mindful about turning toward each other with love and appreciation

Couples who have a poor sex life across the planet are doing these things:

1. They spend very little time together during a typical week
2. They become job-centered (often him) and child-centered (often her)
3. They talk primarily about their to-do lists
4. They seem to make everything besides their relationship a priority
5. They drift apart and live parallel lives
6. They are not intentional about turning toward one another for love and understanding

As you review this information, I want you to compare your relationship with what is found on these lists. Do not compare your relationship with others you may personally know or those you see on various media platforms. Comparing your sex life with others is never constructive. I repeat, comparing your sex life with others is never constructive. It is harmful! The only sex you need to focus on is your own sex life. "Normal" is whatever feels fulfilling for you and your spouse. In large part, your ability to communicate plays a key role in making sure both of you feel fulfilled. As you compare yourself to the list above, make clear goals to do the things that research suggests will lead to a fulfilling and passionate sex life.

Sexual desire and frequency do not need to create contention and dissatisfaction in your marriage. With your spouse, work through this chapter to identify your desire frameworks, the sexual possibilities you share, and your sexual commonalities. Instigate the steps that research has found in sexually satisfying marriages; remember, avoid comparing your sex life with others. As you do this important work together, you will find your sexual desire for one another can increase naturally.

THINK. How does your relationship stack up with the lists above? What is missing? What can you do to experience more sexual desire in your marriage? Make sure to understand the differences between spontaneous, responsive, and contextual desire. Journal how this knowledge helps you better understand yourself and your relationship with your spouse. How can this chapter help you address persistent sexual conflicts?

PAIR. This might be a longer conversation, so create plenty of time to have this discussion. Connect with non-demanding touch. Close your eyes and breathe deeply together for ten minutes. When ready, open your eyes and get started.

SHARE. Discuss what you learned in this chapter. Listen to understand as you share your thoughts from the THINK portion of this assignment. Openly discuss how this information can reduce the frequency and intensity of the sexual conflict you experience in your marriage.

Adding to your Sexual Playbook: Write down what each of your sexual desire frameworks are, taking time to consider contexts that increase or detract from your sexual desire. Then, write down some of your sexual commonalities.

Experiential Activities to Enjoy

Create a Code

With the information you shared together, discuss a plan of action you both agree to use when experiencing the differences in your sexual desire. Perhaps you can create a code word or signal that will quickly inform your spouse of your level of desire. For example, cupping your hand into the shape of the letter "W," while intentionally making eye-contact, could mean, "You doing the Water chores (dishes, bathe the baby, laundry, clean) would help!" Often when couples implement unique relationship codes and nicknames, it can create a practical playfulness that diffuses tensions.

Her Arousal

As a woman, understanding what you find sexually arousing is important information for you to have. All too often I have women say, "Tammy, nothing is arousing anymore!" If that is how you feel, I encourage you to slow down, consciously think of things that your husband does that you really admire, appreciate, and find helpful. Consider how he looks to you. What, specifically, do you find that is particularly attractive or sexy? Are there ways that he touches you that feel reassuring and comfortable? As you think of these things, make a list to remember them. Share this list with your husband. Let him understand the specific, true, and positive (STP) ways that you see him.

His Arousal

Same as above, only the husband is making the list.

Non-Demand, No Clothes Cuddling

At the end of the day, once the house is quiet, come to bed naked. There will be no sex tonight. This experience is for you to emotionally connect. This is a great opportunity for one spouse to let it all out. As you cuddle, the husband asks the wife (then the next day the wife asks the husband) the following types of questions while non-defensively listening to understand:

- What went right today?
- What did not go right today?
- Tell me about work?
- What's happening with _________ (child's name) today?
- How can I be a better spouse to you?
- Is there anything particular you were worried about today?
- Share with me something you were really proud of today/this week.
- Your birthday (or any holiday) is coming up. What would you like?

As you listen to your spouse, think warm and loving thoughts about him/her. Let the conversation go as long as necessary. For some individuals, this can be an opportune time to cry and get reassurance. Don't rush this process. What are some STP (specific, true, and positive) things you could share once he/she is done talking?

CHAPTER 9

Friendship, Consent and Sex

An overarching principle in sex therapy is to *begin* with the relationship. If your sexual relationship is not what you want it to be, I encourage you to assess the friendship you experience with your spouse. Do you know each other's dreams? Are you a trustworthy spouse? Are you aware of his/her needs and wants? When was the last time you really talked and laughed together? How often do you ask your spouse what you can do for him/her? How often do you actually do what is wanted? These are the types of questions and considerations that need to be processed before you start complaining about your sex life.

Please spend a few minutes looking over the image on the next page that was formulated by my colleague, Dr. Jason Carroll, in his textbook entitled, *The Marriage Compass.** There is a lot of information to glean as you study this graphic. See if you can answer the following questions as you review "The Sexual Response Cycle." As you look over this, note how the "Roots" and the "Fruits" correlate with the image of the Ecology of Marriage Tree in *Chapter 7: Understanding your Sexual Soil.*

- What do the roots and fruits represent in marriage?
- What is the relationship between a loving, friendship-founded marriage and a couple's ability to sexually replenish?

* This is the book I use to teach Marriage Preparation courses at BYU. I highly recommend this book for solid doctrinal-based and research-based information regarding the divine institution of marriage.

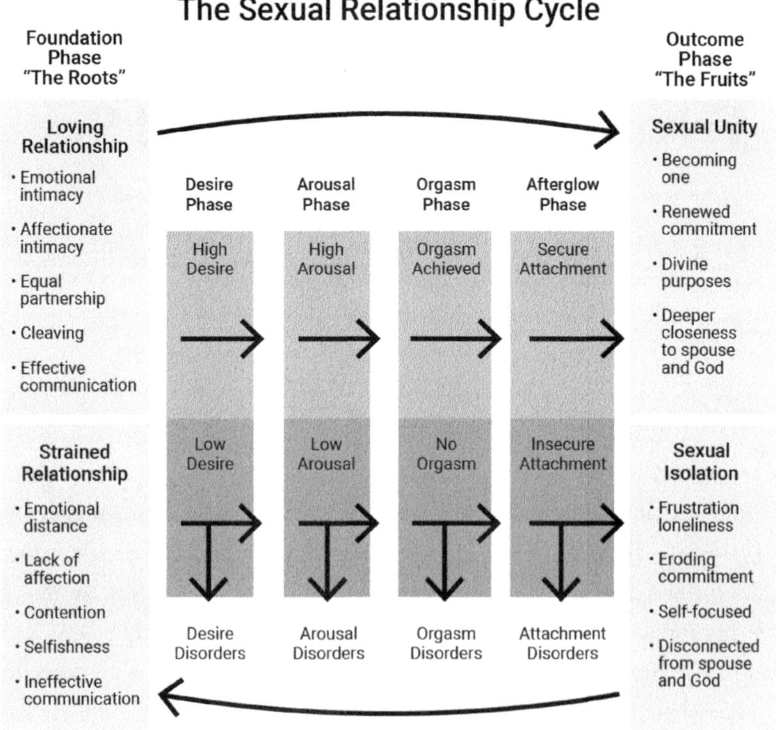

- What is the relationship between a strained relationship and a couple's ability to sexuality replenish?
- In what type of marriage is there more likelihood for sexual dysfunction?
- What characteristics of the relationship contribute to sexual fulfillment?
- What is the ultimate message represented in this graphic?

As a couple improves the friendliness within their relationship, their sexual relationship will also improve. Dr. Blaine Fowers's research on friendships and marriage relationships found that *character friendships* are best suited for marriage. These relationships are enduring because they involve deep commitment, forgiveness, sacrifice, and a dedication to the well-being of the other. Individuals in these types of marriages experience more emotional satisfaction and more meaningful sexual intimacy.[21]

Trustworthiness is an essential aspect of abiding friendships. According to Dr. John Gottman, trust is absolutely central to the success or failure of a relationship. Even if infidelity has not been part of the story, distrust is at the core of every failed relationship. Avoiding difficult conversations and not being fully transparent contributes to a gradual pattern of emotional distancing and distrust. This is one of the key purposes for the THINK PAIR SHARE content of this book! Hopefully it will encourage challenging conversations that might otherwise not be shared. Emotional connection builds mutual trust.[22]

Because of my experience as a therapist, I believe it is necessary to include a conversation on friendship and consent. Occasionally, I will meet with a couple where friendship is difficult to observe. Upon assessing the safety of both individuals, I have discovered that there are times when mutual consent is not occurring within the marriage. Friendship includes mutual respect and consent in decision-making, as well as sexual or physical aspects of the relationship. In healthy relationships, couples work together to help one another become their best individual selves while contributing constructively to the marriage. Unfortunately, for some people there is the misconception that marriage is equivalent to sexual consent. This is absolutely false! Manipulation, by implying one has a duty required to perform sexually for a spouse, is nonconsensual. Although it is the least often reported sexual assault crime, marital rape is, indeed, still considered rape. I believe that until a woman is inviting her husband into her body, a man has no business pushing himself upon her. When the boundaries of consent are broken in a marriage, trust and respect declines, and mental health deteriorates.

Anytime a spouse uses intimacy as a form of power, whether it's withholding or demanding, unequal partnership is occurring. Here are some steps to help couples who are learning to communicate more openly about consent. In any relationship, including marriage, consent is *clear*, *continuous*, *coherent*, and *freely given*.

- **Clear**: Silence, or the absence of a "no," is not consent. No sexual activity should take place without the clear indication of a "yes," whether that be verbal or through body language. "I don't know" means *no*!
- **Continuous**: Consent is needed before every sexual act transpires.

If a person gives consent once, that doesn't establish consent for the future. At any time during a sexual exchange, consent can be withdrawn.

- **Coherent**: Both people must be conscious and capable of giving consent. If someone is sleeping or incapacitated in any way, they are not capable of resisting or giving consent.
- **Freely given**: Consent should be communicated freely. Incessantly pressuring someone to engage in sexual activity until they agree is not consent. Also, if someone agrees to engage in sexual activity under threats, duress or force, it is not consent.[23]

You may still be wondering why I'm including this chapter in the book. Believe it or not, it wasn't until 1993 that every state in the United States of America recognized marital rape. Until then, the rape laws in many states included an exception if the rapist and the victim were husband and wife. Seems barbaric. And yet, in my tiny practice in Utah, this has been a situation that frequently presents in couples' therapy. Being married does not equal consent.

If there is not love, compassion, respect, and mutual consent in your relationship, I suggest that you don't really have a relationship, certainly not a healthy marriage. Please get help! There is no shame in reaching out for support and assistance as you create safety; some helpful resources are included below.

Resources:

Rape, Abuse & Incest National Network - https://www.rainn.org/resources

National Rape Hotline: 1-800-656-HOPE (4673). Available 24/7 in both phone and online chat options.

National Domestic Violence Hotline: 1-800-799-7233. Available 24/7 in English, Spanish, and 200+ additional languages through interpretation services.

THINK. What are some of the thoughts and feelings that you have experienced while reading this chapter? How is the friendship in your marriage? Do you feel that there is mutual respect and consent in your relationship? Are there power struggles between the two of you as you discuss having or not having sex?

PAIR. Find a safe and private place to connect for several minutes before talking.

SHARE. Listen to understand your spouse's feelings about friendship, consent, and sex. How do these three interact within your marriage? Does the husband wait to be invited into his wife's body? What changes need to be made?

Adding to your Sexual Playbook: Write down what consent does and does not look like in your marriage, providing examples for how it will be clear, continuous, coherent, and freely given. Write down some specific goals for improving the friendship in your relationship.

Experiential Activities to Enjoy

Bedtime Rituals

Discuss what bedtime rituals you would like to incorporate into your marriage. Here are some ideas that research shows contribute to healthy marital friendship:

- Leave your phones outside of the bedroom.
- Cuddle and talk before going to sleep.
- Pray and express gratitude for one another before getting into bed.
- If watching television, decide what to watch together and lay close together while watching.
- Clean up the kitchen and bedroom before going to bed.
- Keep work-related conversations and devices outside of the bedroom.

- Cook and eat dinner together before going to bed.
- Go to bed at the same time.
- Alternate giving nightly massages before going to bed.

Jointly agree to create a bedtime ritual. Help each other follow through on doing the ritual.

Read a Book Together

Choose a book that you both want to read. Each day, spend 10-15 minutes reading and discussing what you're learning. This can be any type of book that interests you. On my website (www.tammyhill.com) under the resource tab, I have a number of books on marriage and sexuality that I highly recommend.

Listen to a Podcast Together

Agree on a podcast from which you both want to learn. Listen to the podcast (together or on your own time) and set aside a specific time for discussing your thoughts on the podcast. I host the Live Your Why podcast where many of my conversations involve information about healthy romantic relationships and marital sexuality.

CHAPTER 10

Body Image and Sexuality

As a professor in the School of Family Life at Brigham Young University, I have had countless one-on-one conversations with students about sex. Young men, young women, middle-aged students, married, and single students alike have all asked about body image and the impact it has on sexual desire, arousal, and ability to climax. In a world that not only places an emphasis on beauty, but also has a narrow scope of what is considered beautiful, you can easily guess why this would be a common concern for so many of us.

Body image includes both how you feel about your body and how you think others see you physically. Some of you feel very good about your bodies, and some of you don't. How you feel about your body, and what you actually look like, are not usually the same. Body image is part of your sexuality because the way you see your body has a big influence on the day-to-day decisions you make. Research indicates that people with poor body image make unhealthy sexual decisions more frequently than people who feel good about their bodies. In marital relationships, people with poor body image typically have a more difficult time experiencing sexual desire, arousal, and orgasm. Another interesting fact is when people dislike their bodies, they are more likely to neglect their physical and mental health. This, in turn, negatively affects their ability to truly love and care for others. It's so important to understand that bodies and minds are not two separate entities; they are intrinsically connected. You cannot neglect your body, or think poorly about your body, and expect to fully function.[24]

Body image is a cause for concern especially among females—not just women, but females of all ages. Studies suggest that dieting begins for many children before the onset of puberty. In the United States, dieting, weight concerns, and body dissatisfaction have all been reported in children between 7 to 9 years of age. These reports are more common among girls than boys, with approximately 40% of elementary school-aged girls reporting that they have tried dieting to lose weight. With the influence of mass media, trending fashions, Barbie dolls, and female characters in Disney's fairy tales being front-and-center in many women's lives, the pressure to conform to an ideal feminine beauty starts at a young age. According to marriage researcher John Gottman, in the Western world, by the time a woman is 60 years old, she will have viewed nearly 6 million media messages that describe ideal feminine beauty.[25] Handling the pressure to conform to a certain definition of "beautiful" can have serious psychological effects, such as disordered eating, body dysmorphia, hypergymnasia, depression, and low self-esteem.[26]

These societal pressures don't need to prevent us from working toward a healthy body image or a healthy sex life. As a woman learns to accept her body as an instrument, rather than an ornament, and begins to express her needs and desires to her partner, her ability to wholeheartedly show up in her life, and more specifically in the bedroom, will exponentially increase. Studies clearly show that there are many sexual benefits for women who feel good about their bodies. From an interest in initiating sex, to having more frequent orgasms, to experiencing greater comfort undressing in front of a partner, to being more willing to have sex with the lights on and trying new sexual behaviors, women who feel good about their bodies are doing much better sexually in long-term, committed relationships than women who have poor body images.[27]

For men, be aware that few things hurt a woman more than criticisms of the way she looks. Your wife will feel more beautiful if she knows that you only have eyes for her; a woman's sexual desire is largely dependent on her feeling desirable. Let her know that she is beautiful just the way she is, give sincere compliments, and show her your love in ways that matter to her. In your sphere of influence, do all that you can to change the message that a woman's value is connected to her attractiveness. Recognize that for a woman to feel confident sharing her sexuality, both her mind and heart need to feel secure with the relationship. How you choose to care for your wife's happiness will directly correlate with your sexual and relational satisfaction.

Boys and men are also impacted with body image issues. Recent research suggests that 75% of adolescent boys are dissatisfied with their bodies. Males also make up one-fourth of disordered eating patients. It's clear that body image is more than just a feminine problem; masculinity is also mixed in with the plethora of media messages about bodies. While negative body image issues are not gender specific, seeking help for addressing this issue largely is, as males are much more likely to suffer in silence.[28] Recognizing that a man also wants to feel confident sharing his body sexually, a wife can express sexual satisfaction and pleasure from seeing, touching, and tasting her husband's body. Negative attitudes toward genitals also directly influences sexual dissatisfaction.[29]

Along with the many personal and societal pressures that contribute to struggles with body image, it is essential to acknowledge the damaging role pornography can play. Pornography is one of the invasive tactics of the adversary that can send us spiraling downward when we combine the body-image sensitivities of one partner with the (past or present) pornography viewing habits of the other. It is not good—not good at all! Believe it or not, habitual viewing of pornography is rarely about sex, yet in my work with couples striving to rebuild trust after betrayal, there is nothing as pervasively negative than pornography use in romantic relationships. Combine pornography with the ocean of societal messages on body image that we are swimming in, and it can be very difficult to feel safe getting naked. Does body image impact sexuality? Yes. Does body image impact sexuality in a pornographic world? Absolutely, yes! Many of us are spiraling into marital conflict either rooted in body-shame or shame from sin. Shame keeps us stuck. In my personal experience as a therapist, I have never seen individuals and couples successfully move past this shame without the enabling power of Jesus Christ.

Privately ask yourself the following questions and answer them *honestly*:

- In your life, are there situations you avoid because of the way you feel about your body?
- Do you limit your activities because you fear how others might negatively perceive your appearance?
- Do you avoid having pictures taken regularly because of your appearance?
- How do you react to being in front of a mirror?
- Can you honestly describe ten things that you love about your body?
- Have you thanked God for your body today?
- In your marriage, do you let yourself be seen naked by your spouse?
- Do you make love with the lights on?
- Are you posing in ways to show your best features for your spouse when you're making love?
- Is the negative self-talk about your body cluttering your mind while you're together romantically?
- Can you relax into giving and receiving pleasure?
- Does your body bring you joy?

I encourage you to share your responses with your spouse. This will be a very vulnerable and perhaps, somewhat painful, conversation. However, as you show up more fully in this process, more healing will take place for you individually and within your relationship. Please don't pass over this opportunity to "get naked" about your body.

Self-love, awareness of divine worth, and the importance of understanding true identity are all at the heart of this book. I desperately want you to recognize some important truths that I've learned throughout my life's journey. Your spirit is matter. It has lived forever and it is who you really are. Your spirit is you.

In 2002, I experienced, in a deeply personal way, the profound difference between a body and a spirit. I went to the emergency room at Dixie Regional Medical Center in St. George, Utah after receiving a telephone call that there was something wrong with my husband, Mark Mulford. Upon my arrival, I could tell that whatever was wrong with Mark, it was very serious. I was taken to a small room where a man, I believe a hospital psychologist, told me that Mark had suffered a major heart-attack and was being worked on and that it didn't look good. I only remember a few things from that night, as I'm sure I was in shock. I remember my oldest child, Jordan, being a rock by my side the whole time. I cried like a wounded animal (I can still hear this sound in my head. It haunts me). I asked Jordan, "What are we going to do?" He looked at me and said, "We are going to do this one-day at a time."

I also remember clearly being with Mark's body after I was told that he was dead. I stood there, looking over my husband's perfectly beautiful body, knowing that Mark was not there. His body was a shell for the greater substance, his spirit. It was his spirit that made him Mark. It was his spirit that gave him personality, elasticity, and substance. Who I loved, who I married, who I made covenants with and brought children into this world with was Mark's spirit; his body just happened to be there too. The body can never go anywhere without the spirit. Mark's body wasn't Mark, it was the house that Mark lived in.

My friends, your body isn't you either. Your spirit is the matter that makes your eternal identity as a beloved son or daughter of Heavenly Parents. They know you, dearly love you, and want you Home.

For 28-years straight, I served in my church congregation's primary organization teaching children. From serving as president to music chorister, then nursery leader and back to president, primary was my religious domain. Whenever I would ask the children why they came to earth, their answer was, "To get a body!" Which is absolutely true. We are here on earth to get a body and to become more like our Heavenly Parents by loving and caring for one another.

The great plan of happiness necessitates physical bodies in mortality. Our time on earth is just a slice of all eternity! My friends, you and I, all of us, have waited eons of time to finally come to earth and experience life in a body. How is it going, with your spirit inside of your body? Are you working together or are you at war with one another? I promise you, integrating your spirit and body to work in harmony with one another will make everything so much better. Don't give your power of personal wholeness over to social media trends, ruminating thoughts of inadequacy, incessant comparisons, or fears of being seen. Bring your body and spirit together in a warm, accepting, and grateful embrace. You are beautifully enough, just how you are right now. Hold on to you. You are love—conceived in love, and filled with eternal love. Remember who you are.

If you're wondering how to integrate body and spirit more fully, I have a few suggestions that might help:

- Spiritually connect yourself through deep pondering, study, and prayer. This is an ongoing process that should not be ignored. I appreciate the meaningful way that Brian K. Taylor suggested that we understand our true identity in his talk, "Am I a Child of God?"[30] His suggestion to say aloud the phrase, "I am a child of God" ten times each day, is something that I practice most days, although I have tweaked it a little. In the mornings, ten times I will say aloud, "I am a daughter of Heavenly Parents who love me." I place an emphasis on each word, pause and think about what the emphasized word means to me each day. This practice has changed my life! There are moments when I feel the truthfulness to this phrase. Give it a try!
- It's so important to be aware of the negative messages you have internalized about your body and your sexuality, and to recognize that they are not true. When a negative thought comes to your mind, acknowledge it, and let it go. Choose to let go of negative self-talk. The best book that I know in helping with distorted thinking is written by my good friend, Jody Moore, called, *Better Than Happy*. Indeed, reading and practicing the truths found in this book will help you on your journey to creating personal happiness.[31]
- Do things with your body that help you feel happy every day. Real things that give you energy, like playing pickleball, hiking, swimming, painting, dancing, singing, quilting or playing a musical instrument. One of the ways that we physically connect with our spirits is by practicing our inherent talents or gifts. Read your patriarchal blessing to find some of those for you personally. I also encourage individuals to take the Authentic Happiness Questionnaire (VIA characteristics for adults)[32] where you can identify your natural virtues and then start living them. You have to move and do things to create connected happiness with your body and spirit. Make this a priority in your life, and you will feel the change.

- Take regular breaks from movies, social media or friends that motivate comparisons. Put a clear boundary around your time limits with activities or people who drag you down.

The need to combat the overwhelming negative societal messages about bodies is imperative. Identity and personal value don't come from the way a person looks; they come from who a person is and who a person is becoming. I highly recommend couples and families read *More Than a Body: Your Body Is an Instrument, Not an Ornament* by Drs. Lexie and Lindsay Kite. Understanding and applying the principles found in this book will help create a healthy body image, allowing you and your family to thrive.

I've included several specific ideas to ponder, activities to engage in, and books to read throughout this chapter. I urge you to take the time to review these and complete them. I have also included some additional ideas to THINK about and SHARE with your spouse, along with a couple additional experiential activities. Take your time in thoughtfully completing these! Accepting and appreciating your body is essential to your happiness both in and out of the bedroom.

THINK. Take some time to think about and write down truths about yourself and your body. Use these truths to combat negative self-talk that can sabotage your progress. Next, think of things you can do to better show your appreciation for your body. How can you better take care of your body? Make a goal of one thing to do this week to show your body appreciation (e.g., eat healthy, drink plenty of water, get sunshine and exercise, get enough sleep, tell your body thank you for all that it does, etc.). Finally, write down five things you like about your body. These things can relate to either appearance or what you are able to do with your body. Write down five things you like about your partner's body.

PAIR. Take some time to bond and connect with each other.

SHARE. Share with your partner the things you wrote down. Tell them both about the specific things you like about your own body, as well as what you specifically like about their body! In sharing, do NOT doubt what your spouse says about you! Ladies, when your husband tells you that you are beautiful and that he likes your curves, he's being honest. He wants you to feel his love and acceptance when you are together, both in and out of the bedroom. The one sexual experience a husband is most consistently aroused by is the ability to please his wife. It is not your breast size, not the shape of your butt, not the length of your legs that is most arousing to him. *It is giving you sexual pleasure!*

Adding to your Sexual Playbook: Together, write down some ways you will help each other better love and appreciate your bodies. How will you go to your spouse to let them know when you're struggling with body image issues? What will you do when negative comparisons enter your or your spouse's thoughts? How will each of you graciously accept your spouse's compliments?

Experiential Activities to Enjoy

Body and Spirit Integration

In a full-length mirror, reverently and appreciatively look at your naked body. Take your time as you do this. In your mind, reflect on the many things that each part of your body has done for you throughout your lifetime. As you do so, thank that part of your body. For example, as I examine my belly, stretchmarks and girth, I look for beauty in the functioning this part of my body provided me. Specifically, I think of the opportunities I had to create and carry the lives of my children. Another example would be the 6"-7" vertical scar from my navel to pubic bone where I had colon resection surgery. I reverently thank my body for being able to assimilate nutrients and dispose of waste.

Touch your hands on each body part as you thank it for being part of your life story.

Once you have finished, close your eyes and breathe into a heartfelt prayer of gratitude for the body you have. For the experiences you have had (both good and difficult) as an embodied spirit. After your prayer, pause. Warmly hug yourself.

Do this as many times as is necessary for you to continue to integrate your spirit and body in praise and gratitude.

Lingerie

Find lingerie of your choice. Put it on and stand in front of a full-length mirror.

Observe your curves, your shape, your beauty.

Wear this lingerie underneath regular clothing and surprise your spouse when you undress.

Share the thoughts and feelings you have experienced while wearing the lingerie with your spouse. Listen to what his/her experience was in watching you undress and wearing the lingerie.

Before moving on to other activities, hold one another and express gratitude for your bodies.

CHAPTER 11

Sexual Awareness and Sexual Restraint

Standing in line at the grocery store, it is not uncommon to find magazine covers that advertise things such as "16 Ways to Spice Up Your Sex Life" or "How to Give Her Wild Screaming Orgasms." These articles entice readers to experiment with techniques to improve their sex life, rather than focusing on relationships. The top-selling sector in the US book market is romance/erotica. These books have readers escaping into sexual fantasies and heightening sexual arousal but are not fulfilling the root relational desire to be truly known intimately. Sexual self-help books are also very popular as people look for new ideas to enhance their lovemaking experiences. Relatedly, seeking information on how to perform various sex acts is an ever-increasing website search request. It seems everyone wants to know how to be the perfect lover or to have the hottest sex. Can I tell you a secret? The best way to improve your sex life is to know yourself and to change yourself so that you can better be in a relationship with your spouse! In my work as a therapist, teacher, mother and, most importantly, wife, I have come to truly believe that self-awareness and self-restraint are the greatest tools, techniques, and experiments we can use to become better lovers.

Self-awareness

Self-awareness is a clear understanding of your personality, including strengths, weaknesses, tendencies, beliefs, motivations, and emotions. It is best found by looking at yourself objectively. I believe that being self-aware is much like having personal integrity. Integrity evolved from the Latin adjective *integer*, which means being whole or complete. Realize that your desire to truly sexually connect will require you to become increasingly integrated and self-aware. The following suggestions can help you become more self-aware, in body and in spirit. The process can be humbling, even painful, but will truly assist you in becoming someone you not only love, but also really like!

1. **Put your spirit first**. Remember everything (including all of us) was spiritually created before it was physically created. I have found that spiritually "creating" myself prior to actually living my day strengthens my resolve to purposefully live. Try it! Begin each day by spiritually creating yourself for the upcoming day. Reflect on your responsibilities, self-care plans, and the interactions you may have (especially those relationally challenging interactions). Talk about your spiritual creation in your morning prayer, and ask for strength to live with integrity. As you go through the day, remember your plans, and try to be consistent with them. At the end of the day, report back to God. Tell Him things you're proud of, tell Him things you could have done differently, and pause to listen to Him. This personal creating and living with integrity will bring you great personal satisfaction and happiness.
2. **Journal**. Keep a journal of your progress. It doesn't need to be lengthy, just a line or two or even a number (1-10) scaling your ability to self-reflect.
3. **Listen and learn**. Ask your spouse or trusted friends to describe your strengths and areas where you can improve. This feedback can come from every realm. How are you at work? In your marriage? As a parent? A minister? A disciple of Jesus Christ? These conversations can be enlightening. When done in love, with the

intent to improve yourself by becoming more self-aware, you will grow as a person.

Self-restraint

Self-restraint is our ability to prevent ourselves from doing or saying the harmful things that come naturally to us when we are triggered. We must learn to channel our energy and contain our impulses as we interact, especially in marriage and family life. Initially this will feel like we are exerting extreme self-control by not reacting in the moment. It may seem to require super-human strength! I have found, with time, the implementation of self-control can become easier, especially as my desire to do what is best for another or in a situation becomes more important. I'm not suggesting that you lose your voice in a relationship or certain situations, but rather that your voice become more rational and generous, leading to connection and productivity.

Self-restraint indicates personal strength and character—it brings out what is best in an individual and in their relationships. Demonstrating self-respect by controlling our natural impulses leads to healthy and successful marriages where sexual expression is safe, judgment free, and replenishing. Utilizing the suggestions regarding the development of self-awareness will foster living with greater integrity and love. Many marriage experts have a variety of effective communication tools; recall John Gottman's ATTUNEment process explained in *Chapter 6: Sexual Decision Making as Equal Partners*. These tools do not work without self-restraint!

Truly Listen to Understand

According to marriage researcher, John Gottman, what spouses really want from one another is to be understood. Focusing our attention on what our partner is saying, rather than defending our position, is essential for couples to build a validating, friendly marriage. Often listening to understand requires trying to hear what is underneath the statement. I am going to share an example of a recent argument Jeff and I had when we were both exhausted and stressed (not the best time to resolve things); see if you can "hear" what is underneath both of our words and actions as you "listen" to understand.

> *We had been home a few days from an extended European trip and both of us had mounting career-related responsibilities due to our absence. On top of that, we had college-aged children moving back home for the summer, and we discovered that one of our large freezers had stopped working while we were gone. The first two days at home we balanced our work responsibilities equitably, but the work of the home and family had largely landed on my shoulders. I spent hours cleaning the freezer, more hours on a substantial grocery shopping trip and more hours cooking for our children who had come back home. The third day after our return, we were driving to the gym when I realized that two of our front yard sprinklers were not working. I knew that Jeff had another full day of work at the office, along with a fun game of golf scheduled with friends that evening. I had planned to work from home to get through the pile-up from my teaching assignment. I also had planned to do an activity with the kids at home. Despite all my training and knowledge, I began my rant with, "I know you're going to get defensive, but I wish I could golf today! You have the luxury of going to the office and focusing while I'm home doing everything and trying to get my work done!" Indeed, he did get defensive and within seconds we were arguing, our amygdalas (often referred to as "the reptilian brain") taking over, saying hurtful and untrue things to each other. He left angrily, slamming his golf clubs in the car. I fumed and slammed dishes while making breakfast. We both had a sad, hard day. We made repairs later that evening.*

What did you hear/understand? What is the message each person is trying to have their spouse understand? Jeff felt attacked and unappreciated. I felt overwhelmed and was asking for help. Neither of us listened to understand the other.

Always Make Repairs

After we demonstrate a lack of self-restraint, it is so important to repair the relationship. John Gottman's research says that "the success or failure of a couple's repair attempts is one of the primary factors in whether a marriage is likely to flourish or flounder. It is the secret of emotionally intelligent couples."[33] Repairs can be actions, but should include communication, that take down the wall and open the bridge to a relationship. They include self-reflection and sincere apologies. Coming to an understanding of what is needed does not mean you have to agree; it means you understand where your spouse is coming from. Repairs often involve touch, a hug or kiss, to help with reconnecting.

One easy way to make repairs is to ask the person you are in a disagreement with (while making the repair), "What grade would you give my earlier interaction?" Then listen. Listen to the other side of the conflict and process together how you would respond in the future to a similar situation. For the experience I shared previously, Jeff gave me an F, and I gave him an F minus! Leaving an argument unresolved negatively affects attachment. Every one of us is divinely designed to want to romantically connect. If you are truly wanting to become a great lover in your marriage, it is essential that you make repairs, reconnect, and attach as a couple. Repair. Attach. Repair. *Attach.*

Know When to Take a Break

Learn to recognize when you are approaching the "point of no return!" When you are triggered and the argument is escalating, choose to stop! Push that big red stop sign in your mind and stop! Remove yourself from the situation and let your partner know that you will be back when you have cooled down. Brain science suggests that it takes at least 20 minutes for an amygdala takeover (not thinking rationally) to resolve. For some people it takes longer. Create space for yourself. Get your heart rate up, breathe deeply, or drink ice-cold water. Go for a run or a walk. A combination of these will help force the blood flow from the amygdala to the prefrontal cortex, where you can cognitively and rationally process the argument and your behavior. You will never change the other person;

you can only change you. As you cool down, ponder your own behaviors and beliefs. What do you really want your partner to understand and hear from you? Why do you need your spouse to understand this? When both of you are in a space where you can talk, make repairs and attach. Don't allow yourself to pass the point of no return—it will always lead to regret.

How Self-awareness and Self-restraint Lead to Change

As you incorporate more self-awareness and self-restraint into living consciously, you begin to change. You become increasingly aware that your spirits can, and must, rule over your body. President David O. McKay once said, "True spirituality is victory over self." True sexual connection and replenishment are achieved as you strive to live with integrity. In so doing, you become like our Heavenly Parents.

As you become more centered in behaving in ways that are congruent with who you want to become, you grow more sensitive to your spirit. Remember, the body and spirit make up the soul of man. You have been enculturated to believe that everything of importance happens outside of the body, when in actuality, your body is the home of your intelligence, divinity, creativity, and potential. What makes you so marvelous is what's on the inside. How often do you pause to listen to what's inside of you? Not just the messages coming from your brain, which are often unfairly negative, but to the *truth* of who you are which is felt most richly in the heart? Pause and consider the following ideas:

1. **Speaking prevents you from feeling in the moment.** I've heard that speaking is a bad habit, possibly even a disease. Experiment with *not* talking. Be creative in learning how to communicate with your spouse in loving ways that do *not* include speaking! After a few hours, inwardly reflect on your personal learning from this experience. Share with your spouse what you learned about yourself. Listen to what he/she learned. This can become a delicate and playful way to tune into your spirit and let it take the lead as you lovingly touch and reverence one another.
2. **Focusing on your spirit is nourishing.** Focusing on what your spirit is trying to say could possibly be viewed as selfish, but I

believe it is a way you can nourish yourself. As you give your spirit attention, you provide opportunities for it to find a voice, to grow, and expand. You will recognize greater personal worth and acceptance. You will begin to know who you really are and *Whose* you really are.

3. **Dancing is a fun way for your body to connect more fully with your spirit.** Turn on some fun music (without lyrics), center yourself inside of your body and let your spirit take the lead with movement. In the beginning, this may feel strange and uncomfortable. Don't let that message from your brain stop you from connecting more fully with your spirit. Allow for 15 minutes of playful movement, eyes closed, focused on how you are feeling inside of yourself. (As I start feeling free, my mind will see sparkling lights flashing, and naturally a smile will come to my lips. It has become a highly connecting experience for me with myself. It feels like I am pouring energy into my soul.) Try it daily for a week. See if you notice a change.

As a culture we are always so busy "doing" that we often miss the sense of "being." This happens when we act with our bodies without turning our attention inward, preventing our spirits from fully participating. Integration, or living with body and spirit integrity, occurs as we acknowledge the greatness of who we are. This integrated self-awareness allows one to recognize the spiritual and physical beauty of self and spouse. In marriage, when spirits and bodies consciously make love together, energy will expand in divinely designed ways—Godlike capacities.

THINK. As you have read about the described ideas for connecting your body and spirit for sexual arousal, what thoughts did you have? What is the difference between *doing* and *being* love? Write about any times that you can recall feeling connected in the way described in this chapter. When have you been sexually aware? When have you demonstrated sexual restraint?

PAIR. In a space that is private and comfortable for both of you, hold hands and breathe deeply. Listen to some of your favorite, relaxing music as you decompress together. Hold each other close. Give yourselves over to connecting by being together.

SHARE. Taking turns, share times that you have experienced this deep spirit to body type of love. Try to recall the experiences your spouse describes. Discuss your thoughts on sexual awareness and sexual restraint.

Adding to your Sexual Playbook: Together, decide on and document the ways you will help each other become more self-aware; only write down things you are truly ready to commit to doing! Then, create a plan for how each of you will express sexual restraint in your marriage.

Experiential Activities to Enjoy

Sensual Playlist

Take turns playing songs that create sexual awareness for you. These songs increase your desire and awareness in wanting to touch and be touched. Create an iTunes or Spotify playlist with all your favorite songs. Now you'll have a sexy playlist that you can return to over and over again!

If you like to dance, try having a dance party to your playlist. To further increase awareness, put on something sexy while you dance. Watch yourselves dance in a mirror together. This activity does not need to move into having sex. The intention is to create a greater awareness of your sexual desire and to prolong that desire by practicing sexual restraint.

Awareness and Restraint

This activity involves cutting off two of your senses! Whenever you cut off one of your senses, it heightens your remaining senses. Cutting off two senses makes the experience that much more intense. If there are certain parts of your body you don't want touched, let your partner know beforehand. Husband, blindfold your wife and have her insert a pair of soft foam earplugs or put on headphones. Next, spend fifteen minutes touching and kissing your wife. Not being able to see or hear what's coming next is incredibly erotic. You will find that even the simplest touches feel much more intense. After fifteen minutes, switch places! Bonus—if you are both comfortable, tie your partner's hands together while blindfolded. You can use a silk scarf or tie. Just make sure to tie loose knots or bows.

This activity will increase sexual awareness for both partners, but particularly for the partner who has blocked senses. Sexual restraint is experienced as both of you experience the full 30-minute sensory experiment before moving forward with any genital-to-genital connection.

CHAPTER 12

Sexual Expectations and Becoming Orgasmic

Living in the United States, you can hardly go a day without hearing or seeing something about passion, sex, or the "Big O." With all this hype comes the expectation that most of us are having amazing, head-banging sex, every day of our adult lives! Several years ago, while teaching a Marriage Enhancement course, a young man raised his hand and said, "I'm confused. All my life I was told that sex would be fantastic and totally worth waiting for. My wife and I have been married for a few months. We think sex is actually quite boring. I wonder, what's wrong with us?" With a room full of students, I thanked him for being so brave and vulnerable in sharing his dissatisfaction. I asked the remaining class members to raise their hands if any of them had ever felt similarly. More than half of the students raised their hands. This led to an important discussion about sexual expectations.

Here are some of the expectations offered by my students:

- We would have sex at least once a day.
- Orgasm would come about naturally.
- He/she would know how to sexually touch me.
- We would both be interested in having sex at the same time.
- My mother told me I would hate sex.
- It would only hurt a little the first time.
- Body parts would look different than they actually do.

- He would be aroused and interested in sex all the time.
- Sex would be spontaneous and passionate.

Are any of these similar to expectations you've had? As introduced in *Chapter 7: Understanding Your Sexual Soil,* many of us come into marriage with both idealized sexual hopes as well as some negatively biased expectations too. The most commonly misconstrued sexual expectations are centered in sexual frequency and orgasm. The discrepancies between what we think will happen versus what really does happen are typically the foundation of many sexual problems in marriage. If this is part of your sexual journey, as it is for most of us, a helpful healing exercise is to compare your expectations to your experiences. Talk about these differences with your spouse, and then, together, learn more about the realities of typical married sex. Some of these realities include[34]:

- Only 10-25% of women orgasm with penetration alone.
- Penetration is not necessary for an experience to be loving and sexual.
- Some of the best sex is not spontaneous: rather, it is planned and prepared for.
- Many sexual problems would disappear if we normalized the fact that most sexual encounters start with at least one spouse not feeling interested.
- Communicating about sex while having sex can lead to greater sexual fulfillment.
- Focusing on the quality of the experience supersedes the frequency in which you're having sex.

Throughout my time and experience as a sexual therapist and educator, I have come to believe that normalizing sexual expectations is one of the most straightforward ways to offer sexual hope to a struggling couple. In addition to informing the couple of data regarding what is actually happening sexually in marriages, teaching the difference between having an orgasm and becoming *orgasmic* can be life changing. I teach this process in all my classes at Brigham Young University, in my private counseling practice, as well as in my online and virtual courses. Understanding and practicing this single principle exponentially adds sexual energy and passion into everyday marriages. It revitalizes a couple's life by bringing back much of the positive, sexual energy shared prior to marriage, in the dating and engagement phases of the relationship. If you've ever wondered what happened to your spark, this chapter is for you!

Orgasm is often called the peak of a sexual experience. Through stimulation of nerve endings found in the nipples, penis, clitoris, male and female prostate (G-zone), and anus, sexual energy builds until the body climaxes with a pleasurable, pulsating release of sexual energy. This is followed by a period of deep relaxation and contentment. I give the "Big O" an "A+" because Orgasms feel Amazing! Learning how to give and receive pleasurable orgasms is a wonderful sexual journey that every couple can undertake. As I describe the virtues of becoming orgasmic, just in case you think I don't want you to ever orgasm again, re-read this paragraph. I believe orgasm is a heavenly gift shared with us, mere mortals, to bless us with greater happiness and joy while laboring together on earth.

Did you notice the definition of orgasm included "a release of sexual energy?" Conversely, the process of becoming orgasmic encourages a *retention* of sexual energy. Holding that energy within the body, recycling it throughout the body and creating euphoric feelings of regenerative ascension in the process. Being orgasmic creates more life in a marriage as the erotic energy retention replenishes the couple with more life-giving love. You will discover that this orgasmic journey is often deeply sacred in nature as it transforms from a goal-oriented "doing sex" experience to a timeless, ecstatic "being love" encounter. In many ways, becoming orgasmic is a spiritual state of being what we long for in marriage. Because of sexual conditioning, we "do" sex in a way that often leaves us longing for something more. Our bodies might perform or do sex "right," but our spirits, our whole souls, beg for a connection that feels deeper, more eternal and whole in nature. I fully believe that orgasmic love is the divine, hardwired, intimate knowing that we, as eternal beings created in the image of Eternal Parents, were designed to experience.

So, how do you become orgasmic? Well, like I have said, it's a journey. It doesn't happen overnight. It requires intention, time, and commitment. Sometimes practicing orgasmic love can feel like nothing is happening. I've had clients give up after a few tries, claiming it is just downright boring! Changing a lifelong sexual framework to something so completely different is very challenging. Many of us are doers. We like checklists. We want to know what to do first, second, third, and finally cross the project off the list completely. My mother has told me multiple times that I was born with a checklist in hand, so I'm being honest in telling you, practicing slow sex has been a difficult process of more than a decade for me.

Due to chronic back pain that led to fusion surgery and later foot surgery, I was desperate to learn ways to share lovemaking with my husband that would be less painful for my back, left leg and foot. This, in part, led me to begin an intensive study of tantric sex. Tantric sex includes ancient Hindu and Buddhist sexual meditations, where the goal is healing and the movement of sexual energy, not orgasm (this is distinct and separate from neo-tantric sex, much of which I do not endorse). I don't think it was a coincidence that while visiting Powell's Bookstore on a trip to Portland, I came across *The Heart of Tantric Sex* by Diana Richardson. I read every word and my heart resonated with the message that conscious sex transforms sex into love. I have purchased every book written by Diana, and attended a weeklong Making Love Retreat in Switzerland where she and her partner, Michael, taught couples their approach to tantric lovemaking. I consider Diana not only a colleague, but also a good friend. If you want to begin a journey of practicing more mindful sexuality, I highly recommend the works of Diana Richardson. This will help you discover much more in-depth and articulate information specific to tantric sex. My purpose in this book is to help you recognize and begin to unlock the divine, limitless potential of your sexuality.

Throughout this book, I often interchange the ideas of orgasmic sex, tantric sex, Eastern sex, slow sex, and replenishing sex. Fundamentally, these practices are the same. They focus on slowing down your sexual experiences, being mindful and present, retaining sexual energy, and soulfully *being love* together. If you remember, my recurring and pressing sexual question as a young girl was, "If procreation is a gift from God, shouldn't a couple enjoy it for more than a few minutes?" It has been through much of my slow sex practice that this question was answered. This style of loving incorporates being fully present, bringing your whole self to your lover, consciously experiencing bodily sensations together and finding a transcendent state of unity by being love together. Trust me when I say, there is nothing like it! Once you begin practicing slow sex, the capacity of love you feel, both for yourself and for your spouse, will blossom in beautiful ways that you've never considered. Yoshi, the great Buddhist tantra teacher summed it up perfectly when he said, "If sex is so vital that life comes out of it, then there must be something more to it. That something more is the key towards Divinity."[35]

Countless times, I have witnessed couples transform their sexual relationships by choosing to become more intentional in their lovemaking. As a sex therapist, much of my clientele stems from unmet sexual expectations. By normalizing these unrealistic expectations, and teaching couples how to slow down their sexual experiences, most of my clients find greater love, sexual fulfillment, and connection. They claim the blessings of sexual replenishment, which is a commandment given to us from our Heavenly Parents. Blessings come from obedience, right?!

THINK. Ponder on the idea of becoming orgasmic. Does this make sense to you? How does this idea align with or challenge your sexual expectations? Would you like to experience being orgasmic as a couple? Why or why not?

PAIR. Find a unique place in nature to talk about this chapter. Maybe on a walk or find a hidden bench, rock, or beach to sit on. Breathe and relax. Soak in the beauty of your surroundings as you ground yourself.

SHARE. Discuss your thoughts on becoming orgasmic and how this idea aligns with or challenges your sexual expectations. Formulate a plan of action as you consider becoming orgasmic. Decide on one specific thing you can do to slow down your sexual experiences.

Adding to your Sexual Playbook: Review your sexual playbook; what explicit or implicit sexual expectations have you written? As you've worked through this chapter, would you like to modify any of these expectations? Together, take some time to create new expectations grounded in the research and ideas presented in this chapter.

Experiential Activities to Enjoy

Clarifying your Sexual Expectations

Think about the expectations you had for sex coming into your marriage. List these expectations separate from one another. When you have some time, and are in a good place emotionally within your relationship, share your expectations with one another. Talk about how you developed each specific expectation. Talk about what elements of the expectation you think are rooted in truth, and which you think might be rooted in cultural depictions of sex or other false sources. Take some time to research specific questions you may have. How have these expectations compared to your reality? In what ways have they been disappointing? Better than expected? Totally unrealistic? Discuss how your expectations influence your desire or other elements of your sexual relationship. Be vulnerable and honest as you share these expectations in a friendly way.

Ultimate Massage

This technique is somewhat like an orgasmic meditation. The focus is on receiving love, *not* orgasm. This practice increases love and goodness in the marriage relationship. Couples feel "alive," "young," and "like newlyweds" when practicing this type of lovemaking.

1. Plan for 15 minutes of time together, alone, without interruptions.
2. One partner will stimulate their spouse's genitals.
3. Use a lubricant and a hand—not oral sex.
4. The giver massages pleasurably for 10 minutes.
5. The receiver focuses on receiving pleasure.
6. At 8 minutes, the giver gives a "2 minute" warning.
7. At 10 minutes, the receiver "pulls" the sexual energy inside.

8. Lovingly embrace and kiss. This does NOT lead to sex!
9. Alternate days between giving and receiving.
10. Keep this activity going between you for 6-8 days.
11. Enjoy the goodness of retaining sexual energy. Enjoy the goodness of giving pleasure freely.

Slow Penetration Exercise

- Breathe and feel a consciousness within your genitals. Relax into your penis or vulva. Focus inward, being mindful and aware of your genitals.
- Slow down penetration. Thrusting can be a difficult habit to change; focusing instead on subtle shifts of the penis within the vagina can help. Enter millimeter by millimeter.
- Breathe into the genitals continually relaxing them. Women, focus on opening yourself more fully as you relax your pelvis. Men, focus on relaxing the anus. For men, this often feels like they are making love from the root of the penis. Continually work to release tension from the pelvic floor, breathing into your genitals with an awareness of what they are experiencing.
- In time you will notice the energy exchanged between the penis and the mouth of the uterus, or cervix. You will feel the penis continue to grow as it "snakes" its way further inside of the woman's body. There will be subtle shifts that are worth waiting for as you become orgasmic.
- Making love this way will create a "freshness" in your approach to sexuality, especially as you take the focus away from orgasm as the goal. This type of lovemaking allows for healing, particularly in the vaginal walls.

CHAPTER 13

Having Sex Versus Replenishment

If you're like me in my early years of marriage, you understand that foreplay is the 10-20 minutes of kissing and touching that leads up to intercourse, which is the "main event." It's what you believe men have to do for women to get them "in the mood" for sex, aroused and ready for penetration. I have even heard it called the "outer-play" that leads to inner-play or "intercourse." In all fairness, touching and kissing *do* help create sexual arousal that can lead to having sex. Too often, however, I find the problem with foreplay is that it is short-focused energy by the high-desire partner hoping to claim a future-oriented goal through the low-desire spouse. It begins to resemble a ledger; "I'll kiss and touch you here so that you will kiss and touch me there."

As I work with couples in sex therapy, I've observed that somewhere after the marriage vows are made, touch becomes less about being together in loving, non-demanding ways and more about having sex. This can lead to negative circular dynamics, as seen in the following example:

> *She frequently feels increasingly less sexual desire and begins offering more duty-sex to avoid hurting his feelings. In time, she becomes resentful of having to meet his needs for sex and pulls away from any touch in order to avoid it. He feels increasingly hurt and rejected, becomes resentful of her ability to control their sexual relationship, gets moody, grumpy and is ever on the look-out for any type of touch that could indicate her*

*readiness for sex. In fear that her husband will want to have sex, a wife avoids touching him and pulls away, not wanting to let him get started. Longing for sex, he feels hurt and confused when his wife continually avoids any physical advances.**

As you reflect on this foreplay-for-sex exchange dynamic, it should be apparent that the wholehearted, free-flowing, passionate marriage you have likely always imagined enjoying, cannot be found within this interplay. Growing resentment undermines selfhood, relational trust, and marital replenishment.

However, a marriage need not follow this path. There is a way to interrupt this pattern. Here, I explain three steps to do so:

1. No more self-betrayal
2. Understand the replenishment model
3. Communicate replenishment needs

No More Self-Betrayal

Brené Brown, a great researcher and presenter on vulnerability, has described the benefits of journaling resentments she feels. She humorously calls this writing her *Damn It! Diary*.[36] I encourage you to create your own *Damn It! Diary* or whatever you want to call it. Step back, access your feelings of resentment within your marriage, especially those connected to your sexuality, and journal whatever comes up. It may include thoughts like "I resent that you reject my sexual touches" or "I feel resentful when you only touch me when you want sex." Make a list of these resentful expressions. Do your best to own your feelings of resentment by using I-statements (e.g., "I feel resentful . . ."). This is important because, believe it or not, your feelings of resentment are always rooted in some form of self-betrayal.

As you further analyze each resentful statement, ponder how it's coming from a place where you're not showing up for yourself. Did you say *yes* when what you really felt was *no*? Have you acquiesced rather than engag-

* Recognizing that there are many gendered stereotypes when it comes to sexuality, I used gendered pronouns in this example for brevity. The husband is not always the high-desire partner.

ing in an uncomfortable conversation? Do you point a finger of blame instead of assessing how you failed to speak up for yourself? These are typical ways that all of us self-betray. Normalize the fact that we all, at some point, choose resentment over discomfort. It is much more difficult to value yourself by standing up for your needs than it is to blame your spouse for undervaluing you. In your sexual relationship, choosing to have "duty-sex" instead of talking about your needs in the moment creates resentment. Giving in to performing sexual behaviors you're uncomfortable with in order to prevent conflict is real self-betrayal. Having sex with a spouse that you don't fully trust can also be a way of not showing up for yourself. Choosing to self-betray in the bedroom will always bring resentment and bitterness into your marriage. It is imperative that you show up for you.

Think of ways that you can show up for yourself in the sexual aspect of your marriage. Create time to have these vulnerable conversations with your spouse. Recognize the goodness and strength that comes from choosing discomfort over resentment as you prayerfully and respectfully work together to better understand one another.

Understand the Replenishment Model

In contrast to the exchange model presented at the beginning of this chapter, in the replenishment model, your "foreplay" begins when your current lovemaking experience ends. In other words, as introduced in the previous chapter, you begin focusing on becoming orgasmic rather than focusing on having orgasms, and the lovemaking never really ceases. As you see the truth in this way of living, you will begin to understand the endless possibilities for sexual replenishment in marriage.

There is so much goodness involved in *making love* as compared to *having sex*. In today's vernacular, these phrases are often used interchangeably, yet when you pause and consider the language, doesn't *making love* imply so much more? Lovemaking involves creating goodness, strength, connection, and passion between the two of you. It not only has the possibility of being lifegiving, but it can also generate a transcendent energy that is replenishing to life and relationships.

Consider the ways you make love in your marriage. Remember that there are many ways to make love, and sometimes they include intercourse. Making love must always provide replenishment. Much of the discordance in marriage that comes from differences in sexual desire could be assuaged with a replenishment reframe. As you acknowledge that replenishment involves much more than arousal to orgasm, an awareness of the lovemaking energy you share will abound.

Communicate Replenishment Needs

As you shift from having sex to actively coordinating efforts to replenish the marriage, self-betrayal will diminish along with resentment. There will no longer be the exchange-ledger approach to lovemaking but an overarching goodness that feels free and rejuvenating for both of you. Open and vulnerable communication is essential to this shift. Together, communicate and journal specific ways you can bless your relationship without any strings attached. Remember to continue to use I-statements, as discussed in the section on self-betrayal, and to recognize and reevaluate when you may be choosing resentment over discomfort. Discomfort is a necessary part of growth. As you practice openly communicating your replenishment needs, the comfort you and your spouse experience will increase.

The good energy found in making love adds to the satisfaction, hopefulness, and overall positivity of the relationship. I believe that sexually replenished marriages can become a source of goodness and light to the family, home, community, and world!

THINK. Consider the ideas presented in this chapter. What are you resentful about typically? How do you self-betray? What chapter content areas resonate with you? Are there other areas that you might question? If so, what and why? Journal what you feel is most important for your spouse to understand about you.

PAIR. Come together in a comfortable, neutral place. Get a favorite drink or treat that you can enjoy as you have this conversation.

Once you are both centered and ready, move forward to the sharing.

SHARE. Focus on understanding where your spouse is coming from as you discuss the information from this chapter. What do you both agree about? Are there areas that feel less congruent? If so, can you identify why you feel differently? Are there aspects of this conversation that hearken back to family of origin issues? Continue to process until you feel you can include agreeable ideas to your Sexual Playbook.

Adding to your Sexual Playbook: Write down some specific things you can do together to help move your sexual relationship from an exchange model toward a replenishment model.

Experiential Activities to Enjoy

Likes and Dislikes

It is often uncomfortable to discuss sexual likes and dislikes. These are sensitive conversations that can sometimes go downhill *fast*. Here is a helpful format for discussing your and your spouse's likes and dislikes in a way that fosters understanding. Complete the assessment below individually. At a time when both of you are in a good headspace, share your answers with love and a commitment to understanding each other. The objective of this assessment is not to agree on your sexual experiences, but rather to create a place where you and your spouse feel heard by each other.

1. Overall, my sexual satisfaction is? (1 to 10; 1=very dissatisfied to 10=over-the-moon happy).
2. My satisfaction would increase if I could. . .
3. I would like to contribute to our sex life by. . .
4. I estimate that we have sex _____ times per month.
5. I would like to have sex _____ times per month.
6. I think my spouse would like to have sex _____ times per month.

7. I think I initiate ____ percent of the time.
8. I think my spouse initiates ____ percent of the time.
9. I would like to change our initiation patterns by. . .
10. The activities I enjoy the most in our lovemaking are. . .
11. The activities I think my spouse enjoys most in our lovemaking are. . .
12. If I could wave my magic wand, I would like our sex life to look like. . .

Passion Begins in Her Mind

Recognize that for women, passion begins in the mind. When she feels passionate about something—her work, family, you, exercise, etc.—her body and mind come alive! This is likely the intoxicating feelings you observed in her as you were growing in love. When a woman has positively heightened emotions, she is very capable of experiencing amazing amounts of pleasure! Remember, this pleasure, that can lead to ecstasy, always begins in her mind.

Connection drives desire. Women need to feel emotionally and physically safe before they will ever feel sexually safe with a partner. Together, husbands and wives need to discover what will ignite her mind to passion and her heart to connection. This requires communication. A wife needs to understand what drives her passions (not just sexually, but what makes her feel alive) and then show (not just tell!) her husband what this process looks like. The more specific you are in this aspect of your communication, the more fully she will engage passionately.

Please take a moment to answer these prompts individually, and then share your answers together:

1. You could help me feel more emotionally safe by. . .
2. Some things I am passionate about include. . .
3. Some things that distract my mind when we go to bed together include. . .
4. You could help me bring my "head to bed" by. . .

CHAPTER 14

Mindful Sexual Experiences

I will always remember a therapy session with a young couple who came to see me with some sexual questions. They had a list of discussion points that we started going through. As I answered their questions, the wife was intently writing down my answers. After a few minutes, I asked, "What is the problem you need my help with?" to which the husband directly answered, "We just want to make sure we're doing it right." I remember pausing, feeling quite surprised, before responding with another question, "Are you enjoying being together?"

Unfortunately, this "are we doing it right" focus in sexual relationships isn't uncommon. Messages about sexuality in the Western world are full of patterns that are more conducive to *mind-full* experiences than *mindful* experiences. Think about the typical lovemaking experiences you share. Is your mind filled with some of the thoughts below?

- A mental checklist of repeated sexual patterns
- Worry that something might go wrong, like no orgasm or a premature ejaculation
- Self-doubt in the appearance of your body or body parts
- Anxiety or boredom that it is taking too long
- Behaviors you can do to hurry the experience along
- Feeling let-down because the experience was over so quickly
- Images of other sexual experiences you've had or viewed
- Images of sexual fantasies you would prefer to have

- Pressure to create the best lovemaking experience ever
- Desire to please your partner, even if the experience you're sharing hurts
- Stress that you should be enjoying sex more than you really do
- Focusing on what to do next rather than on what's happening in the moment

I would guess that you're not really enjoying each other if you are this mentally absent in your lovemaking experiences. I call this *imprinted unconscious sex*, where bodies are having sex without the minds being present. In many ways, this type of sex is all about a performance rather than actually showing up for a real-life experience. Routine lovemaking patterns unintentionally develop over time, leading to relational problems such as sexual boredom, dissatisfaction, frustration, and dysfunction. The saddest part of this vicious cycle is that the often-enduring struggles begin with the simple idea that sex needs to be done a certain way in order to be good. These established patterns can create many sexual challenges for couples. Perhaps you can relate to a typical example illustrated below, where a woman's mind is performance-focused during lovemaking:

A woman tends to feel a lot of pressure to sexually please. Her breasts, the most highly sexualized body part in the Western world, are often used to arouse her husband, rather than being enjoyed by the woman. She often accommodates touch that is not pleasurable or comfortable because she wants to make her husband happy. On top of this, her orgasm typically requires more time than her husband's orgasm or ejaculation. The pressure to "come" creates anxiety—particularly when coupled with the thought that her slowness could cause her husband to lose his erection.

This rush to orgasm fulfillment propels the couple to move to penetration much sooner than the vagina is fully ready. Once his penis is inside of her, the thrusting motions begin. The wife, seeing her husband's increased excitement and wanting to please, may have learned tricks to help her husband ejaculate more quickly. Little vaginal squeezes, gyrating in pelvic positions that please him, pretending pleasure by groaning in his ear and faking orgasm are all tools that she might use to speed up the experience. Patterned use of these tricks leads the woman to believe there is a problem with her or that she just doesn't enjoy sex. Over time, this type of sex dramatically reduces the woman's desire for sex as she becomes filled with resentment and apathy.

Such sexual routines don't feel like love at all. While a wife may have the best of intentions in sharing herself this way, this type of sex doesn't contribute to a robust, passionate marriage. It doesn't pressure her to mature and develop sexually either. Men also have challenges being fully present sexually. The following is a common example of a man's performance-focused thinking during sex:

A man feels pressure too. Western society has deemed him the high-desire partner, ready and wanting 24/7. He needs to produce and maintain an erection on demand, with a penis size that defies gravity. He not only needs to be a good lover; he needs to be the BEST lover. His self-confidence is often rooted in his sexual performance, including knowing how, when, where, and what to do to please his partner. When it appears that he's done it right, he believes he's found the "recipe" to lovemaking. If a recipe worked once, it will work again and again and again—right? When he realizes that his mastered techniques are not creating the unbridled, passionate responses he's hoping for, stress develops, cycling into a reduction of sexual self-confidence. A husband's sexual legitimacy is questioned when it appears he doesn't know how to provide sexual pleasure and fulfillment.

Just as in the earlier scenario, performance is the focus. This sexual pattern does not sustain a loving marriage relationship. It also doesn't stretch a man to own and be at peace with his sexuality.

Sexual conditioning leads to an absence of presence. This goal-oriented lovemaking creates a high level of absence, which over time becomes a destructive problem. A wife and husband can't share a physical, intimate, bodily experience if they are not both really there. Repeated, unconscious sex continually nudges your minds forward to the next moment rather than enjoying what you are actually experiencing together in the here and now. This pattern of sex has been taught and learned for generations. As a culture, we have come to believe that sex is mindlessly working towards orgasm. You can challenge your conditioned sexual habits by intentionally being present and aware during your lovemaking experiences. This requires effort as you challenge habits by focusing on what is happening in the moment. This humbling process is very difficult, but I believe it is the only way that something stronger, even something worth living for, can be created.

Mindful sex, or sex with your mind being fully present, is not about what you do or how you do it—there is no "right way" in this free-flowing style of loving *consciously*! For some of you, this may feel boring. For others, it might create mild anxiety because you're not sure what you're "supposed" to do. Others of you will give up, thinking you don't have time for this right now. I have had all these same thoughts myself! Indeed, there may be times or seasons of life when consistently practicing slow sex isn't in the cards, and that's okay. When you realize you're in a sexual rut and want a change, I urge you to turn to mindful lovemaking. Mindfulness increases your ability to empathize with, accept, and securely attach to your romantic partner. Researchers have found that practicing sexual mindfulness is linked to improved relational flourishing, sexual harmony, and orgasm consistency.[37] Choosing to bring a mindful awareness to the bedroom can become a deeply spiritual journey of transforming sex into love.

In being more present-minded while making love, your body will naturally respond in subtle and transcendent ways as you become aware of your spirit within your body as you share yourself with your spouse. While turning inward and consciously assessing what the body is experiencing takes practice and time, it is a perfect foundation for becoming present while making love. The first step in this mindfulness journey is to center yourself, or to connect to what's inside of you! Letting your spirit have a voice, as you feel the love you are, is a process that can be so healing. My mantra for this process is "I am love." As I breathe, close my eyes, mentally scan and relax into my body, and think of this mantra, I begin to feel eternal. I can feel that my spirit was conceived in love by Heavenly Parents. I feel the light, energy, and love of my spirit inside of my body. This exercise has become one of my favorite spiritual processes to become fully centered and present. When my spirit and body feel congruent, I sense my divine worth. It feels as though my soul is light and sharing love. It helps me remember my *why*.

Another way to center yourself could begin with a shower or bath. Getting clean and fresh will add to your pleasure and confidence. Lay naked in bed, close your eyes, and while breathing in through the nose and out through the mouth, try to find points in your body that are tense or painful. Breathe into these points, consciously acknowledging them. This practice will relieve tension as you relax. Continue to scan your body, consciously breathing and becoming more comfortable and relaxed. After 10 minutes or so, turn on your side and face your spouse who has likewise become centered through breathing. During this time, try to not verbally communicate. Allow yourself to be still and quiet.

Take this time to enjoy being naked together. People often think they need to be in the mood for sex before getting naked together. This simply isn't true! When space and time are available, naked bodies like being together. The skin is the body's largest organ, covering 20 square feet. Touch has long been known to decrease the stress hormone cortisol. Even simple touches, like hand holding or touching an arm, can buffer against stressful responses in the body. When we touch through hugging, our brains release oxytocin, a neuropeptide often called the "cuddle hormone." Oxytocin promotes bonding, devotion, and trust, making you feel close and connected to one another. Even without any sexual activities, when a couple lays naked with skin touching, all kinds of wonderful things begin to happen within their brains that can bring them closer emotionally as a couple. When there is trust in the relationship, bodies are always happy to be together, regardless of one's desire for sex![38]

Once you've relaxed into yourself and then into each other, mindfulness practices involve developing an awareness of physical sensations and emotions as they enter and exit your consciousness. Maintain a nonjudgmental attitude as you detach from your concerns, anxieties, and other stressors rather than automatically reacting to them. Doing this helps you create a state of physiological and mental calmness. Breathe and relax into each other with eye gazing, kissing, and conscious touch. These exercises are specified in the experiential activities portion of this chapter.[39]

Remember to absolutely banish rules from your lovemaking experience. If you feel you must do something, or feel you cannot do something, you are not learning through discovery and exploration. Don't miss the opportunity to be the only two people engaging in this unique experience, in this unique space, and in this unique time. You two, together, are working as a team to discover possibilities of love and to reverence the curiosity you create together. Teach one another with awareness and kindly make suggestions as you go along. Embrace the here and now. Become love together.

When you notice that you're distracted, don't fight it; doing so will often make it worse. When you try to ignore it, the distraction can get stronger and become bigger. Instead, take a moment to observe the distraction and then gently let it pass on through the mind. Don't beat yourself up or think that you're a mindfulness failure. Distractions happen to everyone. Learning to let them come in one ear and go out the other while you breathe deeply will help you remain centered as you practice conscious loving.

As you have mindful sexual experiences, communicate with one another about your thoughts and feelings. The THINK PAIR SHARE process below will be most informative if you communicate as the dearest of friends on an adventure of discovering things along the way, with no end goal or objective. You are human *beings*, not human *doings*. There is no right way to be love.

THINK. Ponder and journal about what you have learned in this chapter. Are there aspects of mindful sexuality that really resonate with you? Why or why not? Some individuals are less interested in learning about mindful sexuality. Is this how you feel? Why or why not? What are you willing to try? Can you both decide a location, time and activity that feels bonding to you? If so, get there, breathe, gaze, and have your conversation.

PAIR. When couples I work with are striving to incorporate mindful sexuality into their sexual repertoire, they sometimes experience discouragement because it seems that nothing is happening! I encourage you to choose to look at this type of lovemaking as more purposeful and bonding focused. You both decide a location, time, and activity that feels bonding to you. Get there, breathe, gaze, and have your conversation.

SHARE. Share your thoughts and feelings about this chapter. It might be particularly interesting to explore how mindful sexual creation could connect with the actual physical creation of humankind. Discuss together what you would like to try from the activities listed below. Recognize that as you begin practicing mindful sex, the need to connect and bond is essential for the physical aspects to cooperate in this mind over body experience.

Adding to your Sexual Playbook: Write down some ways you would both like to try to be more mindful and present during your lovemaking experiences. Journal ideas of how you can individually and relationally let go and how you can help your spouse let go of conditioned beliefs around what sex "should" be like.

Experiential Activities to Enjoy

Eye Gazing Experiment

Eye connection is valuable as you meld into one another. William Shakespeare coined the phrase, "The eyes are the windows to the soul." As you eye-gaze, imagine that you are looking deeply into your spouse's soul. It is through the eyes that you can often understand a person's emotions, and even read their thoughts without ever saying a word. When you find yourself getting distracted, simply close your eyes, refocus, and open them again. Together, it is important to understand that closing the eyes to recenter is not abandoning your partner or the eye-gazing practice.

- Lie naked, breathing with eyes closed as you center yourself.
- After several minutes, turn toward your spouse, slowly open your eyes and gaze into your spouse's eyes. You can only focus on one eye at a time, so take time to get to know each eye. You may

discover that each eye has a little "personality" all to itself. For example, my husband's right eye is quite flirty and playful, while his left eye is more intense. Often as we begin our time together, I will focus on the right eye. Then as our time becomes increasingly connecting and passionate, I look more intently into his left eye. As you eye gaze, continue to breathe deeply, in through the nose and out through the mouth, bringing the energy from your spouse's eyes into yourself.

- Now, shift your thinking. Usually, we look outside of ourselves and bring what we see inside. For instance, we open our eyes to look for something specific. The energy is focusing outward to see what you're looking for. With this experience, try having what is outside come inside of you through your eyes. In other words, open your eyes to bring energy in through the eyes. This focus is more on being seen than on looking for something. Remember, this takes time!
- Invite your lover into yourself through your eyes. This can be one of the single most spiritual and connecting experiences, as you see and are seen by your lover.
- Close your eyes when you need to recenter yourself. Breathe. Once you feel rooted again, reopen your eyes.
- At some point, begin genital holding. While laying on your sides, gazing, gently cup your free hand around your spouse's genitals. This needs to feel safe and warm; the focus should be on connecting, not stimulating. Women, allow your hand to hold the length of your husband's penis. If there is no erection, include the testicles in your gentle touch. Men, warmly cup your hand over your wife's vulva. As you both genital hold, continue to eye gaze, breathe, and relax together. Enjoy the warmth of being together in peace and comfort with no expectations. Each of you should close your eyes periodically to connect with your spirit. Allow your self-awareness to increase as you mentally scan your body, making subtle shifts as needed for comfort.
- There is no genital-to-genital contact throughout this non-goal-oriented, extended, and prolonged replenishing phase of lovemaking. This time produces a framework where only the present matters, where husband and wife are literally wrapped

up in each other, immersed in a sensual energy that is truly transforming. Prolonging this replenishment phase of lovemaking heightens feelings of intense love and connection. Your brain is being flooded with hormones and neurotransmitters that drive core emotional bonding. This is the divinely hardwired replenishment that can only be found in deeply committed marriages.

- One day there will be a flickering moment when a door opens, and your souls unite!

Slow Sex with a Mirror

Typically, men are more easily visually aroused than women. This can be important knowledge to have when becoming more conscious lovers. One way to really heighten awareness is to touch and love one another in front of a mirror. Create a romantic environment with soft lighting, music, and a large mirror. Clean up, put on some nice lingerie, then cover it with a silky robe or oversized T-shirt (the idea is to have several layers on so that taking things off in front of the mirror takes some time). As you make eye contact through the mirror, look at one another with love and anticipation for what you are going to share. Slowly undress one another, taking time to look at one another in the mirror while you do so. I encourage you to observe your spouse touching you in soft, romantic ways through the mirror. This can be highly arousing, bringing front and center a deep consciousness of what you are doing and sharing. I really encourage you to go slow! Make this arousal last. Kiss and make love together while watching yourselves. Fill your eyes with one another! Both of you will experience heightened arousal as you take time to enjoy this style of lovemaking. Not only is it a highly passionate experience, but it can also be a deeply emotional experience as your hearts connect through watching yourselves create love with your bodies. This type of encounter creates deep feelings of closeness as you consciously, with great visual awareness, generate love together.

Bringing Food to Bed

Whenever you are slowing down lovemaking, tuning into all your senses can help you become more conscious. Choosing what to eat and how to eat it are important as you incorporate food with sex. Experiment with a variety of foods and food temperatures—warm cheese fondue, strawberries and whipped cream, honey, hot fudge sauce, and yogurt are a few suggestions. As you prepare for this type of lovemaking, decide how to have the environment be romantic and clean. I suggest getting an old sheet or cheap shower curtain to cover your bed, so there are no worries about spilling. Sharing food in a large bathtub might also make for easy clean up.

Set the stage for romance. I think it is fun to start this experience dressed, taking turns feeding one another while emotionally connecting, gazing, and gently touching. Transition to feeding one another with your fingers, gently licking and sucking the food from your lover's hand. As you sit close, look at the arousal you are creating in your spouse's eyes as you slowly savor this extremely sensual and conscious way of loving. This experiment will heighten intimacy if you go slow, keep eyes connected, feed one another first with fingers, then with mouths, and then on to other body parts of your choosing. Afterwards, take time to clean one another off.

Mindful Kissing Acronym

- **Kinetic**: Connect with your inherent energy.
- **Intimate**: Gaze into your lover's eyes, breathing and relaxing together. Remember that this is an intimate, shared experience that is to be enjoyed and savored, not evaluated.
- **Slow**: By slowing down, you can be more present with your lover. Gently explore one another's lips, mouth, and tongue. Be curious as you touch this way. What sensations do you feel within the kiss and within other body parts?
- **Sensual**: Feel the sensuality of the kiss. Spend at least 15 minutes building sexual arousal through your kissing connection.[40]

Conscious Touching Exercise

- Lie naked, side by side, breathing with eyes open.
- One spouse gently touches the other, putting conscious love into the touch. Imagine that your touch is filled with loving energy that is coming directly from your heart into his/her body. Freely touch, moving from side, to back, to side, to front, and back to facing one another again.
- The giver now receives this same pattern of touch from the receiver.
- This exercise is intended to generate a loving energy between you, not necessarily to sexually arouse or stimulate one another. Focus on the emotions you feel driving the touch, allowing your spirit to lead your body in communicating the love it feels for your spouse.
- Often a "sparkle" type sensation can be felt with this light, emotionally-significant touch.

CHAPTER 15

Expanding the Exciting Replenishing Phase

As described in the preceding chapters, when couples focus on orgasm, much of the relational attachment and bonding can be lost. This attitude creates a performance- and goal-oriented way of sexual thinking that heightens the extremely fragile nature of sexual expression. Something designed to create pleasure and connection can develop into either failure or success if climax is the goal. I encourage couples to continually work at prolonging the exciting replenishing phase of lovemaking. Begin with at least 30-minutes, and gradually add time as you continue to practice. In therapy, I have worked with couples who have expanded the exciting replenishing phase of lovemaking to 4-6 hours at times. I have personally spent hours, even days enjoying this replenishment. This is not a comparison; it is a point of reference for you to learn what is possible when you create time and space for love. By focusing on replenishment, or becoming orgasmic, expectations are replaced by enjoying the relational aspect of creating or producing love together as husband and wife.

I believe understanding the value of *creating* love through touch, rather than fulfilling an objective, will result in the passion, rapture, and replenishment we all long for in marital relationships. Building upon the preceding chapters, this chapter provides some practical suggestions on how to slow down and expand the lovemaking process. Chapters in the following section will continue to provide more in-depth, practical knowledge on the different areas of the body that can contribute to replenishing sex.

Pulse Points

A pulse indicates that a person's heart is beating—or that the person is alive! There are some specific points where the pulse can be felt and measured because the arteries are closest to the surface of the skin. Pulse points are an ideal place for intimate touch to slowly start because erogenous zones are connected to pulse points. There are seven points in the human body where nerve endings and blood volume sensuously connect:

- Radial artery (wrist)
- Carotid artery (neck)
- Brachial artery (medial border of the humerus, above the elbow)
- Femoral artery (at the groin)
- Popliteal artery (behind the knee)
- Dorsalis pedis and posterior tibial arteries (foot)
- Abdominal aorta (abdomen)

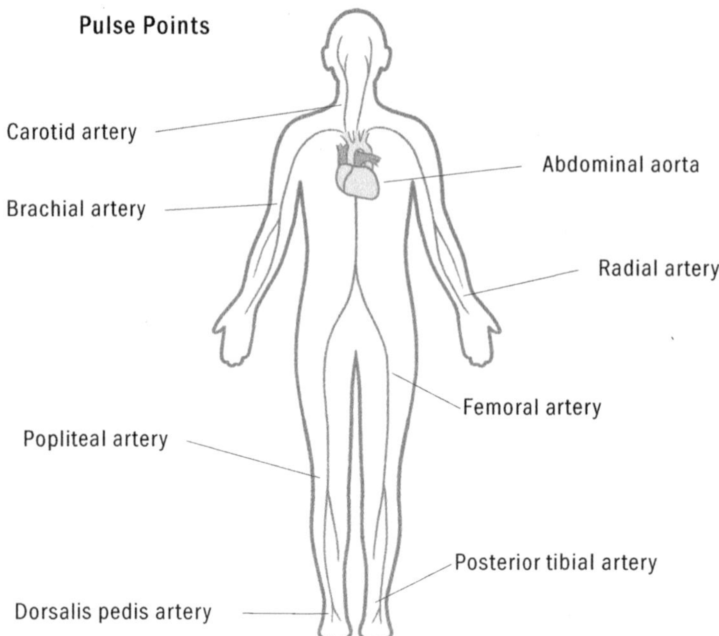

Erogenous Zones

Erogenous (sometimes referred to as Erogenic) stems from the Greek word, Eros, which means erotic desire and love. It includes our basic life force and the dynamism of passion and desire combined with selfless love from the heart. I like to think of the erogenous zones as areas of the body where true romantic love is created or produced. Understanding these zones of the body is helpful in sexual response as these body parts are more sensitive to touch and stimulation. There are three categories of *erogenous zones*, each of which will be explained in-depth in the following section. *Primary zones* include the nose, mouth and lips, the breasts and nipples, and the genitals. *Secondary zones* include the earlobes, the neck, the sacral-lumbar junction, the gluteal fold, and the inside of the thighs. *Tertiary zones* involve the outside surface of the little fingers, the center of the palms, the navel, the anus, the anterior nares, the external auditory meatus, the sole of the feet, the big toes, the thumbs, and the back of the knees.

Expanding the Replenishment Phase Through Intentional Touch

Types of Touch (to and with a body part that both of you decide upon)

Considering different types of touch is an important part of sexual exploration. Here are a few unique types of touch you can consider:

- Feathery, light touch
- Firm, steady touch
- Wet touch
- Blowing, airy touch
- Hot touch
- Cool touch
- Exploratory/experimental touch

Using a combination of these types of touch with the many erogenous zones, you can see that there are countless ways for you to learn about sexual touch. Be creative! One of our faith's beliefs is that we were created in the image and function of The Divine Creator. We are also taught that we, like God, are *creators*. I testify that together, you and your spouse, can create a divine sexual relationship that replenishes your marriage. Utilize your creative faculties as you explore together what types of touch feel good and where they feel good on your bodies. Your sexual relationship is your stewardship; it needs time, effort, and care to flourish.

Remember, individual uniqueness and preferences will vary as you begin this type of sexual exploration. I encourage you to make room for expansion! Much of the excitement comes with learning your partner's preferences and giving room for the gradual evolvement of your own style of sexual expression. This is fun! There is no agenda. These experiences are meant to be playful, connecting, and erotic.

Patterns of Touch

Using a four-beat pattern is a wonderful place to start this type of sexual stimulation. This stimulation is done through touch (with hand, fingers, or other body parts), kissing, sucking, and licking. The four-beat pattern begins with touching a secondary zone, then a primary zone (no genitals yet), followed by a tertiary zone and back to a primary zone (still no genitals). Going through two cycles of the four-beat pattern before ever coming in full contact with the genitals is an extremely powerful technique for elongating the exciting replenishing phase. Always remember, there is no goal other than creating love and connection through mutual touch.

Here is an example of two rounds of the four-beat pattern of erogenous stimulation:

1. Neck (secondary)
2. Mouth (primary)
3. Little finger (tertiary)
4. Breast (primary)
5. Earlobe (secondary)
6. Lips/Mouth (primary)
7. Navel (tertiary)
8. Genitals (primary)

Another, simpler method of expanding this phase of lovemaking is to begin with the secondary erogenous zones. Tenderly and slowly make contact with each zone. Then, gradually move to the primary zones by kissing or lightly touching the lips, breasts, and genitals. Move next to the tertiary zones, stimulating each one. Through this process, the sensuality of the exciting replenishing phase has been created. You are creating love through caressing each other in a free-flowing, carefree space of time. Be mindful of sensations and emotions.

Giving and Receiving Love (Edging)

This is one of my personal favorite ways to make love with my husband. As you expand the amount of time spent in the exciting replenishing phase, passionate energy will ignite and grow as you learn to *give and receive love.* You may have heard it called "edging" before, but I like the way I say it better! This is an easy way to extend your pleasure and intensify your sexual experiences. This touch happens prior to genital-to-genital contact. It involves touching your spouse in pleasing ways and patterns (as described above) that increase arousal. As your spouse gets closer to orgasm, he/she needs to "tap out" or let you know it's time to cool down. Then, it's your spouse's turn to love you in creative ways. As your arousal intensifies, let your spouse know when you need to tap out. Alternate back and forth with this type of loving pattern for as long as possible. You will be amazed at the intense feelings of bonding and true love you can experience for one another when practicing giving and receiving love. Go slow, have fun, and enjoy the journey! Be prepared for intense emotions.

Communicating About Touch

You want to build your sexual connection; this requires heartfelt and honest communication. Because sexual touch and the experiences you share are so private and vulnerable, it is essential that you learn how to communicate about these topics in ways that are helpful to your relationship. I encourage you to use my "hamburger approach" to communicating. As you consider a hamburger, you see that on both sides, there is a bun that is easy to chew and digest. In the middle is the meat, which is much harder to chew and digest, yet it's the real food that will nourish. This approach in communication looks like this:

- BUN—*soft start up*—"Honey, I love when you touch me like this . . ."
- MEAT—*clear message*—"My preference is to try this . . ."
- BUN—*appreciation and love*—"I love learning together about . . ."

THINK. Evaluate and journal about the things you've learned about expanding the exciting replenishing phase. Consider the following questions:

- Why do we have so many erogenous zones?
- Are there types of sexual touch that you're uncomfortable with? Are there sexual touches that you long for?
- Why would it be a good idea to delay touching genitals?
- Do you understand giving and receiving love?
- In what ways would you like to change your ability to sexually communicate with your spouse?

PAIR. Create a private, quiet, and comfortable space to hold each other in ways that feel safe and nurturing.

SHARE. Process and listen to one another as you discuss the ideas from this chapter.

Adding to your Sexual Playbook: Look back to your marital sexual playbook. Did you list anything about your sexual communication? If not, consider adding some guidelines on how you both will approach communicating about your sexual preferences and desires.

Experiential Activities to Enjoy

Your Homework Creation

1. Talk together about ways that you can stretch the exciting replenishing phase of a sexual encounter. Be creative! Make it a unique experience to your relationship.
2. Designate a "Teacher" and a "Student." Each of you will take on your role of instructing/helping and learning/asking questions. These roles will alternate throughout the activity, but try to stay in character as you engage.
3. The teacher shows and tells the student how to touch him/her in an arousing way. The student asks questions and tries to follow the instructions as well as possible. Once the student has earned an A, the teacher now becomes the student, and the roles reverse.
4. Now, the new teacher guides the student in teaching him/her how to provide arousing touch. The new student asks questions and learns how to do this new assignment. Again, once the student has earned an A, the roles reverse again.

    a. *Hint*: Start this type of touch on areas of the body that are tertiary, then secondary, and finally primary erogenous zones. This will fill time in the exciting replenishing phase of lovemaking.

The Alphabet Game

1. Laying clothed together in one another's arms, one spouse will remove clothing, caress, and kiss a body part that begins with the letter *A*.
2. The receiving spouse then does the same to the giving spouse, only with a body part that begins with *B*.
3. Alternate letters between the two of you as you love body parts by using the letters of the alphabet. This can be fun and creative as you can create new (respectful) nicknames for body parts.
4. Usually, the clothes are off long before you run out of letters. If

this is the case, include sensual massage oil, almond or coconut oil, or lube as you caress and kiss each new body part.

a. *Hint*: Remember, the point of this game is to spend more time in the arousing, exciting, replenishing phase of lovemaking. Be deliberate in pacing your arousal.

Find the Soap

1. Get a nice smelling, small bar of soap. Fill the tub full of warm/ hot water. Pour in some bubble bath.
2. Both of you slip into the tub. Breathe, relax, and smile. Make eye contact and flirt as you begin this game.
3. One of you drops the soap into the water. The other person feels around with his/her hands, looking for the soap. (Of course, many other "things" can be found while feeling for the soap!)
4. Once the soap is found, the person gently washes the body part requested by the spouse and then drops the soap back into the tub.
5. Now it is the first spouse's turn to find the soap.
6. Continue this game for as long as you can; remember, the objective is to have sensual fun and to bond, not necessarily leading to orgasm!
7. Refill the tub with warm water as needed.

PART III

The Divinity, Biology, and Sexual Potential of our Bodies

CHAPTER 16

Tertiary Erogenous Zones

These zones are less erotically responsive than the primary or secondary erogenous zones, especially at the beginning of a sexual experience. That said, the touch and stimulation of these areas can still make a significant contribution to the impact of a sensual experience. In tantric lovemaking, it's suggested that waiting to incorporate tertiary erogenous zones until the primary and secondary zones have already received stimulation will enhance the sensory awareness of these areas of the body.[41] I will begin by listing and describing the tertiary erogenous zones in order of sensitivity, going from the most to the least sensitive.

Outer Surface of the Little Finger

The outer surface of the little finger on both hands is a tertiary erogenous zone. Depending on the person, one of the fingers may be more arousing than the other. Gentle stroking, nibbling, licking, or blowing on the outside of the little finger can be pleasurable. It may be that the arousing potential of this tertiary erogenous zone will be best felt once you have already progressed into a state of arousing excitement.

Center of the Palms and Soles of the Feet

There is a point in the center of the palm and foot that is highly sensitive and ticklish. When you start gently massaging or lightly stroking your partner's palms and soles, you will notice responses that will only heighten as arousal increases. Reflexology, a system of massage used to both relieve tension and treat illness, is founded on the premise that the reflex points on the hands and feet are linked to every part of the body. Learning how to massage and touch these tertiary zones is a skill that can help you unwind, release stress, and even create pleasurable sensations throughout the body. Put the palms of the hands and the soles of the feet onto your map for replenishing sex.

Navel

When touched too abruptly, the nerves in the navel can cause a strong abdominal reflexive action that is connected to the functioning of the entire nervous system. Embryonically, the genitals and the navel shared nerve tissue; for some people, this nerve connection continues to exist after birth. Licking, rubbing, or blowing on the navel can be highly arousing for these individuals. For others, it can create a ticklish sensation, or it may lead to the sensation of needing to urinate. Women are more likely to find the belly button to be a sexual hotspot. The female navel lies anterior to the bladder. The area between the bladder and the vagina consists of many nerve endings that connect to the entire clitoral complex. Titillating her belly button and the surrounding area between hip bones can often stimulate responses in the vagina and clitoris.[42] Be curious in discovering what feels enjoyable for you, recognizing that warming-up to this zone is a good idea for an entrance to replenishing sex.

Nasal Openings

Who would have thought the nasal openings have erotic properties? They do! Stroking, kissing, lightly blowing on the nasal openings, just under the tip of the nose, can create a nervous, tingly sensation felt throughout your face. In James Nestor's book, *Breath: The New Science of a Lost Art*, the term "honeymoon rhinitis" is introduced. This condition is when swelling occurs in the erectile tissue located in the nasal passageways during sexual arousal. The swelling can make it harder for you to breathe because it blocks the nasal passageways. During arousal, however, the sympathetic nervous system functioning increases levels of adrenaline which makes blood vessels constrict. This reduced blood flow to the nasal passageway relieves congestion, which can, unfortunately, increase the occurrence of a runny nose and even sneezing during sex.[43] So if you get a runny nose during lovemaking, now you know why!

Ear Openings

The ear has over 25,000 nerve endings, making it a particularly sensitive part of the body. Hearing loving, arousing words whispered in the ears can elicit a double dose of emotional closeness. The words elicit a cognitive, connective response, and the movement of air in ear elicits an erotic, physiological response. The auditory sounds associated with lovemaking also contribute positively to the passion a couple is sharing. For example, most men and women are aroused when their partner breathes heavily, sighs, or moans during sex. Studies document that physical stimulation of the ears with soft whispering, gentle blowing, licking, or massaging enhances sexual arousal and feelings of emotional connection between partners. During lovemaking, caressing your spouse's earlobes to the ear openings with soft kisses and gentle breathing while stimulating other body parts can greatly increase sexual pleasure.[44]

Snuggly inserting wet thumbs or fingers into your ears can cause an induction of the parasympathetic system, bringing you more quickly into a deep and meditative state. This can help with the process of becoming more mindful in your sexual experiences. Deep breathing, along with inner ear pressure, contributes to the ability to be more present and in-the-moment. Listen to each other as you incorporate the ears into your sexual repertoire!

Big Toes and Thumbs

These body parts are called the phallic digits in tantric sexuality. Sucking on the big toe or thumb can create immense genital pleasure for both men and women, particularly when they are in the process of sexual arousal. It is nice to have recently bathed or showered so that big toes and thumbs are clean during this stimulation. Using the pads of your thumbs and big toes when touching can also create some sensitive responses.

Back of Knees

Skin is delicate and stretched thin at the backs of the knees. The major popliteal artery is located here, making it both a pulse and a perspiration point. Light, feathering touches with soft fingers or tongue can feel especially exciting once arousal has begun.

THINK. Journal what you learned about the tertiary erogenous zones. What ideas have you had about things you would like to try/experience? Contemplate your remarkable body! Did you know that you had so much sexual capacity?

PAIR. Get clean, naked, and close. Put on some nice lighting and music. Hold each other while eye gazing for a few minutes. Breathe in your spouse.

SHARE. Listen to understand what your spouse has learned and what he/she wants to try. Then share your own thoughts. How do you both feel as you contemplate the remarkable sexual capacities of the body?

Adding to your Sexual Playbook: After completing the TPS portion, write down what you learned in your sexual playbook, focusing on ways you want to incorporate the various tertiary erogenous zones described in this chapter into your lovemaking!

Experiential Activities to Enjoy

Tertiary Time

Make a list of all tertiary erogenous zones. Separate each one, and put them in a hat or small bowl. Take turns drawing one paper out and asking your partner how he/she would like to try being touched on that area of his/her body. For example, "I would like light kisses on my ear" or "I would like to have my thumb sucked." Spend 2-3 minutes on this spot, and see what responses occur in both of you.

Because tertiary zones are less sensitive, there needs to be more time spent in stimulating these areas. Next, you'll switch places as the spouse giving will now be the receiver. Rotate back and forth until all areas are selected. Then discuss your experience. What did you really enjoy? What was ticklish? What was arousing? What do you want to do again?

Hot or Cold?

One partner will collect as many things as possible that will have a unique texture and/or temperature. When totally comfortable and "warmed up", use these items on the tertiary erogenous zones and see how they feel.

Examples:

- What does a feather feel like on the back of the knees?
- How does an ice-cube feel on the belly button?
- What about rubbing sandpaper on the center of the hands/feet?

You can use the same item on all tertiary body parts to decide what feels best. Another fun twist to this game is to have the receiving partner close his/her eyes or use a blindfold. Guess what is being used to stimulate the various body parts, and discern how much you enjoy this type of touch. Change positions—the giver is now the receiver.

CHAPTER 17

Secondary Erogenous Zones

During a sexual interaction, partners often mutually caress body parts that have no direct anatomical link to the genitals, and the secondary erogenous zones make up nearly 26% of the body's surface area. That's a big canvas for developing your sexual masterpieces! These skin-to-skin caresses without immediate sexual arousal can be very important in transforming intimate activity into replenishing connection. Indeed, some studies suggest that the intentional touching of both secondary and tertiary erogenous zones may play an important role in how the brain maps the emotional connectedness of your relationship. Science tells us that this process, called *pair bonding*, helps to solidify enduring monogamous sexual relationships. Let's look at the secondary erogenous zones and their potential to help you have a replenishing sexual relationship.

Scalp

The scalp contains plenty of nerve endings that can send instantaneous tingles throughout the body. Even the slightest hair caress or gentle tug can create a heightened sexual response. Try giving your partner a slow, sensual scalp massage, moving your fingernails lightly over the scalp and concentrating on the area behind the ears and just above the neck. Deep scalp kneading with your fingers can also create feelings of emotional relaxation. On the nape of the neck, where the hairline begins, lightly pull on the hair to discover little thrills of pleasure. Brushing or combing hair, starting at the scalp and moving to the ends, can feel deeply connecting and may create an emotional response for some people.

Earlobes

For most people, the earlobe can be exceedingly sensitive when kissed, licked, or sucked on. Because of the high concentration of nerve endings, when sexually aroused, the earlobes will flush and become engorged, much like the nostrils, lips, nipples, breasts, and genitals. Although there is not much scientific information connecting sexual arousal with earlobe stimulation, in the tantric world of lovemaking, this practice is encouraged. In a class Jeff and I took, we were instructed to spend 15 minutes massaging and sucking on one another's earlobes as a form of foreplay. Doing this began very playful, but after a while, the practice became quite passionate. I encourage you to explore with your spouse what types of earlobe touch creates excitement for you.

Nape of the Neck

The nerves located where the hair ends at the back of the neck contribute to this particularly sensitive spot. The thin, delicate skin and high concentration of sensory receptors on the nape of the neck also contribute to sensual feelings. Most people are highly responsive to light sensations such as touching, licking, kissing, and gently breathing on the nape of the neck. This type of touch can readily send pleasing, arousing shivers down your partner's back. Don't forget the pleasing touch that can also be created by lightly tugging on the hairline.

Inner Wrists

Locate the inner wrist pulse points with your fingertips by lightly caressing the skin. These nerve endings, found just below the surface of this delicate skin, can quickly ignite with soft, feathery types of touch. Try intertwining your fingers while grazing the skin on your spouse's inner wrists with your lips and tip of your tongue. This touch can create a very passionate response, especially if you include eye contact.

Sacral-Lumbar Junction or Sacrum

The sacral-lumbar junction, or sacrum, is a hidden treasure! The easiest way to locate the *sacrum* is to find the two dimples on your lover's lower back. These indentations, known as the *sacral dimples*, are the place where the sacrum joins the hipbones and where nerves from the spine are connected to the pelvis. The sacrum also has five bone segments that are fused together into one large triangular-shaped bone that ends with the *coccyx*, or tailbone. A reflex, part of the parasympathetic nervous system, called the *cranial-sacral outflow*, is largely responsible for the genital nerve endings found here. Sacral neuromodulation (SNM) studies have electronically stimulated the sacral nerves and found a modestly favorable impact on sexual functioning among women experiencing *anorgasmia*, or difficulty achieving orgasm.[45]

Experiment with your lover to discover what types of touch are especially pleasing for both of you. For some people, the slightest touch of a feather, finger, or tongue can bring about great pleasure. Others seem to enjoy a deeper, more substantial, kneading type of touch that generates feelings of relaxation and releases sexual tension and pressure. Be creative, and try an ice cube or vibrator for some sensory play.

Gluteal Folds

Where the buttocks meet the legs at the tops of both thighs is often overlooked in sexual foreplay. To be fair, some people don't seem to feel much stimulation in this area. Give it a try, and see what happens within your marriage. With your spouse laying on his/her stomach, start touching along this fold by placing both hands on the inner thighs with your fingers pointing toward the genitals. Stroke up, fanning your fingers upward and rotating your hands across the gluteal folds to the outer thighs. Continuing in this fashion, either with a light, feathery type of touch or a gentle, massaging touch, will bring blood to the inner thighs and genitals, helping with the arousal process. Breathing, licking, and kissing along the fold can also be very arousing.

Inner Thighs

The inner thighs are perhaps the most arousing of the secondary erogenous zones. The nerve endings located in the inner thighs are so sensitive that prolonged touch can create highly erotic, pulsating pleasure as increased blood volume pools in the penis and vulva. Stroking upward toward the genitals creates an increasingly erotic feeling. Running your mouth and fingertips gently down the front of the thighs, then slowly moving your fingers or tongue inward and upward toward the groin is especially exciting.

The secondary erogenous zones can provide real pleasure. I hope that you will become intimately aware of them while you and your spouse share replenishing sexual experiences.

THINK. What did you learn in this chapter? List in your journal as many creative ways as possible that you can touch your spouse's secondary erogenous zones. What would you like to try? What would you like to have your spouse try on you?

PAIR. Once again, get clean and naked. Snuggle together in peace with some nice music.

SHARE. Give and receive information that you have thought and journaled about in this chapter. Take turns discovering one another's secondary erogenous zones without the pressure that this needs to turn into penetrative sex.

Adding to your Sexual Playbook: Together, write down some exciting ways you can enjoy and pleasure each other's secondary erogenous zones.

Experiential Activities

Sensual Challenge with Touch

When you're being touched, your challenge is to feel the nuances, decide what you like best, and communicate that to your partner. This simple exercise lays a great foundation for exploring and giving each other feedback. Husband, pick a part of your body that you want your wife to play with. Wife, come up with two different ways of stimulating that body part. Here are some ideas:

- Very lightly stroking with your fingertips
- Moving your fingertips in circles
- Massaging with your thumb
- Feathery strokes, light and airy
- Massaging with your whole hand
- Light, medium, or firm massages
- Light, medium, or firm scratches
- Teasing with your hair
- Squeezing with your whole hand
- Pulsating with your hand

Wife, go back and forth between the two different types of touch, and ask your husband, "Do you like it better when I do this or *this*?" Husband must pick his favorite. Then, switch roles with the wife receiving. Repeat as many times as you'd like as you move to different parts of your bodies.

Water Play

This can be as quick or as involved as you'd like it to be. Take a shower or bath together. Wash each other's hair and soap each other's bodies up, focusing on the secondary erogenous zones. If you have more time (and a tub!), set a romantic scene in your bathroom. Light candles, use a bath bomb and turn on music. Take a long, luxurious bath together, again spending time focusing only on the secondary erogenous zones.

Follow the Leader

This activity can be done with any body parts, but for now I want you to focus on the secondary erogenous zones. You will be imitating what each other does, focusing on touching and kissing. Start off with the husband in the lead. He gets to touch or kiss his wife on a secondary erogenous zone. Then, the wife gets to do the exact same thing to her husband.When you're in the lead, try to keep your moves short, so your partner doesn't have a hard time remembering everything that you did and exactly how you did it. For example, try tracing your tongue against your partner's neck and then having them lick your neck in return. Next, try kissing five times along their sacral lumbar junction and then letting them kiss you in return. You can also talk to each other throughout the exercise. Share when you're just experimenting with something or when you're showing your partner something that you really like. When you're the one following, try your best to copy *all* the nuances of how your partner touched you. Pay attention to their pressure, speed, technique, etc. Take turns being the leader.

Necking!

You get to play with each other's necks for five minutes each! Here are some options:

- Run your fingers up and down your spouse's neck. In particular, try going around to the back of the neck and lightly scratching around the hairline.
- Kiss your spouse's neck with soft pecks or wet kisses.
- Lick your spouse's neck. Try blowing lightly after you lick to give an extra tingle!
- Gently suck on your spouse's neck—be careful not to leave a hickey unless it's wanted!

- Take your spouse's skin between your teeth, and gently nibble on it.

Make sure to stimulate all over the neck. Most people just stick to the sides of the neck, but the back of the neck and hairline can be ultra-sensitive as well. Now, trade places. Talk about your experience.

For more information on secondary erogenous zones, see the reference list included at the end of the book.[46]

CHAPTER 18

The Primary Erogenous Zones—Starting at the Top

The primary erogenous zones are called "primary" because they are the most sensitive of all the zones. These areas are filled with nerve endings that are most directly responsive to sexual arousal. If I were naming the zones, I would call these areas of the body "dessert zones" because I believe in saving the best for last! The primary erogenous zones include:

1. The nose, mouth, and lips
2. The breasts
3. The genitals

Starting at the Top Means that I'm beginning with the nose, mouth, and lips. We'll cover the breasts and genitals in subsequent chapters.

The Nose

The sense of smell is the most primal, evolutionary sense. The neurological pathways from the olfactory nerves go directly to the limbic system, bypassing rational and cognitive processing. This is why smells can evoke memories more quickly than sight, touch, sound, or taste. Psychologically speaking, smell can shock us from reality with an immediacy that is incomprehensible. Smells can often feel sensuous and magical as olfaction is the most direct sensory channel to the genitals and to our most basic sexual drives. Pheromones and scents that resemble sexual secretions are the most powerful olfactory triggers to sexual response. Pheromones are released through perspiration. Humans naturally produce pheromones, which are similar to hormones, but pheromones are secreted outside of the body. The interesting thing about pheromones is that their scents can influence another person's sociosexual behavior. Thus, the smell of sweat can be arousing for both men and women.

Breath also has an important influence on sexual energy. Awareness of the breath creates mindfulness and can help you be fully present in the moment. As I've mentioned, being mindfully present during lovemaking has a profound influence on a couple's bonding connection and validation of one another. Deep breathing can provide relaxation throughout the body, which can be particularly effective in attuning yourself to your body. Any awareness you can bring to your breathing prior to making love will make an incredible difference by creating an environment of tranquility and receptivity. Breathing in through the nose produces a more meditative, cognitive state, while breathing in through the mouth may help clear emotions and engage the pelvic floor for women.

Synchronizing breath during lovemaking can intensify presence and pleasure. This occurs when the breath circulates between partners. As you breathe out through your mouth, your spouse breathes in your air through his/her nose. Your spouse then releases the air from his/her mouth for you to deeply breathe through your nose. The practice of consciously breathing together feels unifying as two lovers create a singular breathing cycle. Breathing intentionally together requires focus and playful exploration. Keep the breathing deep and slow. This practice can awaken sexual energy, especially as you imagine the powerful flow of connection and oneness as you partake of one another's breath.

The olfactory system is directly connected to the mouth through the *cribriform plate*. You can locate the cribriform plate by placing your tongue behind your teeth and slowly moving the tip of your tongue along the roof of the mouth. About two-thirds of the way back you can feel a small, "scratchy" patch of tissue where the soft and hard palates are conjoined. These sieve-like perforations are channels for olfactory nerve filaments coming from the naval cavity. This is the only part of the central nervous system with direct environmental exposure. There is no other location in the human body with such raw exposure because there is a straight connection between mouth, nose, and brain. It has been called the "Oral G-Spot", and there is some evidence that running your tongue on this special spot for a time can create sexual arousal, particularly in the nipples. Personally, I have found that, in anticipation for a sexual encounter, rubbing my tongue on this spot for 10-15 minutes has created a sexual response within my body. While I'm not sure if it is the tongue rubbing or the anticipation in and of itself that creates the arousal, I find it fun to think of my tongue preparing me for a good time.

The Lips

As lips are the most exposed erogenous zone, they are considered very intimate. I believe the lips are also more vulnerable, not only because they are made of soft, sensitive tissue, but also because they are located so closely to the brain. Kissing activates a whirlwind of neurotransmitters and hormones throughout the body that can set the stage for passion very quickly. The abundance of incredibly sensitive, tactile receptors found in the lips is exceeded only by the concentration of these receptors that are present in the clitoris and penis. The mucous membranes on the inside of the lips are also full of sensory receptors which wonderfully contribute to arousal.

Understanding erotic capacities of the upper lip and *philtrum* (the vertical groove that runs between the base of the nose and the upper lip), will greatly enhance the passion found in kissing. Tonguing and sucking on the *lip frenulum* (the soft tissue that runs vertically in a thin line between the lips and gums) and philtrum dilates blood vessels and rapidly increases sexual desire. Stroking your spouse's *lingual frenulum* (the mucus membrane located under the center portion of the tongue) with your tongue in slow back- (where the tongue is anchored to the mouth) to-front (tip of tongue) motions can be particularly arousing.

Tantric anatomy claims that the upper lip on the female has a psychic tube, or *nadi*, that connects to the clitoris and that a male's lower lip is directly linked to his penis. As the husband sucks on his wife's upper lip while she sucks in his bottom lip, a life-force charged saliva passes between them that creates a magical love potion unique to just the two of them. I'm not fully sold on a lot of mystic tantric beliefs; however, experimenting with various tantric sexual ideas has always been enjoyable! Together, as you and your spouse experiment with kissing, take time to explore and taste one another with total awareness. Being present will heighten your emotions of love, as well as create new ways of enlivening your erotic responses. This process can feel strange at first; you might even wonder if you're doing it right. Luckily, there is no right or wrong. Remember, trying something new for the first time can often feel strange. That's normal and okay. Keep trying. Have fun together on your amazing sensual journey.

The Mouth

From infancy, oral reflexes, such as the rooting reflex and the sucking reflex, ensure survival. When the roof of a baby's mouth is touched, the baby will naturally begin sucking. The maturation of the lips also comes about through these reflexes. Sigmund Freud had many views that are not scientifically favorable, yet his work linked both primal needs of survival (eating, sucking, rooting) and reproduction (sexuality). Freud believed that during the oral stage of child development, the relationship between the infant's mouth and the mother's breast was the first experience in eroticism. Though theoretically incomplete, there is truth in the idea that infants learn through oral exploration, particularly as they process new information or stimuli. Studies have shown that both children with ADHD and adults experiencing dementia are self-soothed through thumb sucking. We also know that bodily fluids are produced (saliva) through taste. Certain tastes can create sensory pleasure, which then produces sexual fluids (lubrication). There is undoubtably a strong connection between the mouth and sexual arousal.

Philematology is the scientific study of kissing. There are a few times that I have wondered if this could have been a career for me! I truly love kissing. Studying kissing is interesting to me. Evidence-based research has found connections between kissing, hormones, and sex. In particular, research has shown that saliva has testosterone which increases sex drive. The longer, the wetter and more open-mouthed the kisses are, the more testosterone is shared. Studies also indicate that cortisol, the stress-hormone, decreases after kissing. In my opinion, these are two compelling reasons for couples to kiss more frequently: it reduces stress and improves sexual desire.[47] Research also suggests that kissing is the best indicator of how sex will be. If your kissing is passionate, it's very likely that the sex you share will be passionate as well. A woman will often save passionate kissing for when she is planning to have sex. If she is unsure of wanting sex, her kisses will typically be more platonic.

Kisses are often quick, and quick kisses are generally not mindful or erotic in nature. However, John Gottman says that a 6-second kiss can benefit a marriage by creating a ritual of connection, increasing fondness and admiration within the relationship, and leading to sex.[48] If 6-seconds can do that, imagine what 10 minutes could do! Do you remember the long, passionate kisses you shared before marriage? Creating time each day to kiss passionately without the expectation for sex can work wonders for your marriage. In fact, I encourage couples I work with in therapy to create time to just kiss for a minimum of 10 minutes each day, with no strings attached. This requires the couple to slow down and choose each other which enhances the friendship within the marriage. Because there is no pressure that the kissing needs to lead to sex, it actually allows women, in particular, an opportunity to feel more sexual desire.

Being a good kisser isn't something innate, but it is something that can be learned. If kissing is something that doesn't seem to come as naturally for you, I encourage you to continue practicing. Through practice and time, it can become something you enjoy more fully. One way to start developing this skill is through intentionally getting to know your mouth and tongue. I encourage you to slowly run your tongue all around your mouth. Feel your teeth, gums, and palate. Find your oral G-spot, both your lip and lingual frenulum, and touch your tongue to your philtrum. The tongue is a fascinating organ to me. It is all muscle and no bones, making it uniquely flexible. This versatility makes the tongue particularly good for massaging and stimulating other body parts in a variety of delicate and rhythmic ways. Using your tongue for sucking, licking, and kissing can lead to some of the most pleasurable sexual touching that couples can share.

After becoming familiar with your own, get to know your spouse's tongue and mouth. Taking turns, run your tongue along your spouse's top palate, touching the pressure point just behind the teeth. Continue moving your touch to rub circularly on the oral G-spot. I call this erotic exercise "deep throat kissing." As you explore this style of kissing, be prepared for an all-encompassing sensory connection. Your senses will come alive as you sit naked, straddled together with breasts and genitals touching. Full on kissing is a way that brings noses, brains, hearts, and bodies close together.

Starting at the top with the primary erogenous zones includes learning all about your nose, lips, mouth, and tongue. Most sexual engagement originates here. Spending time to know more about these parts of your body will bring a fuller sensual awareness to your lovemaking. Slowing down and spending time kissing, breathing, smelling, and tasting together are simple ways to improve your sexual and orgasmic connection. It facilitates true replenishment in your lovemaking experiences.

THINK. On your own, journal your thoughts regarding the nose, lips, mouth, and tongue.

PAIR. Get close together and kiss for a few minutes, with no expectations that this kiss will move toward more sexual contact. Simply kiss while being present. Think of the love you feel for your spouse while you are kissing. Try to pour the love you feel into the kiss.

SHARE. Now share what you have journaled. Take time to listen and understand what your spouse is sharing. See if you can come to a place where you both agree to spending more time simply kissing, finding your oral G-spots while paying attention to the nose and ears.

Adding to your Sexual Playbook: Review your sexual playbook and see what you have written about kissing. Together, discuss adding a goal to spend a certain amount of time each day or week in just kissing, with no expectations attached.

Experiential Activities to Enjoy

Deep Throat Kissing

Spend 15 minutes kissing. Get naked with the wife on top, straddling her husband's lap. Explore each other's mouths, and enjoy deep throat kissing together as described in this chapter. Once the fifteen minutes are up, share and listen to one another as you describe your experience, your desires and your ideas for future ways of kissing. If you both want to, keep on kissing and having fun together. This experience does not need to be a precursor for sex.

CHAPTER 19

Primary Erogenous Zones—The Breasts

The breasts and nipples are extraordinarily important to both men's and women's sexual arousal. In general, women are more responsive to stimulation of the breasts than men, but everyone is different. Some women do not like having their breasts and nipples touched while others can reach orgasm through nipple stimulation alone. Stimulation of the breasts and nipples affects nerves that ultimately release the hormone oxytocin, which when pumped through the body not only creates deep relational bonding but can also signal pleasurable uterine contractions. Indeed, it is not uncommon for mothers to experience orgasm while breastfeeding.

Women's breasts are the most sexualized body part in Western culture. Research suggests that women view 400-600 advertisements every day. One in every 11 of these images clearly define what the ideal feminine form looks like with a particular emphasis on sexualizing the female breasts.[49] With these messages being so prevalent in a girl's life, she subliminally equates sex with female breasts, so much so that adolescent girls will often experience insecurities about their breasts—size, shape, fullness, how they hang, not to mention the nipples. In the United States, since 2014 breast augmentation has become a leading high school graduation gift requested by young women. Sadly enough, their parents are obliging. Appearance focused social media platforms used by younger and older women alike, use breast images to allure connection with potential sexual partners. This perpetuates the message that breasts equal sex. As women, this attitude of using our breasts to enhance desire in a partner, can create a disassociation with our own breasts. Too often, these body parts, with their deeply-feminine sexual arousal capacities, become objects for others' pleasure, rather than a primary erogenous zone for women themselves. We must change this trend!

A starting point to changing this trend is recognizing that cleavage, nipples, nipples through fabric, and nipple and breast movement generate sexual arousal for both men and women. Why women? Because, as described above, the Western female brain has been swimming in social messages that breasts are sexy, beautiful, desirable, and even powerful. Ladies, utilize this to your advantage! Find lingerie, bras, and blouses that create sexual stirrings in your mind. When with your husband, wear things that accentuate breasts, show a little nipple, or are otherwise appealing to both of you. This is a wonderful way to more fully share flirty, romantic, sexy time.

Sexual Self-Discovery

An important principle I teach is that a woman needs to understand how her body works sexually. This is an essential part of her sexual maturity and development. If a woman doesn't understand what feels pleasurable, how will she help her husband know how to sexually excite her? Ladies, you have been blessed with beautiful bodies that have amazing sexual capacities. The ability to feel sexually beautiful and whole comes from believing that sexual fulfillment is good, sacred, and replenishing. This aspect of mortality is a blessing that was divinely designed to give you joy. It is an important way to both express and receive love in your life. I believe that a godly woman embraces her body, her curves and her ability to be sensual, passionate and erotic. Dr. Jennifer Finlayson-Fife, a colleague of mine whom I greatly admire, has said, "Learning to love and be loved through the body is foundational to our spiritual and relational capacity."[50]

Knowing and accepting your sexual self allows you to experience something fundamentally divine about yourself. I call this process *Sexual*

Self-Discovery. Unfortunately, many of us have heard that self-touch is sinful. When done in self-serving capacities, especially with pornography, it is sinful. What I'm talking about is very different. Sexual self-discovery is based in goodness because the goal is to bless your life and your marriage. Your ability to accept this part of your sexual development indicates courage as you make a choice to validate your sexual legitimacy. If needed, I encourage you to study the concept of sexual self-discovery and bring it to God in fasting and prayer. Let Him know the desires of your heart. Ask for a confirmation that this principle is right and good. I believe that you will come to know, as I have, that learning the sexual functioning of your body is an important part of your mortal journey. You were created with pleasure in mind.

Women can best come to understand and appreciate their breasts through self-touch or exploration. This is identifying your sexual preferences for the purpose of blessing your marriage with goodness and love. In therapy, I call this *breast work.* This type of practice requires time, privacy, and mindfulness. Relax into awareness by comfortably laying naked, with soft music, soft lighting, and maybe even candles. No falling asleep or thinking about what you are going to cook for dinner, your upcoming work presentation, or your kids. This is *your* time! As you invest in your sexual development, your ability to accomplish things outside of the bedroom will increase. Breathe deeply, in through your nose and/or genitals and out through your mouth. Focus your attention on your breasts. With an easy, relaxed approach, pay attention to your breasts and try to sense what you are experiencing within your breasts. Imagine your breasts as a beautiful symbol of your femininity. With a hand cupping each breast, hug them close to your heart center.

Breathing and relaxing, stay focused on what you are experiencing. Notice the slight stirrings or emotions that come up. This exercise has brought some of my clients to tears as emotions surfaced. Let the emotions come; don't try to stop them. This is healing. As you pull energy from within your chest cavity, let it rest in your breasts. Feel the energy resonating around the nipples and areolas. Touch your nipples, roll them in your fingers, use light-feathery strokes or massage with a firmer hand. As you spend time practicing this exercise, you will begin experiencing radiant energy flowing, like milk, from the nipples. This energy is good! This energy is Godly. The sensitivity of the nipples, as you mindfully pay attention to them, is similar to the sensitivity of the head or glans of the male penis and female clitoral glans.

As you continue with your breast work, take time to cup them in each hand and feel the weight of your breasts. As you touch your breasts, you may notice that they feel larger. This is because sexual arousal increases in blood volume in the breasts which expands the surface area to create more space and room for arousing touch. Lightly caress the sides of your breasts, moving your fingers from the ribcage or armpit to the nipples. With the pads of your fingers, trace the edges of each breast; discover their full width and height. Periodically give your nipples a little squeeze. While you are focusing on the pleasurable, appropriate touch, notice the warmth of your vulva. You will feel an expansion of energy. This sexual energy is naturally causing your body to produce lubricant. You may feel this lubrication begin to pool in your vagina as your body naturally prepares itself for intercourse, which is *not* the objective of this exercise!

This experience will be new for many of you. You may feel awkward, shy, hesitant, or even naughty. I strongly encourage you to take heart and try! Indeed, if I had to choose one exercise as homework for couples struggling sexually, it would be breast work. Why? Because the positive, radiant, feminine energy that a woman can begin to experience as she discovers her breasts for herself will allow her to expand her heart and enhance her confidence and beauty. Breast work will let you get in touch with the goodness in your divine femininity! Increasing your sexual understanding of your body enriches your beautiful feminine spirit and enlivens your body with sexual desire and arousal. Be assertive in claiming the joy your body was created to experience.

THINK. Ponder and journal your impressions of breast and nipple stimulation. Journal your thoughts on sexual self-discovery. How does this process feel in your own life? Reflect on experiences when you have felt sexually empowered and aroused with your or your spouse's breasts and nipples.

PAIR. Get comfortable together while you share this conversation. Make sure to create time and space to foster deeper connection.

SHARE. Share and listen. Decide on a plan of action for your marriage. How will breasts and nipples more fully become a part of your sexual journey?

Adding to your Sexual Playbook: Review your sexual playbook for anything you've written about sexual self-discovery and self-touch. Together, discuss whether you want to modify anything you've written previously and whether there is anything new you want to add. Additionally, write down some ways you can both incorporate breasts more fully into your sexual experiences, focusing primarily on how they can bring the wife more pleasure.

Experiential Activities to Enjoy

Breast Work Together

Ladies, invite your husband to join you. Both of you undress. Breathe there together for a few minutes. There are a few body positions that are particularly helpful during breast work. One very comfortable position is to have the husband sitting spread-eagle, with his back against the headboard/wall, while the wife wedges her buttocks, back, or shoulders against his groin. This creates full access to the breasts. Another enjoyable position involves both of you kneeling on the bed facing each other. Press loins together with the wife leaning back, sharing her breasts fully as her husband continues to provide pleasure. Once comfortable, it is the wife's turn to show him what she finds arousing. Wives, *really* show him how to energize your breasts. First, guide him with his hands on top of your hands. Then allow your hands to be on top of his hands, and gently guide him as he takes the lead. Remove your hands, close your eyes and bask in his loving touch. Kindly describe to him the sensations you are experiencing. It is vital to clearly and lovingly communicate what you enjoy, as well as what you don't care for. Silence is not golden in the bedroom!

As you continue this practice regularly, be mindful of sensing the breasts from within. In time, your breasts can become highly erogenous and sensitive, almost like they have come to life! One client described this feeling saying, "My breasts are so sensitive now. I am aware of them all the time. While mindfully making love, it is almost like my nipples are two headlights! It honestly feels like a bright light is shining from each nipple. It is amazing!"

"Nursing"

Another way to create energy in the breasts is "nursing" engagement. This certainly does not need to include breastmilk, but it can if this is something you both desire. This exercise can generate orgasmic energy that enhances your erotic passion exponentially. Get naked and comfortable together. Usually laying on your sides facing each other works best. The husband should warm up the breasts and nipples with light, fluttery touches and soft kisses. When the wife feels ready, she will invite her husband to gently suckle from one breast. Find a cadence and pressure that feels comfortable for the wife. After 5 minutes, the husband changes to the other breast, where he suckles again for 5 minutes. Rotate again to spend an additional 5 minutes on each breast. Both of you can bring your heads to bed by focusing on the beautiful energy that comes from this experience. Breathe and relax into the nursing process. For some couples, both husband and wife will imagine that milk is being produced during the nursing. They claim this adds a grounding, nourishing experience to their lovemaking. Typically, after 20 minutes of nursing, couples are either fully relaxed and ready to drift off to sleep or fully aroused and ready to have intense, erotic sex. As couples incorporate nursing into their lovemaking sessions, they can experience an amazing connection with nipple-suckling stimulation.

Nipple Stimulation

Both men and women are usually pleased with nipple stimulation due to the abundance of nerve endings located there. Sucking the nipples is often the best way of producing pleasure, but light touches with the fingers are also good. Most people will respond to gentle strokes moving inward from the areola. Rotating an erect nipple with a wet palm is another effective way to provide sexual pleasure, as is flicking and lightly biting the nipple. Spend time discovering what type of touch is most pleasing to both you and your spouse. Experiment with new sensations like rubbing an ice cube around the breasts and nipples or simultaneously sucking on a nipple and a peppermint. This type of playfulness can add dimension, friendship, and a sense of freedom as you work together to learn more about pleasuring breasts and nipples.

CHAPTER 20

Primary Erogenous Zones—Genitalia

The genitalia are the most erotically stimulating of all the erogenous zones. In many cases they are thought of as what constitutes sex. While I hope that through this journey of tertiary, secondary, and primary erogenous zones, you have discovered there is a whole universe of erotic treasures just waiting to be found beyond just the genitalia, I also hope that you can come to better appreciate the divine beauty and power of both male and female genitalia.

I find the miracle of fetal development absolutely fascinating! Isn't it incredible that a sperm and an ovum can come together to create an entirely new human body? A body that will house a unique spirit offspring of our Heavenly Parents. This creative power, given to us, is mind-boggling, to say the least. Not only do our Heavenly Parents give us the capacity to create new life, but They also trust us to *nurture* that life. I have a hard time trusting that my children will load the dishwasher correctly! The trust of our Heavenly Parents in us is truly remarkable.

Did you know that early in embryonic and fetal developmental stages male and female anatomy is indistinguishable? The genital tissues look exactly the same. Undifferentiated embryonic tissues develop into different structures in male and female fetuses. Structures that arise from the same tissues in males and females are homologous; this is called *embryotic biological homology*. Around 5-6 weeks, an embryo has reproductive struc-

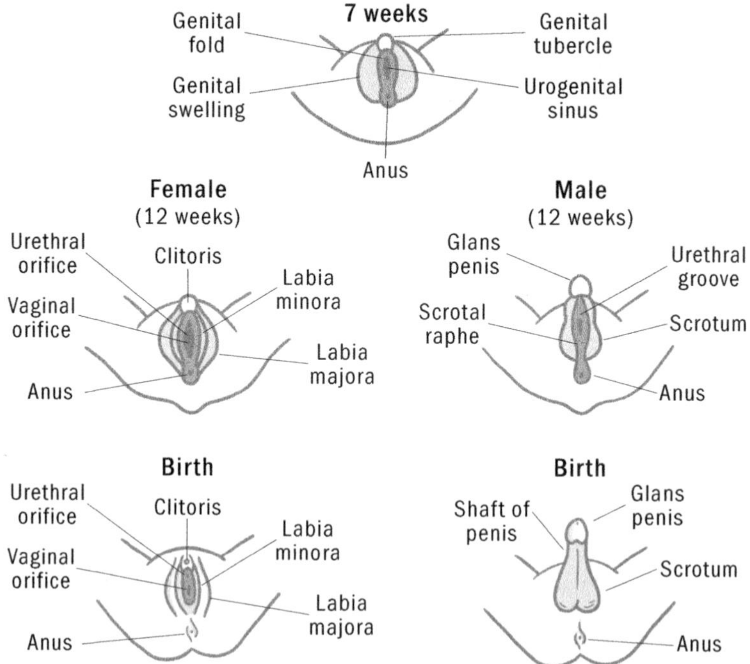

Embryonic Biological Homology

tures, ducts, and gonads that can develop into a female or male reproductive system. Although the chromosomal sex of the child is determined at conception, it isn't until the genes determining sex are activated that the appropriate structures will remain while the others degenerate (this occurs between 7-12 weeks).

Ovaries and testes develop from the same gonads. A similar glans area, with a concentrated number of nerve endings, develops into the penile glans or the clitoral glans. The bulbourethral glands in males are homologous to the Bartholin's glands in females. Female labia majora develop from the same tissues that create the male scrotum. The embryonic tissue that becomes the vagina in females, degenerates in the male embryo. The male penile foreskin is the female clitoral hood. And the list goes on. So, why is this information important to your sexual relationship? Because, believe it or not, sexual research is continually teaching us about the intricacies of anatomy and development that relate to male and female sexuality. I'm especially intrigued by the fact that in the last 20 years, science has made dramatic progress in understanding female sexuality. In particular, recent research has discovered the true size and shape of the clitoris. There is so much more pleasure that can be found when you know how much more clitoral stimulation is possible. And did you know that a male's prostate gland is homologous to a female's prostate gland or G-spot? Discoveries are continually being documented as we learn the facts around male and female genitalia.[51] These discoveries can give you perspective on your journey to creating a replenishing sexual relationship.

The study of language and linguistics has always interested me. Studying etymological root words can occasionally provide "aha" moments. Such is the case with the word genital. The root word is genius, which is also the root word for genesis (beginning) and progenitor (ancestor). Pondering these words heightens my spiritual understanding of the sanctity found in genitalia. It is in the union of male and female genitalia, along with the divine evolution that occurs within a marriage relationship, where we express the fullest capacity of our human potential. It is within this genital sexual encounter, or life-giving power, that every individual soul (body and spirit) begins. The next time you hear the vulgar terms that are so widely used to describe the genitals, I hope you will pause, reflect, and teach the beautiful sanctity found within these Godlike body parts. The foundation of the entire plan of happiness rests upon their proper use and functioning.[52]

I encourage you, as a couple, to set aside significant time to learn about your own and your spouse's genitals. One of the important sexual principles taught by the late sexual researcher, Dr. David Schnarch, is the concept of "eyes-wide-open sex." [53] I suggest you keep your eyes wide open as you learn more about the genitals by really looking at them, touching them in a variety of ways, and sharing what feels good, better, and best. This exploration can feel awkward due to the high-level of vulnerability you experience by being fully naked and unashamed together. In time, however, as you continue to trust and learn together, these can become some of the most sexually bonding moments you share as a couple. There is relatively new sexual research that shows evidence of mirror-neurons playing a crucial role in sexual interactions. Touching your partner while mutually looking at each other's bodies positively impacts sexual arousal for both of you. I don't believe it is by coincidence that sexual responses of both spouses are enhanced when direct touch of one partner is being observed by the other. This process of interpersonally getting to know one another's erogenous zones is a multisensory way of creating relational sexual arousal. I strongly encourage you to utilize the efficiency of mirror neurons as you share time together and become increasingly proficient in knowing your own and your spouse's genitals.[54] As you do so, sexual intimacy will become more replenishing.

Consistent with the transcendent magnificence of creating a new life, our reproductive systems are intricately complex! To address the complexity inherent in our powerful reproductive systems, I have included several anatomically correct images and quite a few definitions in this chapter. This chapter may feel denser or more difficult to comprehend than other chapters. Take your time as you slowly read about the distinct parts of your own and your spouse's genitalia. Flip back and forth between the text and the images, and use this chapter as a reference when a refresher is needed on specific terms in later chapters. Whenever I define a new term, I have used italics.

Male Genitalia: *Observe the illustrations and identify the different parts of the male genitalia.*

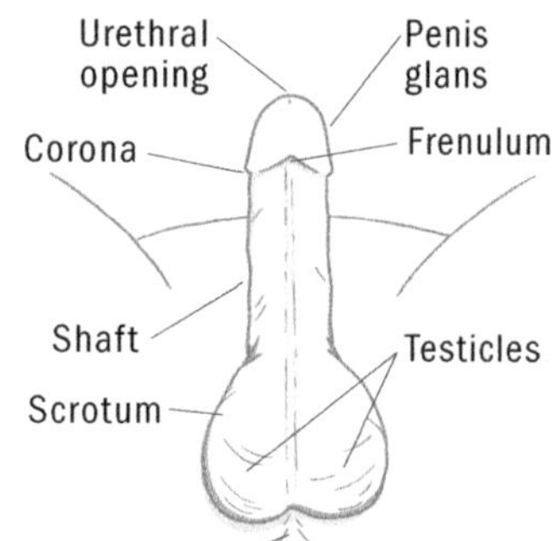

The *head of the penis* is also called the glans of the penis. The opening of the urethra is found here. The *urethral opening*, or the very tip of the penis, is where urine, pre-ejaculate, and semen come out of the body. It has about 4,000 nerve endings which makes it the most sensitive erogenous zone of the male body. The *frenulum* (the upside-down v-shaped underpart of the head of the penis) is another extremely sensitive part of the male primary erogenous zone. Manually and/or orally stimulating this part of the penis is usually very exciting. The *shaft* of the penis extends from the root of the penis (found near the lower belly) to the urethral opening. It consists of 3 lay-

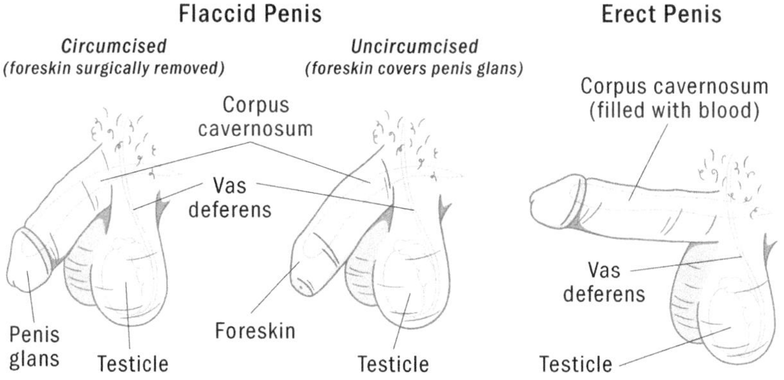

Flaccid Penis

Circumcised (foreskin surgically removed)

Uncircumcised (foreskin covers penis glans)

Corpus cavernosum

Vas deferens

Penis glans

Testicle

Foreskin

Testicle

Erect Penis

Corpus cavernosum (filled with blood)

Vas deferens

Testicle

ers of spongy tissue. The urethra is also located within the shaft of the penis. Nerves, hormones, muscles, and blood vessels all work together to create an erection when a man becomes sexually aroused. Nerve signals, sent from the brain to the penis, stimulate muscles to relax which allows blood to flow to the tissues in the penis. This entire process makes the penis hard and is called an *erection*. The average size of an adult erect penis is 4 ⅔ inches in length. When a penis is flaccid or soft, it lies snug against the scrotum.

The *scrotum* is the sac of skin that hangs below the penis. It holds the *testicles* or *gonads* and keeps them at the right body temperature for sperm production. When it's cold, the scrotum pulls the testicles closer to the body to retain heat. If it's too warm, the testicles hang loose and away from the body. Often when a male is sick and feverish, the scrotum is noticeably loose around the testicles, allowing for excessive heat to dissipate. The scrotum is covered with wrinkly skin and some hair. It's not uncommon for one testicle to be larger than the other, thus having an uneven hanging scrotum. The testicles and scrotum are both super sensitive, so any hitting or twisting can be very painful. Touching or licking the scrotum gently during sex can be pleasurable.

The *perineum* is the erogenous zone that I believe is most frequently left out of sexual fun. Both men and women have a perineum. For men, it is the vertical cleft found between the scrotum and anus. It has many nerve endings that, when massaged, can create quite a bit of pleasure. Gently slide your finger in and up-and-down or circular motions to determine what feels best. As you do so, blood flow increases to the prostate, which will enhance this erotic massage. You may have heard of a man's *G-spot,* which is technically called his *P-spot.* This refers to the external massage of the prostate gland through the perineum. Some men experience sexual pleasure from anal stimulation and prostate massage. I will teach more about male prostate massage in a different chapter.

Female Genitalia: *Observe the illustrations and identify the different parts of the female genitalia.*

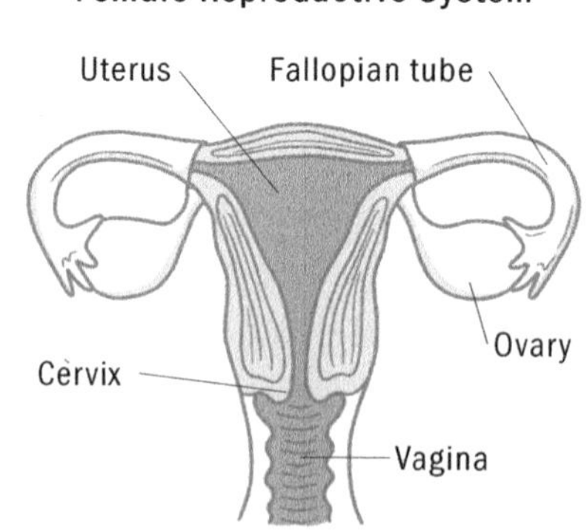

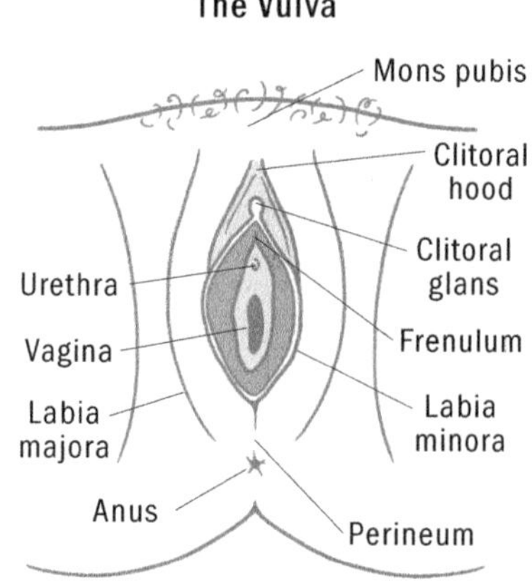

The female *vulva* consists of all the genitalia that are outside of the body, which includes the mons pubis, labia majora, clitoral glans, and urethral and vaginal openings. Sexologists encourage teaching children that boys have a penis, and girls have a vulva. Many of us grew up with the knowledge that girls have a vagina, which is true but not complete. In fact, most women (75-90% depending on what research you are reviewing) do not orgasm with vaginal penetration alone. Including the sexually responsive parts of the female body in describing genitalia is much more accurate, hence, using the term vulva is preferrable. Interestingly, in Latin, vulva means "wrapper" or "covering." A veil is something that covers, conceals, and protects other things. Indeed, the vulva covers or veils the internal female genitalia, much like veils in religious ceremonies cover holy places. Personally, I find this imagery incredibly beautiful. The reverence involved with the meaning of vulva truly encapsulates the significance of divine femininity and sexuality.

The mound of fatty tissue, located anterior to the pubic bone that is naturally covered with pubic hair, is called the *mons pubis*. This is often referred to as the *mons*. It contains sebaceous glands that produce pheromones which contribute to sexual attraction.

Below the mons are two sets of genital lips: The *labia majora*, the visible, larger fleshy, hair covered external lips, and the *labia minora*, the smaller, more sensitive set of lips tucked beneath the protective labia majora. Labia can be short or long, wrinkled, or smooth. Often, one lip is longer than the other. They can vary in color from pink to brownish black. The color of labia often changes during sexual arousal and as women age. Some women have larger outer lips, while many women have larger inner lips. Both the labia majora and minora fill with blood during sexual excitement. When the labia majora is folded open, you can see the labia minora. It looks like vertical folds of tissue starting at the clitoris, where the folds encircle the clitoris to make the clitoral hood. Directly underneath the clitoral glans is the *frenulum*. These folds continue to descend, forming the borders of the vestibule bulbs. Eventually, the labia minora ends as the lips are joined together by a fold of skin called the *fourchette*.

The *vulva vestibule* is the area found between the two smaller lips of the labia minora. This is a smooth surface that begins below the clitoris and ends at the fourchette. The vulva vestibule contains the opening to both the urethra and the vagina. The bulbs of the vestibule (also known as the vestibular or clitoral bulbs) are made of soft erectile tissue that becomes engorged with blood during sexual arousal. They are homologous to the root of the penis. (However, during the embryonic stage, the developing bulb is bisected by the vaginal opening to form two halves.) The vestibular bulbs and the clitoris are believed to function very similarly. Spending time with gentle, exploratory touch of the vaginal vestibule and the vestibular bulbs greatly enhances sexual excitement, as these external parts of the female genitalia lay anterior to the internal clitoral complex.

The *clitoris* is a sensory organ, meaning that its only purpose is to provide pleasure, specifically sexual pleasure! As the clitoris is only created in females, I view this as important evidence to the reality of our Heavenly Parents' desire for Their daughters to enjoy and be replenished through sexual touch. The tip of the *external clitoris*, also called the clitoral glans, is located near the top of the vulva, where the labia minora meet and is covered by the *clitoral hood.* It can be the size of a small pea or as big as a grape. It is estimated that the clitoral glans, the only visible external part of the clitoris, has roughly 8,000 nerve endings, making it a hotspot of sexual pleasure. A very important part of a woman's, and couple's, sexual development is found in the journey of clitoral stimulation. This process, over time, will largely determine the ability for a woman to orgasm during sexual arousal and stimulation.

Due to the high nerve intensity found within the clitoral glans, it's no coincidence that there is also a clitoral hood. This loose covering can either completely or just partially fold over the clitoral glans. Start this exploration by lightly pressing your well-lubricated finger on the clitoral hood. Discover what types of touch feel most pleasurable. Try a circular motion, move to figure 8's and zigzagging. What happens when you tap? By beginning this discovery on the clitoral hood, you are stimulating the very sensitive clitoris underneath. As this becomes increasingly pleasurable, move your lubricated finger to the round bulb or clitoral glans found underneath the hood. Some women find this too sensitive; if so, move your finger back to the position on top of the clitoral hood. If all of it is too sensitive, try starting this exploring by touching through panties. Often silky underwear can provide the perfect buffer for extreme pleasure to be felt. In time, and only if both spouses desire, stimulating the clitoris with the husband's mouth and tongue can often bring about the most pleasure. You can start this on top of your underwear too, spending time determining what type of touch is most enjoyable. Never move directly to the clitoris until the wife is wanting more. This insures further consent and clarity in this significant shared experience.

There is so much more to the clitoris than just this "little button of pleasure." Believe it or not, it wasn't until 2005 that a female scientist, Helen O'Connell, published the internal parameters of the female clitoris. Another full decade of research was conducted until 2015, when the first 3-D imaged clitoral structures were created, giving a clear, visual picture of the size, shape, and diversity of the internal clitoral complex. I find the history of female sexual research both disheartening and thrilling. In the BYU *Healthy Sexuality in Marriage* course that I co-created,

I spent an entire lecture discussing the ramifications of centuries of insufficient research conducted on female sexuality. My heart often aches, and I have even shed a few tears, for women throughout the history of the world who were shamed, thrown into mental institutions, and even sent out West to "tame the savages" largely due to diagnosed "hysteria." This female condition stemmed primarily from insufficient acceptance and knowledge of feminine sexuality. Had I been born in a different era, I am convinced that with my natural curiosity about sexuality, along with my unabashed willingness to research and explore, I very well could have been one of those "crazy" women. I also believe that you, my friends, with so much new information, will be the first generation of couples with the resources to truly understand the capacity of female pleasure. Utilize this knowledge and embrace the freedom you have while creating a marriage relationship that fully recognizes the depth of female erotic power. We are so very fortunate to live now, with a wealth of information available in both normalizing and enhancing female sexuality.

With the latest research, we know that, much like an iceberg, 90% of the clitoris cannot be seen as it extends inside of the body, back and down both sides of the vagina for about five inches. The *internal clitoris* is divided into two parts. First, the wishbone-shaped shaft and legs. The legs are located directly underneath the labia majora, with the shaft sitting underneath the mons pubis, just above the clitoral hood. Second, the *crura*, the root or bulbs of the internal clitoris, are teardrop in shape. They surround the vagina, connecting at the clitoral shaft, with their full width

Aroused Versus Resting Clitoral Complex

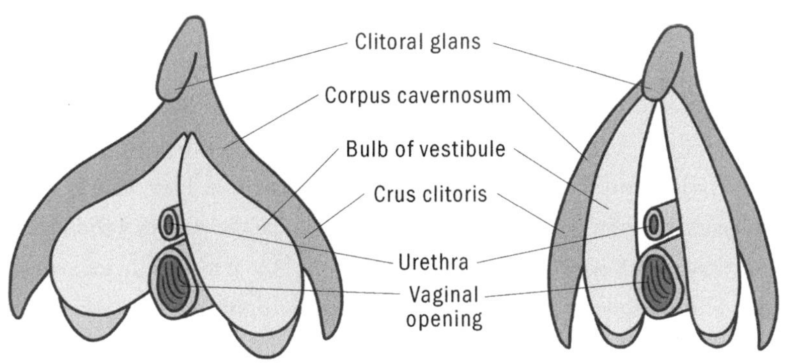

found directly underneath the labia minora. This internal part of the clitoris is most frequently referred to as the clitoral root, clitoral body, or clitoral complex. As you touch and stimulate the labia majora, labia minora, vestibule, vestibular bulbs, clitoris, mons, vagina, and urethra externally, you are also contributing to the pleasure experienced by the internal clitoral complex. I cannot emphasize enough the immense contributions that spending time and using a variety of touches on the entire vulva (external female genitalia) has to female pleasure.

The *urethra* is an extension of a tube from the bladder to the outside of the body. It is the tiny hole located just below the clitoris where a woman urinates. The *vaginal opening* is right below a female's urethral opening. This is where menstrual blood leaves the body. Typically, the distal opening of the vagina is partially covered by a membrane called the hymen, which often stretches or tears when a woman first has intercourse, though other activities can also cause it to rupture. A variety of things can go inside the vagina, including fingers, a penis, sex toys, tampons, and menstrual cups and discs. When babies are born, the vaginal opening is called the birth canal. Once aroused, running a finger, penis, or tongue around the vaginal opening can feel pleasurable; this can also be a great segue to penetration.

Another reason to call female external genitalia the vulva, rather than the vagina, is that the penis and the vagina are not equivalent sex organs. In the embryotic homologous stage, the tissue that creates the vagina in a female, degenerates for a male fetus. The female vagina is an elastic, muscular tube connecting the cervix to the vulva. Because it has muscular walls, the vagina can expand and contract, allowing it to accommodate anything from a finger to a penis to a baby. The walls of the vagina are lined with protective mucous membranes, which keep the walls moist. Normally women have a clear, white, mildly-scented discharge, known as cervical fluid, that uniquely varies. It is generally more noticeable prior to ovulation and the week before a menstrual period. Historically, your female ancestors were encouraged to *douche* (flush the inside of the vagina with fluid, often squirted from a bottle or bag) for feminine hygiene purposes and to prevent pregnancy. This process is highly discouraged today, as is the use of scented products to clean the vagina. A vagina naturally cleans itself.

Vaginal tenting (pictured perfectly in the previous illustration) is the process of the vaginal walls nearly doubling in size and shape upon sexual arousal, creating space for comfort during penile penetration. The first third of the vaginal region—closest to the vaginal opening—has nerve endings that feel pleasurable with various touch. The region found in the back two-thirds of the vagina has little-to-no sensory pleasure points, but it does still feel pressure. When the penis, or possibly a sexual tool or toy, is placed in the back of the vagina, the pressure provided can create erotic enjoyment while the clitoris is being stimulated.

The *perineum* is the vertical-running crevice found between the vulva and the anus. Like men, this area of the female body can be intensely pleasurable when stimulated in pleasing ways. I think it is interesting to note that in tantric lovemaking, the perineum is located near the first shakra, or *mool shakra*, where sexual energy is stored. Located halfway between the length of the perineum is a pulse point; you may want to slow down to find it.

Anal Stimulation

The *anus* is the opening to the rectum and has many sensitive nerve endings. Some people, both men and women, experience sexual pleasure from anal stimulation. If this is something you are both interested in exploring, please consider the following precautions:

The lining of the anus is vulnerable to tearing because it is fairly thin and lacks natural lubrication. Using lubricants can help, but it doesn't completely prevent tearing. Any tears or fissures can allow viruses and bacteria to enter the bloodstream. Anal intercourse significantly increases your risk of getting human papillomavirus (HPV), which can lead to the development of both anal warts and cancer.

The anus was designed to hold feces. It is surrounded with the anal sphincter, a ring-like muscle that tightens after you have a bowel movement. When this muscle is tight, sexual anal penetration is painful. Repetitive anal sex may weaken the anal sphincter, making it difficult to hold in feces. Overtime you may become incontinent.

The anus is full of bacteria, which can potentially infect the giving partner. Having vaginal sex after anal sex can also lead to vaginal and urinary tract infections. Oral sex after anal sex puts both partners at risk for hepatitis, herpes, HPV, or any other sexually transmitted infections.

Though serious injury from anal sex isn't common, it can happen. Anal tears, fissures, and hemorrhoids can be very painful and frequently require medical attention.

We have now completed our journey through the erogenous zones with an in-depth look at the most sexually arousing part of the human body, the genitalia. I hope you stand in awe of these masterpieces of creation, which foster our ability to both multiply by having children and replenish our relationships through healthy sexual connection.

THINK. What have you learned about your genitals? What about your spouse's genitals? What are you going to do with this knowledge? This is a great time to journal.

PAIR. Spend time close together. Consider keeping your clothing on, so there is not undue pressure felt by either partner to need to explore in the moment. As you are close, I encourage you to pray for guidance and clarity as you discuss the thoughts you've had while reading this chapter.

SHARE. Taking turns, share information you have learned about your own genitalia and your spouse's genitalia. Looking through the italicized words, take time to explore and discover each body part. Work together to come up with some activities or experiences that will help you to continue learning about the primary erogenous zones.

Adding to your Sexual Playbook: As you reflect on this chapter, consider writing down some of the new information you learned and how you will incorporate it into your lovemaking. Discuss and document how you show love and respect for your own and your spouse's genitals in your language and actions.

Experiential Activities to Enjoy

Show and Tell

In this activity, both of you should clean-up, get naked, relax, and lube up well. As you have read this chapter and looked over the illustrations, see if you can identify all the parts discussed on your spouse's genitalia. Change positions, letting the other spouse identify genital specifics. While you're looking, explain to (or tell) your spouse what you are seeing and feeling: colors, textures, nooks, and crannies. Once you are finished, lie on your sides facing one another. Talk about your experience. Describe what you were thinking *and* what you were feeling, both while touching and being touched. Discuss if there are other types of touch you think you would like to explore. There is no pressure to have sex, though it is not off the table if both spouses agree to it.

Slow Genital Stimulation

Turn on a playlist of romantic music and spend the length of the first song simply cuddling and talking and the length of the second song kissing with light touch. When the wife is ready for vulvar stimulation, spend at least three songs engaging in vulvar stimulation. Husbands, really open your eyes while massaging, tapping, and rubbing your wife's vulva with your fingers, penis, and tongue. Wives, communicate your pleasure while kindly guiding your spouse in his exploration of your vulva. On the following day, switch places and have the wife slowly explore her husband's genitals.

CHAPTER 21

The Orgasm Gap

Historically the definition of sex has been a linear process that places the focus on vaginal penetration and male ejaculation. Similarly, our culture's definition of sex has largely been focused on the important function that male orgasm/ejaculation plays in procreation. For all inclusive purposes, regardless of where a woman is in the process of sexual response and irrespective of her capacity to orgasm, the male orgasm has been the definitive description of the sex act. As described in *Chapter 20: Primary Erogenous Zones—Genitalia*, we have just recently begun to understand the female potential for sexual pleasure. In research, as well as in society, we are taking important strides to be more inclusive of the female experience in our understanding and definitions of sex; I hope this chapter will help you in your efforts to better include female pleasure and orgasm as part of your personal and relational understanding of sex.

By far, the most common sexual issue I personally work with in couples therapy is the infrequency or lack of female orgasm. It is disheartening to hear the stories of wives desperately wanting to know what to do differently and husbands feeling at a loss, not knowing how to help their wives. From newlyweds to "nearly-deads," this is a universal struggle both in and out of Church membership. This chapter is going to be very straightforward and detailed with specific sexual information to help couples work together for orgasm success. That said, I want to first remind you that once we turn our sexual encounters into goal-oriented exchanges, frustration can become the watchword. Being together sexually needs to be about blessing the relationship with goodness, connection, and pleasure. It is about replenishment, not just a plan of action ending in orgasm. Achieving orgasm takes practice! Husbands and wives both need to be patient with themselves as they work together to apply the material included in this chapter and connect together along the way.

The two greatest keys in helping a woman achieve orgasm are knowledge and time. Knowledge is something that both husband and wife need, but more specifically, a wife needs to get comfortable with the practice of sexual self-discovery. Sexual maturity and development come from learning and understanding your sexual functioning then relaying that information to your husband. You need to get your head around this idea by prioritizing self-discovery and clear communication. Now, let's talk about time. The first orgasm is the "hardest" to achieve because of everything you are learning. The synapses in your brain are relaying information from one brain cell to the next as your brain-to-genital connection takes place. If a woman is worried about how much time it might be taking to feel aroused to achieve orgasm, she will be unable to relax, which will prevent the orgasm from taking place. Plan for plenty of time and space as you explore and learn together how to create an orgasm.

For most women, receiving oral sex, or *cunnilingus*, is reported as the most effective way to achieve orgasm. As men become increasingly sensitive to the importance of the female orgasm and recognize that penile-vaginal intercourse alone is often ineffective in achieving one, they can increasingly utilize cunnilingus in their sexual experiences. I know that some people may feel a little squeamish about oral sex. I respect your agency and differences in sexual preferences. As a couple, as a team, and as equal partners, you can decide together what activities to incorporate into your sexual relationship. Your responsibility is to make decisions based on good information and spiritual guidance, recognizing that these decisions can be revisited in the future.

Sexuality is at its best when the woman's sexual needs are being met. The fact that orgasms come easily for men was clearly documented in Masters and Johnson's claim that the male sexual experience is "ejaculatory inevitable." Historically, Dr. Alfred Kinsey, a famous sexual researcher who interviewed thousands of individuals about their sex lives, stated that

75% of men typically ejaculate within two minutes of penetration while only 33% of women regularly orgasm at all. This means that two out of every three women are consistently not climaxing during sex.[55]

Researchers from the *Archives of Sexual Behavior* assessed the sex lives of over 52,500 adult Americans and discovered that a large contributing factor to the orgasm gap is a lack of understanding the female anatomy, by both men and women. When labeling a diagram of female genitalia, 59% of men and 45% of women could not accurately label the vagina. Over six in ten men and 55% of women didn't know where the urethra was, and 43% of women and 52% of men failed to label the labia. Studies have also found that among women whose partners spent twenty-one minutes or longer on foreplay, including passionate manual and/or oral touching of the vulva, only 7.7% failed to reach orgasm consistently. What an amazing closing of the gap! From two out of three women not being able to consistently reach climax to nine out of ten achieving orgasm. This is the difference knowledge and time can make![56]

Although approximately 90% of women report having an orgasm from some form of sexual stimulation, most women do not routinely (and some never) experience orgasm solely from penile-vaginal intercourse because the clitoris is not directly involved with vaginal penetration. A very likely reason that women do not typically orgasm with intercourse is due to the distance between the clitoris and the vaginal opening. If the clitoris-vagina distance is less than 2.5 cm, orgasms are reliable during penetrative sex. A greater spread in distance will typically require direct clitoral stimulation. Either way, understanding that the clitoris needs sexual stimulation for female orgasm to occur is essential.[57]

The chapters in this book that include information about female genitalia, in particular the clitoral complex (*Chapter 20: Primary Erogenous Zones - Genitalia*) and female G-Zone (*Chapter 25: Female G-Zone*), provide adequate information for you to learn where organs are and how they contribute to female pleasure. The remainder of this chapter is largely directive for husbands as it will discuss techniques to achieve female orgasm, including tactile and oral touch, or cunnilingus. Just like trying anything for the first time, this practice may feel strange at first. I encourage you to not give up after the first few attempts. Continue to try, communicate, evaluate, and try again as you experientially learn how to give and receive pleasure this way.

Pointers for Manual Clitoral Stimulation

- In preparation for lovemaking, I encourage couples to shower, shave, brush teeth, and trim nails. Your feelings of confidence and freedom to explore and touch one another will be greatly enhanced by coming to bed clean and shaved. I understand the busyness of life with a large family and young children, so I know this isn't going to happen every night. Still, I encourage couples to come to bed clean and ready for pleasure as frequently as possible.
- This is a journey of bringing pleasure to the wife, which in turn is highly satisfying for the husband. Gradually make love to all of her by spending plenty of time with light touching, eye gazing, kissing, loving her breasts, and talking. There is a 20:20 rule to lovemaking I like to teach. The first 20 minutes is spent in emotional and non-sexual touch while the second 20 minutes is directed toward sensory-building sexual touch. I strongly encourage at least 40 minutes of time lapse in this type of connection prior to penetration and/or direct clitoral stimulation. This slow approach to orgasm will increase the probability of climax occurring, but even more importantly, it will build connecting pleasure within the relationship.
- Once you begin touching her vulva, make sure you have adequate lubrication. You may touch your finger into the opening of her vagina to get some of her natural lubricant. I also suggest using other lubricants to help with this process of arousal. Your lubricated finger can rub her labia majora, pulling back the folds to expose her labia minora, vagina, and clitoral glans. Start by massaging the clitoral glans through the clitoral hood before moving directly to the clitoral glans. Take your time on and around the clitoral glans, rubbing, tugging, tapping in vertical, zigzag, circular, and figure-8 motions. Speed and tempo can also vary, with the tendency to accelerate as excitement builds.
- Take note that it is not uncommon for this type of touch to feel extremely pleasurable one time and too intense another. It is imperative for a wife to gently communicate to her husband how she pre-

fers to be touched. (Unless she learns this by sexually maturing and understanding her own arousal, this will be challenging for both of you.)

- With increased arousal, a wife often likes a finger, or fingers, inserted vaginally. Pressure in the back region of the vagina is very pleasurable to many women. Also, locating the cervix is a good idea. As you reach a lubricated finger or two inside of your wife's vagina, gently feel straight back from the vaginal opening. Your finger will reach the cervix (i.e., opening of the uterus). It will feel much like the tip of your nose. All around the tip of the cervix are nerve endings that can provide a lot of pleasure. Putting pressure on these points, softly rubbing them, or running your finger around the cervix are ways to ignite these nerve endings. Again, communication is essential! For some women this vaginal exploration won't feel good. For others, it can lead to ecstasy!
- If vaginal penetration and pressure feel good, and with clitoral stimulation necessary for orgasm, this is a time when a wife may want to reach down and begin stimulating her clitoral glans while you go to work on the internal clitoral complex and female prostate. She may want to grind on your thigh, play with her own breasts and nipples, or experiment with different sexual accessories to help with this process. Spend time doing what feels best, which will likely involve the continual need for massaging the clitoral glans, as you work together with loving communication to steadily provide increasing sexual pleasure to your wife.[58]

Pointers for Practicing Cunnilingus

- Women may feel anxious that they might smell or aren't clean enough to receive oral sex. Of course, as mentioned previously, showering and coming to bed clean can provide more confidence and freedom in your lovemaking. Still, it is helpful for a woman to be reassured that she smells fine and that you enjoy the way she smells.
- This is a journey of bringing pleasure to your wife. As stated earlier, gradually make love by spending plenty of time with light touching, eye gazing, kissing, loving her breasts, and talking. Then slowly move to teasing with light kisses and caresses from the inner thighs to flut-

tery, light genital kissing. Nibbling or blowing through underwear can also feel really nice. Once she is naked, before ever bringing your tongue to the clitoris, breathe while kissing her pubic mons and labia majora. As she lays on her back, with legs open wide, gently spread the labia majora and look at her vulva, while lightly touching all of her with your fingers and tongue. You can sense her arousal as she guides your head and face while lifting her buttocks toward your mouth. Experiment together to find the touches that feel exciting, arousing, and orgasm producing. Circular, up-and-down motions, and tapping on or near her clitoris, will likely create the most pleasure. Some tongue around and in-and-out of the vaginal opening may also be pleasant, but remember that the clitoral glans is the external pleasure-center. Using a steady stream of stimulation is usually the best way for her excitement to build. Approaching orgasm, then backing away from climax is a delightful way to expand the replenishing stage of lovemaking. This giving and receiving pleasure is a way to create erotic passion together. Typically, the more prolonged this experience is, the more intense and pleasurable the orgasm climax will be.

- As your wife climaxes, stop moving the finger or tongue. Hold steady on the clitoral glans to enhance the power of the orgasm. Then watch, pull back, and lightly touch the clitoral glans again, avoiding overstimulation, to ascertain her desire for another orgasm. If your wife communicates desire for further stimulation, start slowly again, building the pressure and rhythm of your touch as you provide more pleasure. Having multiple orgasms is a possibility for most women but not for all. The following chapter provides detailed information on multiple orgasms for both men and women.
- As any sexual experience concludes, take time to hold one another to experience the important "afterglow" phase of lovemaking. This time spent cuddling and gently communicating after having sex contributes positively to your relationship satisfaction. A recent study found that due to the activation of dopamine and oxytocin in the brain, for many couples, the feelings of love, friendship, and goodwill lingered for 48 hours after sex.[59]
- If giving and receiving oral sex is something you want to learn more about, I highly recommend the book, *She Comes First: The Thinking*

Man's Guide to Pleasuring a Woman by Ian Kerner. Here you will find intensive and detailed instructions on the art of cunnilingus. It has a wealth of knowledge for couples looking to learn more.

THINK. Individually, journal the thoughts and feelings that you have had while reading this chapter. Label the emotions specifically. Anxiety? Excitement? Dread? Then ponder and write the root cause of these emotions. For example, you may write something like, "Fear—I am afraid to receive oral sex because my mother told me that oral sex is sinful."

PAIR. This time get warm and comfortable in a bath, hot tub, or shower. Get clean and then just hold on to one another and breathe deeply for 10 minutes or so. Try to match breaths as you breathe in through the nose and out through the mouth.

SHARE. Once you are clean and dry, lay together and discuss the journaling experiences you had separately. Listen to understand. Hold each other while talking and making eye contact. Finally, I want you to discuss your thoughts about the following sentence: *Female pleasure is a worthy pursuit.*

Adding to your Sexual Playbook: Review what you've written previously in your sexual playbook about giving and receiving oral sex. Would you like to make any modifications to what you've written previously? Note specifically whether cunnilingus is something one or both of you want to explore now or at a future time.

Experiential Activities to Enjoy

Tongue Tapping

Once clean and comfortable, try a little experiment that I call *tongue-tapping*. Taking turns, rub or tap your tongue on your spouse's neck, lips, nipples, inner wrists, navel, big toes, behind the knees, along the gluteal fold, and finally spend some time tongue-tapping different parts of the penis, testicles, and scrotum, or labia majora, labia minora, and clitoral glans. Tapping in a variety of ways adds excitement and understanding of what types of touch you find more enjoyable.

Clitoral Rolling

Once you have emotionally connected as a couple and the wife feels clean, confident and is becoming increasingly aroused, you can practice this exercise. Never go directly to the clitoral glans. It is too sensitive and will not feel pleasurable.

Gently pull back the labia majora, and look at the clitoris. Touch gently with your fingers and thumb. Then lovingly explore the clitoral glans with your tongue. Lick in different motions: up and down, side to side, or figure eights. Now suck the clitoris between your lips, and gently roll it on your lips and tongue. Keep your teeth away! This is making love to your wife with your mouth and tongue. As you practice, this type of pleasure will become increasingly comfortable for both of you. Know that this type of lovemaking is often the most exciting and pleasing for women. The moisture and delicate texture of your tongue and lips are a perfect complement to the intensely sensitive clitoral glans.

Pleasure Evaluation

This is not about giving your husband a grade (unless it's an A+)! This is about giving your husband feedback. As sexual experiences need to happen for couples to really learn how to pleasure each other, having feedback is essential for continued learning and ultimate sexual fulfillment.

CHAPTER 22

Multiple Orgasms for Men and Women

Central to this book is the concept of replenishing sex in marriage, where both husband and wife connect emotionally as well as physically. I have emphasized that there are many ways to make love. Enabling both the husband and the wife to have an orgasm is just one of those ways. This chapter will focus on having multiple orgasms. However, when having multiple orgasms becomes your goal, it can take some of the pleasure out of your sexual experiences, much like having orgasm-focused sex can often decrease the enjoyment couples share together sexually. If having multiple orgasms is something that you want to try, counsel together. Is this something you want to work on together? Or is this something you feel more comfortable trying first alone? It's so important to remember that once the experiment becomes frustrating to one or both of you, the connection you are longing for can be interrupted or diminished. Clear communication will be necessary as you explore these possibilities together. Also, as you read the material presented in this chapter, it is important to recognize that multiple orgasms have not been researched extensively; most of the information available on multiple orgasms comes from self-reported, personal stories.[60]

Multiple Orgasms for Women

It has long been known that most women have the capacity for multiple orgasms because there is typically not a refractory period after a woman orgasms. As long as a woman has interest and energy, without clitoral hypersensitivity, she can typically continue to orgasm. A common description of multiple orgasms for women is that once the first orgasm ends, there is a short period of time when the woman is not having an orgasm. Soon after, due to continued or renewed stimulation, another orgasm happens. Typically, the first orgasm is the most intense with subsequent orgasms decreasing in intensity.

If attempting multiple orgasms, realize that continued stimulation of the highly-sensitive clitoris can become unpleasant. When this happens, stop touching the clitoral glans, move to the labia, vaginal opening, female prostate and/or perineum, then circle back to touching the clitoral hood before directly touching the clitoral glans again. This process is one that I recommend a woman does by touching herself as she learns about her own arousal and pleasure. She can include her husband in the journey, perhaps as an observer. She can also guide his touch or involve him with passionate kissing or nipple stimulation.

There are a few things that might help if you choose to learn how to experience multiple orgasms. Frequently, there is a continued tingly clitoral glans sensation after the first orgasm which indicates the desire for further stimulation. Pause to pay attention to that sensation. Reapply lubricant generously and, using fingers, palm, mouth, vibrator, or other tools, continue to stroke the clitoral glans, along with other sensitive genital areas. Pay attention to your own sensory cues as you determine what feels most pleasurable. Breathe deeply while your excitement increases. You can also engage your pelvic floor with contractions while your arousal is growing. Take your time—it isn't a race. This is a learning process so be patient. Remember, some women don't experience multiple orgasms, and that's okay! The purpose of sex is replenishment, not multiple orgasms.

Multiple Orgasms for Men

For men, orgasm and *ejaculation* are frequently used interchangeably. However, they are actually separate physiological processes. Orgasm is the peak intensity of sexual pleasure that occurs 3-7 seconds prior to ejaculation. It can create an altered state of consciousness or a dreamlike feeling of pleasure due to the secretion of oxytocin. The release of this hormone also leads to the rhythmic contractions that occur with ejaculation as the body expels semen. Once ejaculation takes place, the brain is flooded with both dopamine and endorphins, creating feelings of relaxation and sleepiness which contribute to the refractory period. Isn't it wonderful that men are created to receive the pleasure of these varied hormones in a way that will naturally bond them to their spouse, with whom they have a covenant relationship? How sad when these hormones are wasted when orgasm and ejaculation are coupled with pornography and/or masturbation!

Currently, there is only subjective information regarding multiple orgasms for men. Historically, the thought has been that men are unable to have multiple orgasms because of the refractory period, where the body goes through a period of rest from sexual arousal. Depending upon the amount of oxytocin released during ejaculation, as well as the age and health of the man, the refractory period can last between 15 minutes to as much as a few days. However, there are self-reported instances where some men claim to have multiple orgasms. A 2016 review article explained that for men, multiple orgasms occur within a span of 20 minutes, and the ability to have them declines after age 30.[61] By learning to delay ejaculation, a man can enjoy sexual pleasure for longer periods of time.

The first step to enjoying multiple orgasms requires a knowledge of pelvic floor muscles. Muscles that stretch from the tailbone to the public bone, *called the PC sling*, are involved with sexual arousal, erectile function, and orgasm/ejaculatory capabilities. The strength of these muscles, coupled with the ability to conscientiously relax these muscles, is key to controlling arousal and having multiple orgasms. Isolating these muscles, as described in the following chapter (Chapter 23: Pelvic Floor Therapy), and exercising them regularly, will enhance your ability to delay ejaculation. Unfortunately, there is not specific data on which pelvic floor techniques lead to multiple male orgasms and self-reported experiments are varied. Trying each of the techniques listed below can provide an opportunity to learn what works uniquely for you:

- Some men report that squeezing or flexing the pelvic floor muscles for a few seconds when reaching the point of ejaculation will stall ejaculation while experiencing orgasmic sensations.
- Other men report that short pelvic floor squeezes or pulsations will prolong orgasm.
- Other reports suggest that one long squeeze in conjunction with deep, purposeful breathing, while pressing firmly into the perineum, leads to orgasm without ejaculation.
- Finally, other reports claim that pelvic floor squeezing sensations make ejaculation more powerful but do not delay ejaculation.

Engaging in these processes requires a man to have arousal awareness. The body follows a predictable pattern from an arousal threshold to an orgasm threshold. During sex, arousal builds to a point and may plateau for a time. After enough stimulation, the arousal level leaves this plateau, rising quickly towards the orgasm threshold.

For men, the peak of the orgasm threshold is also known as "the point of no return" or more scientifically, *ejaculatory inevitability*. Once

Arousal to Orgasm Threshold

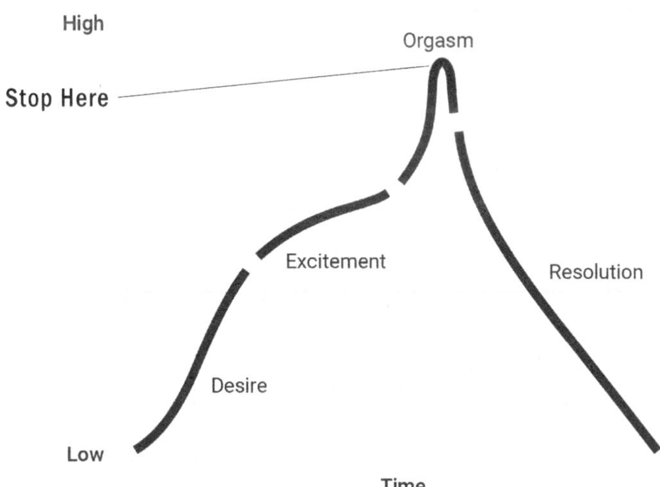

this point is reached, the pelvic floor muscles begin to involuntarily contract, and semen is ejaculated. For a man to experience multiple orgasms, he needs to be keenly aware of his arousal pattern and able to identify the point immediately prior to reaching ejaculatory inevitability.

An arousal scale, developed by sexologist Dr. Barbara Keesling, is a helpful tool to use when becoming aware of your arousal pattern. Learning to recognize your arousal pattern on this 1-10 scale can help you learn when to "cool down" to prolong pleasure and experience orgasmic sensations without ejaculating.[62]

Arousal Level	Description
0	No Arousal. A completely flaccid penis.
1-3	Arousal and sexual interest. The body responds with blood flow to the genitals, and the penis begins to get erect.
4-6	Increased arousal leading to a full erection.
7-9	Feeling highly aroused and desiring more stimulation. Touch is increasingly pleasurable.
9-10	The point of ejaculatory inevitability.
10	Ejaculation occurs.

Remember, learning a new skill will take time. Hitting the point of no return is going to happen as you work together to learn this new love-making technique. Enjoy the experience of learning together with an attitude of exploration and awe.

Identifying sexual energy, and understanding how to direct it, is an important part of being good at controlling your arousal. It's an erotic energy or sensory force that can be directed with the mind to different body parts. Often this sexual energy, or the sensations felt when "turned on," will begin at the tip of the penis or in the testicles. Through breath-work exercises, pelvic floor exercises and mindfulness, you can learn how to move this sexual energy away from the penis to other parts of the body. Learning to channel this energy will greatly increase your ability to prolong ejaculation.

Once you're at a 7-8 on the Keesling arousal scale, relax your body and breathe in deeply. Focus your awareness on the tip of your penis. Identify how it feels and what types of sensations you're experiencing. Shift that awareness to your testicles, and identify the sensations there. Now, become aware of the sensations in your perineum and, next, your anus. Do you feel energy in these areas as well? As you analyze the sexual sensations throughout the genitals, identify your arousal epicenter. While continuing to breathe deeply, with your mind's eye, move the sexual energy from the epicenter towards the center of your body, below the navel.

In time, and with continued practice, you will discover the ability to absorb sexual energy into the body by slowing down the arousal with deep breathing and pelvic floor exercises. While you inhale, intentionally contract your pelvic floor muscles. Imagine the sexual energy flowing into your body as you slowly exhale. Continue this practice for several minutes. You will notice that as your arousal and desire to ejaculate declines, the sexual energy "settles" into the body, creating an expansion of passionate, loving emotions in the heart. Your whole body can become fueled with sexual energy, allowing you to have more powerful sexual experiences. Once your breathing has become regulated, start again to become sexually aroused with loving touch. Continue with this pattern of arousal awareness and sexual energy as long and frequently as possible. With these exercises, you can begin to experience multiple orgasms and delayed ejaculation.[63]

THINK. What are your thoughts regarding multiple orgasms? How important is this for you during this season of your life? Is this something you feel comfortable trying first alone, or would you prefer sharing this journey with your spouse from the beginning?

PAIR. Come together in a comfortable way. Relax into one another without speaking for several minutes. Breathe together, fully clearing your mind of other matters. Take a deep cleansing breath before you begin sharing.

SHARE. Discuss openly your thoughts about this chapter. With equal voices, create a plan of action that will work best for both of you.

Adding to your Sexual Playbook: Together create and write down some guidelines to help you remain focused on replenishing your relationship when you are also trying new experiences, such as achieving multiple orgasms.

Experiential Activities to Enjoy

Identifying and Strengthening Your PC Muscle

This activity is great for both men and women! Halfway through urination, stop or slow the flow of urine by squeezing your lower pelvic muscles. Don't tense the muscles in your buttocks, legs, or abdomen. Don't hold your breath either. When you can successfully do this, you've identified your *pubococcygeus* muscle (PC) muscle. Of note, the PC muscle works as one of the deep muscles in the pelvic floor that also supports the spine. The pelvic floor, sometimes called the pelvic bowl, looks much like a bowl of muscles that fills the space at the bottom of the pelvis between pelvic bones.

Now that you know what contracting your PC muscle feels like, it's time for an exercise regimen! The PC muscle contracts along with other muscles that make up the pelvic floor. Begin by lying on your back on your bed with your knees bent or leaning back in a chair with your legs stretched out and ankles crossed. Begin squeezing then relaxing your PC muscles, doing 2 sets of 20 repetitions. It's critical to completely relax your PC muscles between every contraction. Once you get comfortable with 2 sets of 20, try holding the contraction longer (for two to three seconds). Then fully relax between each contraction. Consistency is the goal. Like any muscle-strengthening exercise, listen to your body, and use wisdom so you don't overdo it. Occasionally test your progress by stopping, starting, then stopping the flow of urine.

Methods for Delaying Ejaculation

These are all wonderful practices when wanting to delay ejaculation, either for the experience of multiple orgasms or for men experiencing premature ejaculation.

Penis Squeeze

Once you are aroused to a 7 or an 8 on the Keesling arousal scale, squeeze the tip of the penis. Place the thumb on the underside of the head of your penis, near the frenulum, with your fingers on the top side and squeeze hard. If done correctly, this action will decrease arousal.

Scrotum Pull

Once a man becomes aroused, his body will naturally draw the testicles up closer to his body. The scrotum will also stretch and become tighter across the testicles. Wrap your hand around the base of the scrotum, where it is attached to the body, and squeeze it gently while pulling the testicles away from the body. Pay attention to how this method affects arousal.

5 Senses

This mindfulness technique helps you remain aware of your arousal. Once aroused to a 7-8 on the Keesling arousal scale, pay attention to each of your five senses. What do you see? Hear? Taste? Smell? Feel? As you intentionally focus on each sense, notice how becoming mindfully present in your environment affects arousal.

"Million Dollar Spot"

Once you are aroused to an 8-9 on the Keesling arousal scale, apply pressure to the slightly indented area on the perineum, about halfway between the testicles and anus. Using the pad of your middle finger or thumb, push upward towards the body while still stimulating the penis. Recognize how this touch affects arousal.

CHAPTER 23

Pelvic Floor Therapy

By small and simple means, great things are brought to pass. Learning about and strengthening your pelvic floor may be a small and simple tool that can lead to great results on your journey to claim a replenishing sexual relationship with your spouse. I first learned of the importance of the pelvic floor ten years ago after having back surgery. I had lived over half a century not knowing about the pelvic floor, nor how it might contribute to healthy sexual functioning. I want you to learn about the pelvic floor now so that you can start enjoying the benefits that come from having a healthy one. Read this carefully and apply it to your life. You'll be glad you did.

What Is the Pelvic Floor?

The pelvic floor supports the bladder, rectum, and prostate in men and the uterus and vagina in women. It includes all the tissues, muscles, ligaments, and nerves that support these organs. While both men and women have a pelvic floor, women are more likely to suffer from pelvic floor dysfunction (PFD) due to pregnancy, labor, and delivery of infants. The frequency of PFD increases with age, with PFD found in 10% of women under the age of 40 to nearly 50% of women over 80. The prevalence of PFD is higher for overweight women, those suffering from chronic bowel issues, women experiencing menopause and/or women who have had a hysterectomy.

Male Pelvic Floor

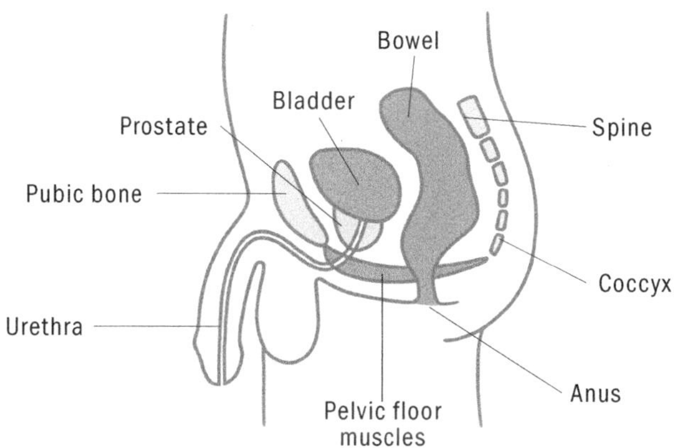

Female Pelvic Floor

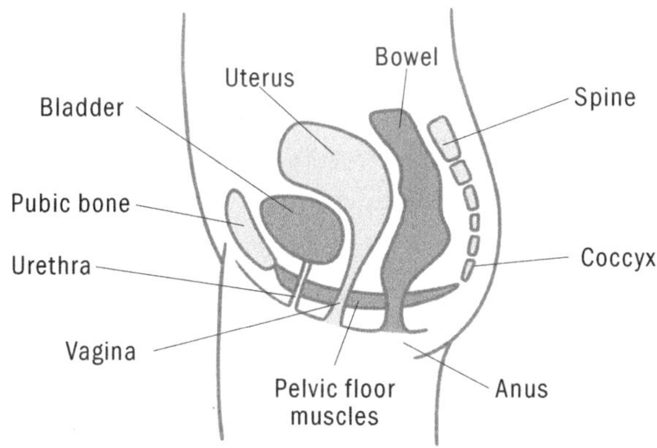

The pelvic floor has been described as a "hammock" for all the organs located in the pelvic region. Problems occur when the pelvic floor hammock doesn't contract and relax as it should. The failure to relax causes muscle spasms that result in urinary or fecal incontinence, lower back pain or sexual dysfunction. A weak pelvic floor hammock may lead to a reduction in vaginal and clitoral sensations, resulting in weak and less-fulfilling orgasms, leaking urine and gas, difficulty tightening and contracting the pelvic floor muscles in Kegel exercises, and contributes to tampons, menstrual cups or discs, and diaphragms not staying within the vagina. The health of the pelvic floor is strongly correlated with women's sexual functioning.[64]

When to Seek Pelvic Floor Therapy

When an individual experiences incontinence, chronic pelvic pain, or difficulty with bowel movements or urination, he/she is an excellent candidate for pelvic floor therapy. While men may be treated for premature ejaculation and painful ejaculation, when it comes to sexual issues, pelvic floor therapy can be a lifesaver for women seeking treatment for *dyspareunia* (painful vaginal sexual intercourse) or *vaginismus* (inability to relax vaginal opening to allow for penetration). While many factors can contribute to painful intercourse, there is typically a physical component to the situation—this is where pelvic floor therapy can make a world of difference. Consensual, loving sex in marriage should be pain-free. I have seen so many couples in my office whose sexual lives have transformed in just a few months by getting a pelvic floor therapist on their team.[65]

I believe that pelvic floor therapy should involve a holistic, full body approach to health, as everything in the body is connected. Pain or dysfunction in one area is very likely contributing to pain or dysfunction somewhere else in the body. For instance, jaw and pelvic floor muscles are connected through embryological development and fascia tissue. When you are clenching your jaw, you are also clenching the muscles in your pelvic floor. Nerves that begin in the neck control diaphragmatic breathing, which in turn affects the mobility of pelvic floor muscles. The lower back is stabilized through pelvic floor muscles, so pelvic floor therapy can also work wonders in reducing lower back pain. The list goes on and on. Finding a pelvic floor therapist or physical therapist who will approach pelvic floor therapy with a holistic approach is the best advice I can share when talking about the importance of seeking help for PFD. I encourage you to look into a provider within your insurance group that specializes in pelvic floor therapy. It can make a world of difference not only in healthy sexual functioning but in all-around wellness.

Signs of a Healthy Pelvic Floor

The health of your pelvic floor will impact your bladder, bowels, and sexual experiences. Listed below are signs of a healthy pelvic floor in each of these areas.

Bladder:

- Urinating every 2-4 hours during the day
- Sleeping through the night without waking up to urinate unless pregnant or older than 65 years
- Emptying bladder without pushing or straining
- Freedom from painful urination, leaking or uncomfortable urges to urinate

Bowel:

- Bowel movement at least once a day (no constipation)
- Feces that look like a sausage or soft-serve ice-cream
- Feeling satisfied after a bowel movement
- Freedom from pain or straining during a bowel movement
- No incontinence nor uncontrolled passing of gas
- No hemorrhoids

Sexual:

- No pain with intercourse or orgasms
- No unwanted orgasms
- Little difficulty attaining or maintaining an erection

If you are experiencing challenges in one or more of these areas, I encourage you to seek medical help and perhaps a referral to a pelvic floor therapist. Pelvic floor challenges stem from having either an overactive or an underactive pelvic floor.

Overactive Pelvic Floor

An overactive pelvic floor means that your pelvic floor hammock is contracted and ascended, leading to difficulties lengthening and relaxing. In this situation, doing Kegel exercises is not a good idea as they will make these muscles tighter. Signs of an overactive pelvic floor include:

- Lower back, hip, groin, sacroiliac joint (SIJ) or tailbone pain

- Urgency to urinate
- Constipation
- Hemorrhoids
- Painful intercourse
- Painful vaginal insertion (penis, tampon, menstrual cup, vibrator, etc.)
- Incomplete bladder emptying
- Straining to urinate or have a bowel movement.

Underactive Pelvic Floor

An underactive pelvic floor means that the pelvic floor muscles do not voluntarily contract appropriately. In this situation, Kegel exercises are essential to strengthen the pelvic floor and increase tone, endurance, and coordination of the pelvic area. Signs of an underactive pelvic floor include:

- Urinary incontinence
- Fecal incontinence
- Vaginal and/or anal prolapse
- Vaginal pressure and discomfort
- Lower back, hip, groin, sacroiliac joint (SIJ) or tailbone pain

Pelvic Floor Resources

If you are experiencing pelvic floor challenges, you are not alone! Overall, nearly one quarter of women in the United States experience pelvic floor disorders.[66] Get the help you need. There is no shame in this! There are great online resources to help with pelvic floor dysfunction when waitlists or other factors delay or prevent you from seeing a pelvic floor therapist. I really appreciate the videos, articles and products that can be found at intimaterose.com and at thevaginawhisperer.com. Additionally, *Beyond the V Women's Health* has a wonderful YouTube channel and Instagram account, full of videos that provide helpful information about various pelvic floor assessments and exercises.

If you are experiencing any symptoms, I strongly encourage you to get some help. If you do, your quality of life may be greatly enhanced both in and out of the bedroom. As you understand and strengthen your pelvic floor muscles, you are acquiring a valuable tool on your journey to a more replenishing and connecting sexual relationship with your spouse.

THINK. In reviewing the listed pelvic floor health indicators, how healthy is your pelvic floor? Do you think you might benefit from pelvic floor therapy? Does your current health insurance cover pelvic floor therapy?

PAIR. In a quiet and comfortable place, get close, and be still for several minutes before you start sharing.

SHARE. Discuss your THINK responses. Determine if a plan of action is necessary for pelvic floor therapy. Act on the plan, supporting one another in this process.

Adding to your Sexual Playbook: Write down your thoughts on maintaining a healthy pelvic floor and how you will reach out for help in this area if it is needed.

Experiential Activities to Enjoy

Identify your Pelvic Floor

Unless you have a conscious awareness of your pelvic floor muscles, you will not be able to strengthen them. Here are some ways you can identify them:

- Imagine you are urinating. Contract then relax the muscles you would use to stop the stream of urine. Do this several times.
- While you are actually urinating, stop and release the stream of urine several times.
- Contract the muscles you use to hold back a bowel movement or keep yourself from passing gas, but don't contract your buttock,

abdomen, or inner thigh muscles. When doing this correctly, your body shouldn't lift at all. Pay attention to this.

- For women, insert a finger or vaginal dilator into your vagina, then contract your pelvic floor muscles around your finger or the dilator. You should feel your vagina tighten and your pelvic floor move upward.

Try not to use your abdomen, leg, or buttock muscles when you contract and relax your pelvic floor muscles. Exercising these other muscles won't help you strengthen your pelvic floor muscles. To find out if you're also contracting your abdomen, leg, or buttock muscles, you can place one hand on your stomach and your other hand underneath your buttocks or on your leg. Squeeze your pelvic floor muscles. If you feel your abdomen, leg, or buttocks move, you are using the wrong muscles.

Be sure to relax your pelvic floor muscles completely after you contract them. If you're having trouble identifying your pelvic floor muscles, please get help from a medical professional who can refer you to a pelvic floor therapist.

Kegel Exercises

Once you learn to correctly contract your pelvic floor muscles, do 2 or 3 sessions of Kegel exercises (contracting and releasing your pelvic floor muscles) every day to get the best results. It's best to spread the sessions throughout the day. Get into a comfortable position, either laying down or sitting in a chair, so your body is relaxed. Once you're familiar with the exercises, you should be able to do them in any position and in any place, such as standing, waiting in a line and even driving. You don't have to go to the gym. It's nice because you can stealthily do these exercises literally anywhere!

Get comfortable and follow these steps:

- Breathe in deeply through your nose, letting your abdomen rise as it fills with air. Keep your pelvic floor muscles relaxed as you breathe in.

- Breathe out slowly and smoothly through your mouth as you gently contract your pelvic floor muscles.
- Keep your pelvic floor muscles contracted for 3-6 seconds (until your muscles start to get tired) while you breathe out. This is called a contraction.
- Breathe in and release the contraction. This relaxes your muscles.
- Relax your muscles completely for 6-10 seconds. It's very important that you relax fully between each contraction and that you don't hold your breath. Always spend the same amount of time or longer relaxing your muscles as you do contracting them.
- Repeat this exercise 10 times each session.

CHAPTER 24

Male Pleasure and Prostate Massage

The first part of this chapter focuses on understanding and pleasuring the male prostate, while the experiential activities focus on the penis. I know some of you are going to pass by the first part of this chapter; that's totally fine. For those who are interested, there is quite a lot of pleasure that men can experience through prostate massage. This is something both spouses need to get on board with. One should never pressure or manipulate the other into performing sexual activities, no matter how much you may want to try them. Remember, making sexual decisions as equal partners comes from independent places of maturity. Two wholehearted people coming together is what makes sex fun, fully connecting and mutually fulfilling.

In tantric reading, the male prostate gland has been referred to as the "hidden penis" because over one-third of the penis is actually found inside the body. It is about the size of a ping pong ball and is internally located just below the bladder, surrounding the urethral tube. The prostate produces about 20-30% of the seminal fluid which both nourishes sperm and makes semen more fluid for easier transport in the female body. Another interesting fact is that during ejaculation the prostate contracts, closing off the opening between the bladder and urethra. This makes it impossible, in healthy situations, for semen and urine to be ejaculated simultaneously.

Prostate massage can ease inflammation. It can also be sexually stimulating. Although there is limited research on sexual prostate massage, and there is no evidence that it assists with sexual dysfunction, it is known that prostate massage may enhance the intensity of ejaculation.[67] If this is something both husband and wife want to explore, this chapter can help you with this process. Before starting, I encourage husbands to defecate and thoroughly clean themselves. I also recommend using a latex-gloved hand (to protect the delicate anal membrane from fingernails and as a lubricated rubber surface will glide more easily than skin) as you learn together about prostate massage. You will not be touching the prostate directly, but rather through the rectal wall, where the lobes of the prostate can be felt. This area is very sensitive to pressure, so be gentle and slow as you learn together what feels nice. Always use a water-based lubricant in this situation.

If desired by both spouses, set the environment to be romantic with low lighting, soft music, and plenty of time. The husband should sit with his back against pillows, pull his knees up to his chest and angle his buttocks forward slightly, breathing deeply and relaxing into this position. This creates an exposed, open area for his lover to kneel or sit cross-legged in front of him. The wife should start by massaging the feet, legs, thighs, and abdomen before coming near the genitals. As you begin this type of lovemaking, I encourage couples to get familiar with the husband's perineum. As you explore, you will find an indented patch, about the size of a pea, along the perineal fold that runs vertically between the anus and testicles/scrotum. This is sometimes referred to as the "Male G-spot" or as his "sacred spot" in tantric writings. If this area has not been previously touched, you will want to go slowly because the sensations are felt so deeply inside of him that it may initially feel uncomfortable. In time, massaging the penis with one hand, while massaging this spot with the other, can become highly sexually satisfying and deeply emotionally connecting, even healing. From this place, gently cup the penis and testicles with both of your hands as you maintain eye-contact for several minutes. This experience is a perfect place to start anal and prostate massage.

When the husband feels fully relaxed and ready, the wife should put on a latex glove and generously lubricate both the finger and anus with a water-based lube. Gently massage the anus with the pads of your gloved fingers in circular motions. Focus on touch that creates sensual pleasure to the anal opening, which is full of nerve endings. It is helpful if the husband communicates what feels nice, so that his wife has clarity in what type of touch is preferred. Don't poke your finger into the anus, but rather as you massage, with plenty of lube and time, the anus will relax and allow the finger to enter.

Once inside, allow the anal sphincters to adjust to the finger intrusion; don't move the finger in and out, but hold it there for a few minutes. While waiting, with the other hand, cradle the length of the penis and testicles snuggly against his body. This provides a warm, secure feeling. The husband should breathe deeply and talk lovingly to his wife as she comes to more fully understand how to touch him in this deeply intimate and vulnerable way. If necessary, slip the finger out of the anus to apply more lubrication, then gently return it inside, holding it steady as the anus relaxes around it.

Now it's time to find the prostate. There will be a variety of sensations felt by the husband, with the most pleasurable being the increased feeling of impending ejaculation. Slowly crook your finger upward about two inches inside the anus where you will feel a roundish, egg-shaped protrusion. With the husband communicating how much pressure feels good, the wife can provide an internal massage while externally holding and massaging the penis, testicles, and perineum. When the husband is on the brink of ejaculating, the wife can extend his pleasure by lessening pressure on the prostate. The wife can begin to move her finger partially in and out of the anus, stimulating the nerve endings found in the anus and creating an ebb and flow of arousal. This arousing combination can continue for as long as you both desire, recognizing that ejaculation is not the goal of this experience, although it is likely to occur as this internal and external simultaneous touch can create great pleasure. If desired, at some point, the wife can remove her finger and her glove, straddle the erect penis, and share a wonderful culmination to the experience.

Whatever way you decide to finish the prostate massage, I encourage you to hold each other closely with loving care. Look deeply into each other's eyes; this is a replenishing time where souls can connect through the eyes. Deeply felt emotions can often surface with male or female erotic prostate massage. I believe these emotions can provide the deeply-bonding intimacy we are divinely created to experience in marriage. These are the moments that are all-to-often missed in lovemaking. Slow down and savor these special, sacred moments you create together.

THINK. Independently consider what you felt while reading this chapter. Can you identify the emotions that came up? What were your thoughts? Were you able to stay present and focused on your thoughts and feelings rather than worrying about what others might think?

PAIR. After you've both had time to read and process the chapter, come together.

SHARE. Thoughtfully listen to each other's experiences. Ask questions and listen to better understand. What parts of this chapter are you interested in and ready to integrate into your lovemaking? Are their parts of this chapter you're not interested in currently trying? It is totally okay if it's not the right time or if this is not appealing to you.

Adding to your Sexual Playbook: Write down how you would like to include male prostate massage in your relationship and whether there are elements of this process you're ready to try now or would like to consider trying at a future time.

Experiential Activities to Enjoy

Penile Familiarity

I have heard several times in therapy a wife saying that the penis is ugly, gross, disgusting, or "Ewww, I'm not going to touch that thing!" Ladies, this is an important part of your husband's body that is frequently associated with masculinity and manhood. Don't "demasculinize" your husband by these types of comments. Boys and men typically love their penises. This is a body part that brings them great pleasure. Your husband's penis is external, so they have had a lifetime to get familiar with this important, erotic body part. Now, as a wife, it is your turn to also become familiar with your husband's penis, testicles, perineum, and anus.

1. With your husband naked, learn about the different parts of his genitals. Discover what parts are more or less sensitive. With plenty of lubrication, try touching with various strokes or taps. Discover what types and intensities of touch feel best.
2. As your husband's penis becomes erect, move it back and forth with your hand. Touch him this way until he gets close to climaxing, then pull off the penis, and let things cool down. Continue to do this several times without bringing him to ejaculation. This is an excellent way to help prolong pleasure, delay ejaculation, and give you information as to how to sexually touch your husband in ways that create sexual pleasure for him.
3. Communicate together through this experience. The husband may need to guide the wife's hands as she learns to touch him in ways that feel good.

Ever Ready!

You may have learned by now that a man's penis frequently becomes erect, even if you shared a long, leisurely lovemaking experience a few hours ago. There isn't a schedule as to when a penis should or shouldn't become erect—it just happens! Your husband can control what he does when this happens, but he cannot control when it will happen. Fifteen minutes before church starts to midnight after an exhausting day, a man can be ready to sexually connect. As visual desire is normal for men, it often just takes a glance, a wink, or working around the house without a bra for his penis to be standing at attention, ready for connection! Knowing this fact is important, especially as I often hear wives shaming their husbands for this "ready" response. I want to challenge couples to decide on a mantra, or fun exchange, that can happen between them when an erection happens and the wife feels some type of sexual response is necessary on her end of things. Instead of making this a sore spot or source of conflict, create positive energy with this natural, difficult-to-control bodily response. How can you make the ever-ready penis fit into your conversations with humor, anticipation, understanding, and love? Could it be that a quickie or hand-job could fit into the schedule occasionally? A fun, sexy mantra or a quickie are both ways that a wife can practically and lovingly contribute to her husband's well-being, as he tries to manage his normal bodily responses.

As I work with clients wrestling with this ever-ready dynamic, I have found that when a wife has a willing, non-shaming, loving attitude, she can help her husband feel like the luckiest man alive! Cutting, emasculating remarks, repeated refusals, resentment, and lack of understanding can make your marriage feel miserable. Men were created in this ever-ready fashion intentionally by loving Heavenly Parents. Think about that as you work to increase generous kindness in your marital sexual dance. As you do so, you will enhance bonding and replenishment within your marriage.

CHAPTER 25

The Female "G" Zone

I imagine there will be some readers who find this chapter frustrating, while others will read it and try new things with excitement. As I have stated before, this might not be for you, and that's totally okay! You get to choose what your sexual relationship becomes over the course of your marriage. My hope is to teach you things that can add depth and passion to your lovemaking experiences and to help you claim the sexual replenishment that you were wonderfully designed to enjoy.

Cultural and Scholarly Perspectives on the G-Zone

There's a lack of clear and conclusive research on the female prostate, better known as the G-spot (named after the German gynecologist Ernst Grafenberg), and female ejaculation. "A lot of mixed messages" is the easiest way I can describe my experience researching this topic. The first book on the topic, *The G-Spot,* written in 1982, talks about a very sensitive area on the front wall of the vagina that, when stimulated, can lead to intense sexual pleasure and orgasm for some women. This book also classified three different types of female orgasms—clitoral, vaginal, and blended (a combination of clitoral and vaginal); however, published research today still suggests uncertainty of three distinctly unique types of orgasms, as described in more depth later in this chapter. Unfortunately, the cultural take-away from this book was the idea that if you're not having G-spot orgasms along with female ejaculation, you're missing the "main event" of sexual pleasure. The 1980s and 90s hype on the G-spot and female ejaculation resulted in expensive and ineffective G-spot collagen injections and multiple new sex toys designed to help women achieve this goal-oriented style of sex.

A new dimension of vaginal sexual pleasure was introduced in 1997 when Chua Chee Ann, a physician and researcher, published her findings on the "A-spot" or anterior fornix erogenous zone, also referred to as the AFE zone. This is an area of sensitive tissue on the anterior vaginal wall to the opening of the cervix through which the G-spot (at this time period, researchers were just beginning to study the G-spot as a possible female prostate) can be pleasurably stimulated. This news brought on a frenzy of female sexuality research which, fortunately, created the gateway for many of the advancements in female sexual science we appreciate today. However, with technological advances creating widespread access to information, female orgasmic possibility soundbites and clickbait sent a much less helpful message to women regarding their sexuality. Many women felt sexually inept, even broken, when they could not experience G-spot, A-spot, or AFE zone arousal, pleasure, and orgasm. This cultural framework effectively progressed the 1960s scientific suggestion that women's sexual capacities were inferior to men's sexual possibilities.[68]

Pornography has also contributed to inaccurate beliefs regarding what is considered "normal" in sexual experiences. Along with staged female ejaculations or squirting, exaggerated male penis sizes, and female pleasure being directly tied to the thrusting force of the male penis, pornography misinforms and ultimately harms one's ability to discern helpful sexual information. This trend leaves couples confused and highly frustrated as they struggle to have relational sex where both partners are giving and receiving pleasure.

Do you experience a quandary of how women should understand and relate to their sexuality? If so, you are not alone. With much of female sexual science being inconclusive and society being lied to by the porn industry, where can you find helpful answers to questions such as:

1. Is there a female prostate or G-spot?
2. Can women ejaculate?

3. How can we incorporate the female prostate and ejaculation into our lovemaking?
4. Can sexual exploration and discovery be fruitful to our marriage relationship?
5. Will this exploration contribute to increased frustration and disconnection in our sexual relationship?

Let me give you my opinion on all of this. Clitoral orgasm, vaginal orgasm, and female-ejaculation-focused sexual experiences will prove frustrating and less than connecting when couples are making this the goal of their sexual experiences. I repeat, expect to share aggravating sex if your lovemaking is achievement focused. These exchanges will not be replenishing. However, if both of you can approach this style of loving with open-minds, straight-forward communication, and a sense of adventure, you may share some pleasurable discoveries. Read through this chapter, and then decide for yourselves what you want to do with the information.

Understanding the G-Zone

As you may imagine, the many differing opinions regarding the G-spot, A-spot, and overall female sexual pleasure can make writing about this topic somewhat challenging! Even today some educators are claiming the "G-spot is a myth" while concurrently researchers are suggesting it is not a spot, but more of an area. Other scientists consider the G-spot to be part of the clitoral root or clitoral complex. Epidemiologists often refer to the G-spot as the female prostate because in the embryonic biological homology of humans, the male prostate is the equivalent to the female G-spot. Medically speaking, the G-spot is also sometimes referred to as the *Skene's glands*. Can you understand why there is such great confusion!? Despite the various opinions of what the G-spot is or is not, the fact that so many scientific domains are exploring this controversial, elusive spot clearly suggests evidence that somewhere inside the vagina women can experience intense sexual pleasure!

Literally days before sending this book to publication, I virtually attended a conference where an exciting recommendation was encouraged by researchers of female sexual health. The suggestion was to update the term "G-spot" to "G-zone" for a more accurate description of this area of the female anatomy. Instead of searching to locate a specific or singular *spot*, recognize that there are five distinctly different types of tissues that make up a *zone* where, with appropriate stimulation, a female can experience pleasurable sexual sensations, swelling, and fluid ejaculation. These five tissues and the distinct contributions each make to female pleasure are:[69]

- The *corpora cavernosa* of the clitoral crura are two spongy masses of highly sensitive erectile tissue which swells with sexual arousal.
- The *corpora spongiosa* of the vestibular bulbs are two bulb-shaped masses of sensitive erectile tissue distributed on each side of the vaginal opening and around the anterior vaginal wall. These contribute to pleasurable swelling with sexual arousal.
- The *prostatic glandular* tissue surrounding the urethra contains nerve endings contributing to intense pleasure and fluid ejaculation.
- The *urethra*, upon stimulation, will also contribute to sexual pleasure and arousal.
- The *anterior wall of the vagina*, the tissue located on the upper wall of the vagina which is densely connected to the urethra, will add sensual pleasure upon stimulation.

The G-zone includes tissue found in the clitoral complex (clitoral crura and vestibular bulbs), it also contains tissue found below the bladder that surrounds the entire length of the urethral canal (roughly 1.5-2 inches in length). This particular prostatic glandular tissue begins at the urethral exterior opening and extends towards the cervix. Since 2009, it has been scientifically referred to as the female prostate. To create sexual pleasure, you do not directly touch the female prostate, but feel it through the anterior "roof" of the vaginal wall. Upon sexual stimulation of the prostate gland, with time and increased sexual arousal, it can produce a white, viscous secretion which exits the body through the urethra. This fluid is not urine but has a similar composition to male seminal fluids. It is frequently referred to as "female ejaculate."

For simplicity in writing this chapter, I will refer to this part of the G-zone as the female prostate.[70]

Exploring the G-Zone and Stimulating the Female Prostate

Before I describe how to find the female prostate, I want to acknowledge that not all women can feel their prostate gland, and not all women who can find their prostate find it sexually arousing. Indeed, Dr. Laurie Mintz's research found that 37% of women could not find their prostate gland, 17% found it, but it gave no pleasure, and 46% found their prostate gland and found pleasure or orgasm through stimulating it. My goal in writing is to give women more information in hopes that they can better claim the pleasure and joy that they are divinely designed to experience. I encourage you to experiment to find out for yourself whether this is something that will bring you pleasure and replenishment!

In my experience, having helped countless women and couples understand this part of the female body, the best way to get acquainted with this body part is for the woman to find it first, and then verbally guide her husband as he strives to understand how to bring her greater pleasure. If you want to use a mirror, it is often easier to see what it is you're touching. Ladies, first things first, go to the bathroom before you get started. Then, with a lubed-up finger, gently spread your labia apart and find your urethral opening. You will notice a thicker area (about ½" in diameter) around the urethral opening. Now slide your finger into your vagina, keeping your palm facing upward, insert your index and/or mid-

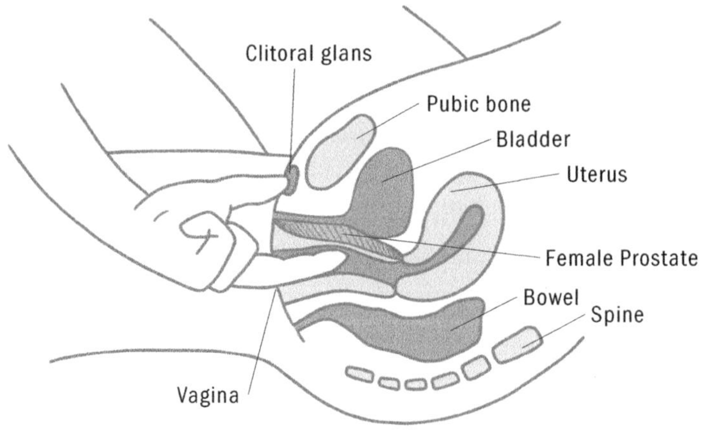

Finding the Clitoris and Female Prostate

dle finger into your vaginal canal up to your finger's first knuckle joint. Press upward, toward the roof of your vagina, and you will feel a patch of tissue that feels different, more textured. Keep your finger on this spot, and identify that this is where your urethra is connected to your vagina. Tap, press, rub circularly, explore, and breathe into any sensations that you might feel as you become familiar with the "head" or beginning of your female prostate.

Recognize the intricacies of the G-zone, including the female prostate, as you slowly slide your finger deeper inside your vagina, until you get to your finger's second knuckle. Remember, you should be touching the roof of your vagina; your palm needs to be facing upward for you to understand what I'm describing. Through the vaginal roof tissue, you will feel the textured ridges of your prostate gland as you explore. Go slowly so that you can become familiar with this part of your body. You may feel that you need to urinate. This sensation is normal; breathe and relax into it. This can be the start of newly-experienced erotic pleasure. Slide the pads of your fingers all over this area, from one side to the other, feeling the ridges and the texture. Feel the "ledges" that surround both sides, and run your fingers gently along each side; all of this is the body and connective tissue of your prostate gland. Stay here awhile as you touch gently and discover more definition. When you're ready, gently move back further with your finger, toward the cervix.

The tip of the cervix feels just like the tip of your nose. If you have gone back that far, move your finger backwards, where you have already been touching. Then slowly, so you can learn more fully what this area of your body feels like, continue with your palm still facing upward to the third finger knuckle joint. Identify the back end or "tail" of your prostate gland; it may feel round and firm or it could feel more like a ramp, flattening out at the end. Either way, curl your finger upward around the tail or end of the prostate gland. Gently use a "come hither" motion with your finger. If you cannot reach this part of your prostate gland, it's totally okay. Continue to touch the area you have already explored.

Now that you've found and become familiar with your prostate, invite your husband to learn about it too. He will insert his fingers and repeat the steps you have taken in discovering aspects of the G-zone, including the female prostate. Locate the external urethra, move to the patch where the urethra is connected within the vagina, touch the textured ridges of the prostate gland through the vaginal roof tissue, and the tail or end of the female prostate. It will likely be easier for him to reach the cervix and stimulate the sensitive nerve endings with the "come hither" motion of his finger. Take your time together as you learn and identify these pleasure centers. Try having him place two fingers on either side of the prostate, or the ledges, and run his fingers front to back. Breathe and open yourself to this touch as your prostate gland is rolled between gentle, squeezing fingers. Move the fingers side-to-side (in a windshield wiper motion) across the width of the prostatic tissue, feeling the ridges while changing the tempo of the touch, enhancing pleasure with each stroke.

You both may notice, with continued stimulation of the prostate gland, some swelling as it enlarges, much like a balloon. Bring a finger outside of the vagina and feel the urethral opening, running the finger in circles around this tissue, then come back inside and continue to feel the full length of the prostate gland. This time as the prostate is being massaged, the wife can practice lightly squeezing her pelvic floor and buttock muscles. Continue this action for as long as it feels pleasurable. She must communicate kindly with her husband as to the touch that feels pleasurable and erotic versus touch that feels uncomfortable. Stick with the pleasurable touch! When needed, add more lubrication.

The sensation of feeling like she needs to urinate will continue to grow as her prostate gland is stimulated. Push through the sensation, noticing that it ebbs and flows with the variety of touch being given to the prostate. Now slow down with circular or side-to-side motions, continuing to breathe and relax as stimulation continues. Touch every spot of the prostate, from head to tail and everything in between, focusing on the most pleasurable spots. For many women, the tail of the prostate is full of nerve endings that are especially erotic. Relax and continue to breathe into the pleasure. As husband and wife, work together and notice how your emotional connection can be greatly enhanced. As a team, united in giving and receiving pleasure, you are learning together how to sexually replenish. Over time the prostate will feel full and swollen, juicy, and erotic as she savors his loving touch.

Along with an increased feeling of needing to urinate, a wife may also experience soft streaks of pleasure that pulsate through her body. Sometimes this feeling will run down the length of her legs and out through the bottoms of her feet. Don't try to make any of these sensations happen—it doesn't work that way. Instead, just continue to relax, breathe deeply, and receive the goodness and pleasure that comes from loving, erotic touch. As excitement increases, she may have an increasing desire to achieve orgasm with clitoral glans touch. Female ejaculate expert, Deborah Sundahl, suggests that you breathe in fully and ask yourself three questions:

1. Do I feel aroused and very excited?
2. Do I feel like I need to urinate?
3. Does my prostate feel swollen? (It can begin to feel engorged, much like a plump grape.)

If the answer is "Yes!" to all three of these questions, it is an indication that she's close to ejaculation. She should lift her bottom off the bed, as the husband removes his finger from the vagina, then she can firmly push her pelvic floor as if she is trying to urinate. Hold a few seconds, then return to his stimulation of all areas of her G-zone, including the prostate. As pleasure increases, repeat the steps of removing his finger from the vagina while she lifts her buttocks up and pushes her pelvic floor as if trying to urinate. In time, she may either feel warm ejaculate spray or ooze from the urethra. If this happens, together you have stimulated her prostate to ejaculation!

Just as anything good in life requires time and practice, this exercise does as well. Recognizing this orgasmic pleasure and goodness comes from stimulating arousal to which encompasses all five areas of tissues that comprise the G-zone, many women report that female ejaculation feels like what is called a vaginal orgasm. Orgasms that occur through prostate stimulation are often felt deeper in the body and can be more emotionally interactive because they are connected to the pelvic nerve, which is a bundle of nerves (called the *sacral plexus*) located on the back of the pelvis. Clitoral orgasms are connected to the *pudendal nerve*, which is part of the greater sacral plexus bundle of nerves. The couples I work with who are committed to learning and enjoying this aspect of lovemaking, often experience a deeper, more loving bond than they felt prior to learning about the female prostate and ejaculation. I am convinced that this process can truly lead to some of the sweetest sexual replenishment shared in marriage.

Considering the newly proposed referencing of the female G-zone, the debate between calling an orgasm an orgasm based on where it originates versus what is being stimulated (the clitoral glans or the female prostate) in determining whether the orgasm is clitoral or vaginal, could be considered old information. The idea that "it's all part of the whole package" seems likely to be more accurate. However, over time sexual findings have defined a "blended" orgasm as one occurring when both clitoral glans and prostate are stimulated simultaneously. Personally, through years of study, effort, and therapeutic coaching, I know many women who have experienced all three types of orgasms. I understand that not all women have this experience, and that's totally okay. I don't think it matters where an orgasm originates or even if an orgasm occurs. What matters is the replenishment or pleasure and emotional connection that is experienced as husband and wife learn more about female sexual possibilities together.

Some women do not ejaculate. Please don't get frustrated if this doesn't happen for you, especially as you start this journey. I suggest that you ask yourself this question, "Was this experience enjoyable?" If you answer affirmatively, then you have succeeded in having a wonderful, replenishing lovemaking experience! I urge you to not get discouraged. This practice personally took me years to understand and experience. Any sexual experiences that are not enhancing love, goodness, and feelings of connection are *not* the type of sexual experiences you were created to have in marriage. This time should be enjoyed and reverenced by both of you.

Female Ejaculation Q&A

Here, I have included answers to a few common questions that I get from clients, that I suspect you may be having as well:

Q: What is female ejaculate?

A: Let's start by saying what it is not! It is not vaginal lubrication or urine. It is prostatic, seminal fluid mixed with glucose and trace amounts of urine. It looks like watered-down skim milk, tastes sweet, and does not smell.

Q: How much does a woman ejaculate?

A: Most women ejaculate about a teaspoon of fluid at a time. There are non-documented claims that women have ejaculated as much as 6 ounces at one time, soaking bedding in the process. Again, your experience will be unique to you and reverenced by you.

Q: What if my experience is different?

A: Why rob yourself of the joy you were sexually designed to experience by comparing your sacred experiences with those claimed by others? There is nothing good that can come from comparing your experiences with another's. I urge you *not* to do so. One of the fastest ways to discourage yourself is to compare yourself to others. Theodore Roosevelt has been attributed as coining the phrase "comparison is the thief of joy." When you were created in the image and function of Heavenly Parents, the plan was for your sexual experiences to be cherished within your marriage relationship. I implore you to choose to keep a sacred boundary around this important aspect of your mortal stewardship. Enjoy what you have, using helpful sources to learn together how to improve upon the experiences you sacredly share. In doing so, you will find greater joy and happiness.

THINK. Alone, process what you learned in this chapter. Honestly ask yourself if learning more about the G-zone is part of the journey you want to explore together. Assess the level of frustration that typically occurs when experimenting sexually. If frustration and irritation are more of the norm, then I suggest holding off on female prostate and ejaculation exploration. Decide to first focus on firming up the emotional connectedness of your relationship.

PAIR. Together in a location you both enjoy, breathe deeply and relax into one another for several minutes. Practice eye gazing for 10 minutes or so, until both of you feel connected and relaxed.

SHARE. Alternate sharing the things you thought about while reading this chapter. Listen to understand. Decide if this is a good season of your life and marriage to spend time exploring the female prostate and ejaculatory possibilities. How emotionally connected do you feel to do this work? Is there a desire for both of you to learn together? Jointly, make a decision regarding this aspect of your sexual experiences. It is totally okay if it's not the right time or if this is not appealing to you.

Adding to your Sexual Playbook: Write down what you both feel good about for now regarding this chapter. Make a notation regarding whether this is a topic one or both of you want to explore at a future time.

Experiential Activities to Enjoy

Finding the Female Prostatic Tissue Together

1. With plenty of time, I encourage you to come to bed clean, naked and ready to communicate clearly with one another as you make love. It will be very necessary to talk kindly and directly as you learn more about the G-zone, particularly the female prostate. This experience will need to be focused on the wife's pleasure. The husband will become aroused and possibly lose and regain an erection several times throughout the activity. That's normal. It will be more enjoyable and relaxing for the wife if she knows that this experience is focused on learning together without the need to provide sexual pleasure for her husband.
2. It might be helpful for a woman to use a heating pad or bag

between her legs as you get started. The warmth will help increase blood flow to the pelvic region.

3. Make certain that you have plenty of lubricant. It may be necessary to reapply lube several times throughout this exploration.
4. Emotionally connect. Talk and lightly touch without demand. Kiss and enjoy making out. Make this time enjoyable and replenishing for both of you.
5. With the wife guiding the husband, follow the steps outlined in the chapter as you both become familiar with the female prostate. Don't worry or stress if this doesn't go as you hoped. Remove any pressure to obtain any result beyond a loving connection! You are not earning a grade here! The objective is to enjoy learning together.
6. Don't give up too soon. If it starts feeling disappointing, pull back and enjoy other types of sexual touch. You can try this again another time, or you can calm and center yourselves and try to learn some more.
7. Make this experience positive and connecting. The work you are doing is sacred to your relationship. This needs to be a way of replenishing one another.

Orgasm Discernment Exercise

As I start explaining these exercises, I want to again emphasize that there are mixed opinions about female orgasms. Many scientists say that an orgasm is an orgasm is an orgasm, meaning regardless of where the orgasm originates, all orgasms are the same and use the same body parts. These scientists have more credible research and education than I do, so if you want to stop here, I completely understand and respect your decision. My own years of study and exploration, however, have me fully leaning in toward the second camp of orgasm researchers, described next:

Some sexologists and researchers talk about three different types of orgasms that a woman can experience: external clitoral glans (i.e., vulvar), vaginal (female prostate/G-spot, uterine, or A-spot), and blended (external clitoral glans combined with vaginal). Understand that all of these orgasmic experiences are occurring in the female G-zone. Before I describe each of these, I want to clearly state that all orgasms are good and satisfying. One orgasm is not better than another. I'm offering this spectrum of orgasms to provide differentiated clarity of what you may be experiencing, as well as the ability to put language around your experiences as you communicate about them with your spouse. In working with couples, I have also found that once a woman begins to understand her orgasmic possibilities more fully, especially by awakening the female prostate, she will often experience a growing desire for more full-bodied orgasms.

1. **Clitoral orgasm:** Clitoral orgasms are achieved through stimulation of the external clitoral glans leading to rhythmic contractions of the pelvic floor. This can be achieved without any stimulation of the internal clitoral compound.
2. **Vaginal orgasm:** As I have described the female prostate at length, and acknowledged that the combination of these body parts comprise what scientists are recommending be referred to as the G-zone, I will focus here on another vaginal pleasure spot. The A-spot, or the *anterior fornix*, is found deep within the vagina, right around the neck of the uterus or the cervix. Because of the role of the uterus in this orgasm, vaginal orgasm may also occasionally be called uterine orgasm. This area is about 4-5 inches inside the vagina and is rubbery in texture. The pressure applied with a finger, dildo, or penis needs to be in direct contact with the cervix. As touching the cervix can be very uncomfortable for some women, go slow as you learn more about this exciting body part. The pressure alone can enhance pleasure. By pressing, intense rubbing or slight jostling motions, a woman can orgasm deeply. Her body will begin to quiver and shake: often there will be muscles twitching throughout the pelvic floor into the inner thighs and even all the way down the legs through the feet. This movement is all indicating extreme pleasure. This type of orgasm is often more emotional in nature, leading to deeper bonding and connection.
3. **Blended orgasm:** This is a combination of clitoral and vaginal

> stimulation. There is a combination of sensations that are found in both types of orgasm, including the emotional component experienced with vaginal orgasm. Characteristic to a vaginal orgasm is an apnea response, characterized by the suspension of breath followed by an explosive exhale, which can be followed by laughter, sobbing, or screaming. The pleasurable pelvic floor contractions that coincide with clitoral stimulation are also present. A suction-like sensation of the cervix and uterus occurs and is immediately followed by deep relaxation of the entire pelvic floor. This type of orgasm can so completely release tension that feelings of sexual saturation may be experienced for several days.

As you read through these descriptions, you might recognize that you have experienced some or all of what is described. These orgasms are not separate, but more of a G-zone continuum. On one end of the spectrum is the clitoral orgasm with the blended or vaginal orgasm lying at the other. Strong pelvic floor muscles are essential to progressing toward vaginal orgasm (pelvic floor therapy can be very helpful here; see *Chapter 23: Pelvic Floor Therapy* for more information). A strong pelvic floor is also associated with the likelihood of experiencing female ejaculation. Think of where you are on this spectrum, get excited, and recognize that more pleasure awaits you.

CHAPTER 26

Sexual Fantasy

The preceding chapters have focused on providing detailed and accurate information on the amazing and divine ways our bodies have been created to experience and share sexual pleasure in marriage. Our bodies are amazing, but our brain remains the most important and powerful organ in creating a replenishing sexual relationship. This is seen in many ways, including being mindful and bringing your head to bed as explored in Part 2; it is also seen in our ability to create and share sexual fantasies with our spouse. However, this can be a difficult concept for some members of the Church to understand, as illustrated by my experience co-creating and team-teaching the first healthy sexuality course taught at Brigham Young University. The course was provisional and observed closely to meet appropriate requirements. Perhaps you can imagine the hours of preparing university-acceptable lectures, while also including instructive, helpful information. I felt like I was walking a tightrope in every lecture until the class was formally approved. Two of my lectures seemed to create some kickback for being contradictory in nature. One of them was entitled *Erotic Discipleship,* and the other *Healthy Sexual Fantasy*. In both cases, the lectures felt too contradictory for some students' way of thinking. It seems difficult for many deeply spiritually-minded individuals to embrace and nurture the goodness of sexuality. These two parts, spiritual and sexual, can feel incongruent. Yet, as discussed in previous chapters, these two parts are essential in the development of wholehearted people.

Your sexuality is yours, not your spouse's. You get to determine how much joy this aspect of your existence will bring you. Unfortunately, eroticism is often only tolerated. Throughout childhood, adolescence, and into adulthood, we often don't know what to do with this aspect of our mortal, physical experience. Our sexuality is always there, it is part of who we are, but out of fear and shame we suppress this part of ourselves. Then, once married and in a sexual relationship, we are often unsure how to make room for eroticism in our lives. Bringing this aspect of yourself into your marriage will contribute greatly to the happiness and success of your relationship. Despite the discomfort, to fully claim the joy of human love, you must be willing to work at giving attention to the sexual part of yourself. This process is imperative if you wish to become a wholehearted human being.

In church settings, I understand that people often want to believe that your sexual, erotic self is awakened on your wedding night. This is a false notion. In reality, each of you have been sexual since birth. While the fullest expression of your sexuality is best shared in a committed, covenant relationship, throughout life you have developed erotically with sexual thoughts, attitudes, and beliefs. You share what you have sexually cultivated inside of yourself when expressing physical intimacy in marriage. Good sexuality is about unselfishly blessing your own life, and the life of your spouse, through this deeply vulnerable and passionate human capacity.

Here are a few simple questions that you can consider when pondering the idea of sharing your sexual self in your marriage:

1. Is this behavior delightful and enjoyed by both of us?
2. Am I using this behavior to connect with my spouse more fully?
3. Does this bring us closer together as a couple?
4. Am I getting to know myself and my spouse better through this experience?
5. Overall, how do our shared sexual experiences impact our relationship?

Monogamous couples can keep the romantic spark alive by creating a relationship that provides replenishment through regular erotic, playful and connecting sex. This type of sex doesn't just happen—it requires intentional novelty. Sharing sexual fantasies is a form of erotic play that can provide variety, while also allowing for personal sexual development. Understanding basic principles of healthy sexual fantasy can help guide your behavior as you integrate activities to increase variety and playfulness in your lovemaking experiences. Principles of healthy sexual fantasy include:

- **Erotic knowing is the highest form of knowing.** A wholehearted, differentiated person allows being intimately known to foster his/her progression toward personal integrity. There is nothing more replenishing than making love as two wholehearted individuals, intentionally showing up for each other. No wonder the verb *know* refers to sexual intercourse in the scriptures.
- **Sexuality does not control you.** You are not acted upon, but rather have the agency to act in ways that contribute to wholehearted sexual living. You have the choice to act or not act on the possibilities that come into your mind. You also are accountable for the consequences of the choices you make. You are a sexual being with the freedom to choose how to use your sexuality to bless your life and the life of your spouse.
- **There is not "a right way" to do sex.** As a husband and wife, together you can equitably decide how to share your sexuality. No one else should ever be in the bedroom with you, in real life or within your mind. Open the gift of your sexuality with one another, and as a team, choose to be erotically good together. Remember, anxiety and guilt kill arousal.
- **Along with the commandment to multiply, you are also commanded to replenish in marriage.** The labor involved with family life is essential to maintaining and sustaining the human race. These obligations and responsibilities can also squelch sexual desire. Just as the earth was created with variety for the benefit of mankind, sexual replenishment is found in a variety of creative ways, including fantasy.
- **It is together, as husband and wife, that we claim the promised blessings of eternal life.** Choose not to do anything that is a threat to your spouse or to your relationship. Your sexuality must line up with your covenant commitment to care for your spouse, yourself, and your core values.

Sex plays many roles in a marriage relationship. Sometimes it is deeply spiritual, other times primarily playful, and sometimes it is all about making repairs and forgiveness. Bishop William Swing, retired bishop of the Episcopal Church in the United States, said this about the various components of marital love, "Where there is an ongoing relationship of caring, where there is a sense of humor, where there is a sense of mutual mercy, where there is a sense that God has given sex to you, . . . there is nothing livelier."[71] *Lively*! Would you describe your sex life as lively?! This says volumes to me about the value of a covenant sexual relationship created by two wholehearted lovers, coming together to play, share erotic passion, and replenish each other. This is just a little bit of heaven on earth!

Developing sexual fantasies together requires collaboration, vulnerability, and a need to let go. There will be feelings of awkwardness and discomfort as you try something new. That's just life! Calm your mind from the distracting chatter that disconnects you from your bodily sensations and from each other. Staying focused and mindful will increase your ability to feel pleasure, humor, bliss, awareness, and so much more. In other words, "Hold on to yourself." When you slow down and breathe through anxieties, you will discover parts of yourself and your relationship that, in time, will invoke feelings of peace and a deepened, abiding sense of security. Sexual fantasy will make your relationship grow and feel less humdrum, all while tapping into your often unknown and unseen erotic, sexual self.

In this experiment, remember the importance of living morally and spiritually aligned with your core values. Because some sexual fantasies can include illegal, unethical, or sinful components (often due to pornography use), it's essential that I include the caution to remember who you are and what you really value, even in sexual fantasy. Images, fantasies, or ideas that move toward perverse, anti-social, degrading, or strictly selfish behaviors are not constructive in a healthy marriage. This is a place you do not want to go! Remember, sexuality does not control you.

As you explore fantasy role plays, various sexual positions, and erotic storytelling as partners, you get to choose together what to try. Perhaps you will not feel interested in any of it. Maybe your spouse will want to try all of it! This is when you go back to the sexual decision-making and sexual stewardship chapters, and utilize the tools outlined in these chapters to work as a team. There needs to be a lot of trust and goodness in the relationship outside of the bedroom, before you can expect it to happen in the bedroom. If you're hesitant, work on building trust and friendship in other ways before moving forward with this chapter.

Sexual Fantasy Dynamics

Some common sexual fantasy dynamics include:[72]

1. **Innocence**: Being clueless, needing instruction, being taught, and finally being brought to pleasure
2. **Novelty**: New experiences, new places, and unexpected or surprising sexual encounters
3. **Forbiddenness**: Against the rules, illicit experiences that feel intoxicating and enticing
4. **Opposites Attract**: Primal attraction, largely contrasting masculine and feminine traits
5. **Reckless Abandon**: Surrender to another's unbridled passion for you

Some research suggests that "fantasy training," or doing a guided sexual imagery involving you and your partner, contributes to positive relational outcomes. When you think about your partner, recalling sexual experiences that you've shared, it makes your partner seem more appealing. This type of fantasy contributes to a happier and healthier relationship.[73] As a clinician, I encourage the couples I work with to reflect on special times they have shared, including sexual experiences. I believe this fosters a sexually positive mindset, encourages fidelity, and strengthens emotional connection. In covenant marriages, we promise to share our romantic, erotic, sexual selves with only one person; both fantasy training and remembrance can enhance the sexual dynamic within the marriage.

THINK. Individually journal thoughts and impressions you had while reading this chapter. What stood out to you? What sexual fantasies do you have (everyone has them!)? Consider writing one of your fantasies down to share with your spouse.

PAIR. This time I want you to be alone, rested and without any distractions. Once you get to this space and time, get naked and hold one another. Breathe deeply. Make eye contact and kiss.

SHARE. As you listen to understand your partner, observe his/her ability to talk about fantasy and ability to listen to your fantasies. If there is discomfort, go slow, and be kind. Together, decide what you want to incorporate into your marriage at this time.

Adding to your Sexual Playbook: Together, journal your thoughts on exploring your sexual fantasies, including how you will prioritize your friendship as you work through the vulnerable feelings that may surface as you share and explore your sexual fantasies with your spouse. Write down what fantasies you have decided together you would like to try. Write down what fantasies you may want to revisit trying in the future.

Experiential Activities to Enjoy

My Sexuality Exercise

Find a private space to write or type for 8 minutes. Write whatever comes up for you as you consider the following questions:

- What does my sexuality want?
- What turns me on?
- How do I tolerate my sexual anxieties?
- What does it mean to be erotic?
- Am I enjoying the sexual part of me?
- How does my sexuality align with my values?

Once you've written this for 8 minutes, read through it. Pray to understand your sexuality more fully. Do this experience again the next day and on the following day (three days total). Then journal responses to these questions:

- What have I learned about my sexuality?
- Do I feel differently about my erotic self today than I did on Day 1? How? Why?
- Did I have any spiritual enlightenment during this experience?

Sexual Positions

Different positions can bring variety and fun to your sexual relationship! Look through the following pictures and descriptions and then discuss with your spouse which positions you'd like to try.

Missionary Position

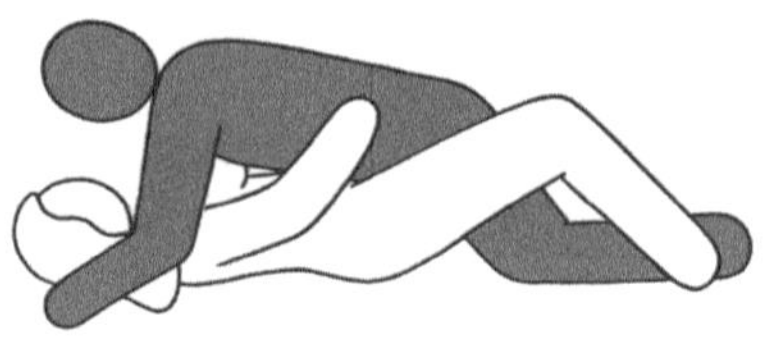

The missionary position, or man-on-top position, is a sex position in which, generally, a woman lies on her back and a man lies on top of her while they face each other and engage in vaginal intercourse. The missionary position is often preferred by couples who enjoy the romantic aspects of ample skin-to-skin contact and opportunities to look into each other's eyes and kiss and caress each other. This position is also believed to be a good position for reproduction. During sexual activity, the missionary position allows the man to control the rhythm and depth of pelvic thrusting. It is also possible for the woman to thrust against him by moving her hips or pushing her feet against the bed. It also allows her to squeeze him closer with her arms or legs. The position is less suitable for late stages of pregnancy and for when the woman desires to have greater control over rhythm and depth of penetration.

Cowgirl Position

The husband lies flat on his back with his legs out straight. The wife sits on top of him, straddling him and facing his head. While sitting up straight, wife inserts husband's penis into her vagina. Cowgirl also works if the wife bends slightly forward over her partner, allowing the clitoris to rub against the husband's pelvis. She can also touch her own clitoral glans with a finger

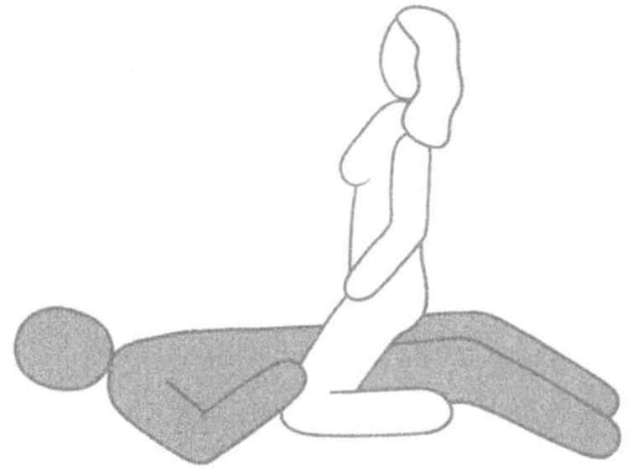

or vibrator. She can rock her hips back and forth or bounce up and down. If the penetration feels too deep, she can put pillows under her knees to prop her up a bit higher.

Reverse Cowgirl

The husband lies flat on his back with his legs out straight. The wife turns around so that she's facing his feet. While straddling her husband, with her knees or feet on either side of his legs, the wife inserts his

penis into her vagina. During reverse cowgirl, the husband's penis will penetrate at a different angle, allowing for female prostate or G-spot stimulation. The wife controls movement, as well as the depth and angle of penetration. Leaning slightly backward will give her extra room to stimulate her own clitoral glans using her hands or vibrator.

The Magic Bullet

The wife lies on her back with her legs in the air, resting them on her husband's shoulders. The husband kneels in front and inserts his penis into the vagina while pulling her buttocks snug onto his knees. They both have full access to clitoral glans stimulation. He can use her legs to go as

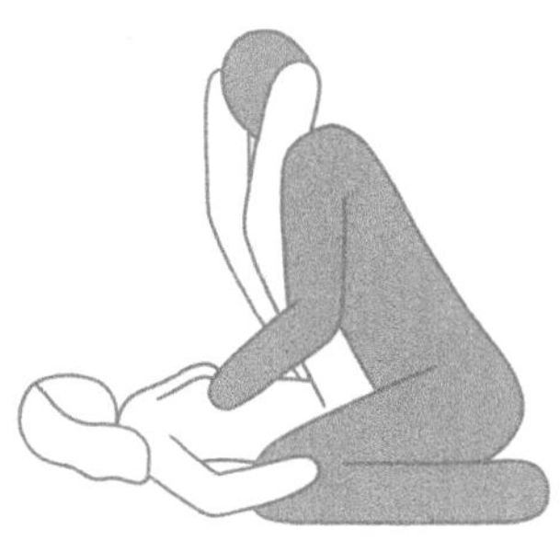

fast or slow as desired, while pushing the legs together for a tighter feel. His penis can have more contact with the G-spot. This is also a good position for later pregnancy.

Modified Missionary

The wife is on the bottom, and the husband is on top, just like in the missionary position. Once the husband has penetrated the vagina, the wife brings both of her bent legs to the husband's sides. He can use his arms and legs to support his weight as he thrusts. In this closed missionary position, she can stimulate her clitoral glans while thrusting. With the wife's legs bent tight against his body, her vagina will feel tighter, making the experience even more pleasurable for both of them.

Yab Yum

The husband sits upright with his legs folded. If he finds it uncomfortable, he could sit on a chair, or the edge of the bed instead. The wife sits on his lap, penetrating her vagina with his penis, wrapping her legs around his waist and her arms around his shoulders. He can wrap his arms around her waist and rock back-and-forth slowly. Try thrusting up and down, side-to-side, or the wife can arch her lower-back while rocking rhythmically onto his pelvis. Get as close as possible to stimulate each other's bodies with hands, lips, and tongue. This is also a perfect position for eye-gazing experiences.

Queening

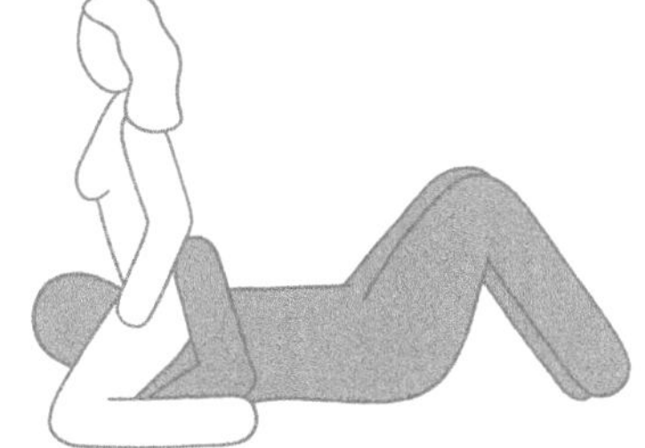

This position refers to a woman sitting on her husband's face to be orally stimulated by him while his hands are free to roam and touch other body parts.

Face Sitting

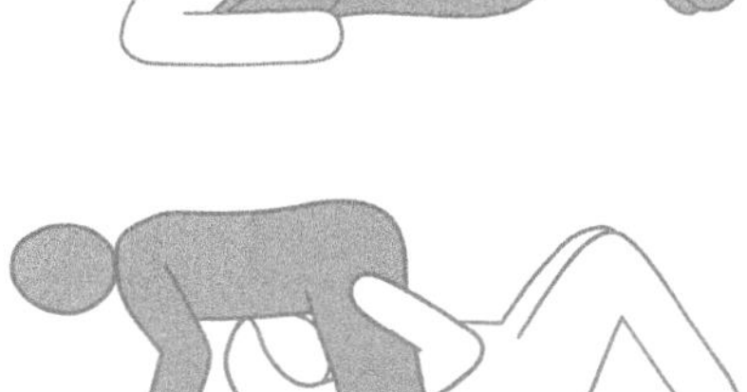

This position refers to a husband sitting on his wife's face to be orally stimulated by her while her hands are free to roam and touch other body parts.

69 Position

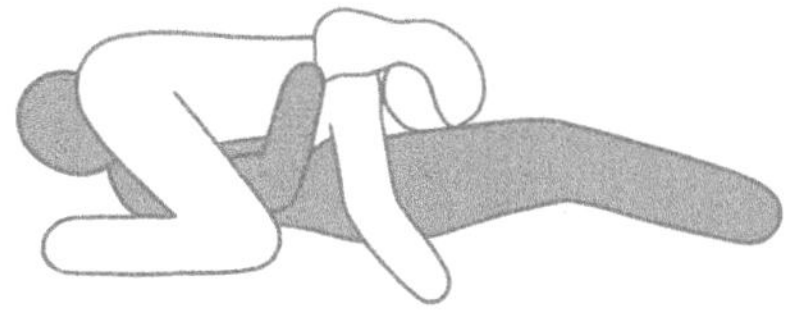

This is a mutual oral sex position so named because each person is curved against the other, face to groin, making the shape of the number 69.

Role Play Scenarios

Choose a role play. Get dressed up for the fun! You can do as much or as little with each of these scenarios. Personally, I encourage you to go all in! It's lots more fun.

1. **Innocence**:
    a. It's the first time you've made love. He needs to show her everything to do.
    b. She needs to dress only in a white dress shirt with a tie, then ask him to teach her how to tie a tie. She doesn't know anything about ties!

   c. She teaches him how to cook a recipe. He is wearing only a pair of jeans and has never cooked before.

2. **Novelty**:
   a. Try a new sexual position in a new location.
   b. Greet him at work, the airport, or school wearing only lingerie underneath a long coat.
   c. Plan a getaway to a place you've never been before.

3. **Forbiddenness**:
   a. Imagine you're not married yet and make out. Keep it chaste for at least 20 minutes.
   b. Pretend your spouse is serving his/her mission and you snuck into the bedroom.
   c. He is a police officer giving her a ticket for speeding. She talks him out of the ticket.

4. **Opposites Attract**:
   a. Focus intently on the parts of your spouse's body that you're especially fond of; no touching for at least 20 minutes, eyes only.
   b. Slip into the shower with your spouse. Bring some ice. Play around with the hot and cold sensations on various body parts.
   c. She's home from the gym all sweaty and gross. He is showered and dressed up, looking and smelling fine. Tease, flirt, and see what happens.

5. **Reckless Abandon**:
   a. With consent, he picks her up and brings her to bed and ravishes her.
   b. With consent, he is blindfolded while she gets her way!
   c. While driving home together, start touching, talking, looking, and being excited to get it on. Rush into the house. Start unbuttoning clothes while kissing. Act like you can't get to the bedroom fast enough. (This one can start out feeling forced, but by the end there is only desire.)

CHAPTER 27

Sexual Accessories

This chapter is called "sexual accessories" because for some individuals the term "sex toys" feels inappropriate. Personally, I see the products introduced in this chapter as "tools" more than toys. Depending upon a couple's joint decisions, these tools may or may not be chosen to enhance the replenishing nature of their sexual relationship.

As I introduce various types of products in this chapter, be assured that I am not affiliated with any of them. I am simply providing information you may find helpful should you choose to integrate products into your lovemaking. This is a choice you have to make unitedly as a couple, recognizing that you can revisit the conversation countless times as you move forward together on your sexual journey. It is very common for ideas a couple shares early in marriage to fluctuate and adapt through the years. For example, a couple I recently worked with had been totally opposed to using vibrators throughout their 29-year marriage. Both of them were on the same page in not feeling the desire or need to introduce them into their lovemaking. For whatever reason, the wife became curious about using a vibrator and expressed her desire to her husband in an important, vulnerable conversation. They came to see me to process this decision. Their teamwork and collaboration were remarkable! The depth of their shared sexual maturity, as well as their ability to work together as equal partners in making this decision, is layered with evidence of true marital health. Making informed and progressive changes to your shared sexual experiences over time can revitalize your erotic energy. This couple began to use a vibrator and found the experience very pleasant. As their therapist, it is thrilling to watch them continue to progress sexually together, even after 29 years of marriage.

Before I jump into specifics of various sexual accessories, I first want to encourage you to spend time working together in communicating various arousal thresholds without the use of tools. Why? Because there is knowledge that comes from direct sexual touch. A husband's finger or tongue stimulation of his wife's clitoral glans, while she clearly communicates to him what she enjoys, is neurologically informing him of what pleases her. He is getting to know her. It is the same for a wife as she comes to sexually know what arouses her husband when she directly stimulates his body with her fingers, hands, breasts, mouth, or tongue. When a sexual tool is being used, the body-to-body data and awareness is modified. Deeply intimate and directive sexual communication between spouses can be stunted. In my own experience, personally and professionally, I find the deliberate, brain-to-body, husband-to-wife processing of arousal requires couples to sexually stretch as they become one another's passionate soulmates. This idea might feel frustrating to some of you because you prefer your tools and are sexually satisfied using them. I'm happy for you. There is no need to change unless you want to adjust to sexual encounters without tools. I still hold firm in my position, however, that there is a depth of knowledge that is not neurologically communicated or learned when couples do not intentionally slow down to figure out one another's sexual thresholds and preferences through tactile or oral touch.

Using sexual products, accessories, tools, and toys is like any other aspect of your sexuality. It is your decision as a couple to choose what you want to incorporate into your lovemaking. It is no one else's business—ever! If there are medical precautions that you have received from your doctor, follow those guidelines. Otherwise, you get to choose and explore what works best for both of you.

Lingerie

I heard once that lingerie can make you feel emotions you typically keep hidden beneath your clothes. There is a sensual awareness that comes when wearing bras, panties, teddies, baby dolls, and other styles of lingerie. As I've personally become increasingly comfortable with the goodness of sensuality, I find that these "secret emotions" contribute to feelings of anticipation, self-confidence, and an overall heightened sexual awareness. Knowing that I am wearing something beautiful, attractive, and sexy feels freeing, provocative, and empowering. In my experience of working with extremely devoted, faithful, Christian wives and mothers, I've seen a tendency to overlook, ignore, or shun practices that encourage sexual integration. In part, the development of divine femininity includes holding on to the erotic, wholehearted, passionate self. A very simple way for women to begin embracing their beautiful sexual parts is to incorporate more sensual experiences into their everyday living, such as warm baths, revitalizing showers, rich-smelling lotions, arousal oils and creams, as well as lingerie.

Is sensuality an idea that creates discomfort for you? Perhaps because adults in your life never comfortably talked about it? Or is it because sensual means pleasurable and you wonder if it is righteous to feel pleasure? Maybe you view sensual products as a waste of hard-earned money or not worth your time?

Whatever the reason, I encourage my clients, students, and you, dear reader, to become more comfortable in accepting the goodness and enjoyment that comes from feeling sensual. When all five senses are involved with living, deeply-fulfilling sensual experiences can be shared and *remembered*. Every waking moment, your sensory receptors are receiving sensual input that play a crucial role in information retention. Memory is greatly enhanced when an experience intentionally focuses on multiple senses—sight, sound, taste, smell, and touch.[74] These senses were given to us by our Heavenly Parents. Being intentional in choosing to key into each of your five senses, or in removing one or two to better focus on the others, can add a wonderful dimension to your lovemaking experiences. For example, using a blindfold is an easy way to add some suspense and fun in the bedroom by increasing your focus on smells and sounds along with your anticipation of touch. When one sense is removed, the others make up the difference!

Embodiment theory claims that language and emotions affect each other. Scientific data supports the idea that there are changes in bodily responses, including facial expressions, heart rate, or skin conductance, during the mental evaluation of emotionally-descriptive words and sentences.[75] With this in mind, I want you to do a little experiment with each other. Alternating turns, read each descriptive word aloud. Share with each other the thoughts and feelings each word evokes. Thoughts and feelings are different! A thought is a cognition while a feeling is an emotion.

- Silky
- Lacy
- Sheer
- Creamy
- Erect
- Luxurious

I find this experiment fascinating. Most people will connect sexual experiences and ideas with sensual words and have both emotional and physiological responses to the same words. Your divinely designed brain and body are sensually connected on purpose! Wearing lingerie has a unique way of helping women tap into their femininity. As you incorporate more sensual experiences into your day-to-day living, you will be pleasantly surprised by the enhanced sexual awareness in both your mind and body.

Lotions, Oils, Waxes

For those who are currently less inclined to invest more than a few dollars into your sexual experiences, these types of products are a great solution to frugally create more eroticism in your marriage. Conveniently, many of these types of products can be purchased through Amazon.com. There are literally hundreds of these types of products on the market; I am only including the names of actual products that I have both used and enjoyed. Not all of the specific brands I've listed can be found on Amazon; type the names into a search engine or go to the references at the end of the book to see some website URLs.[76]

- **Nipple creams:** These products awaken the nipples with essential oils (e.g., Jo; Exsens).
- **Sensual massage oils**: These products can be used all over the body for relaxation, warmth, and fragrance (e.g., Almond or coconut oil; *Maple Holistics; Bloomi*).
- **Erotic candles:** These products provide 4-in-1 enhancement with romantic lighting, sensual fragrance, a heated massage oil, and most contain arousal oil (e.g., Kama Sutra; *True Pheromones; Skinny Dip; Lelo*).
- **Arousal oils:** These products contain compounds that stimulate blood flow. I often call these types of products "liquid libido" (e.g., *FORIA; Zestra*).

IMPORTANT NOTICE: Never use flavored creams, oils, or lubes for penetrative or oral sex. These products contain sugar alcohols, glucose, or glycerin that can cause yeast and urinary tract infections.

Lubes

Two Bartholin glands are found on each side of the vaginal opening. Their function is to release vaginal fluids during sexual arousal. There are several factors that can contribute to insufficient lubrication, including lack of arousal, stress, medications, and age. When needed or wanted, adding lubrication can provide increased sexual pleasure and comfort for couples. Lubrication reduces friction in the penetrative process, which also makes it less likely for a condom to break or come off during sex. There are a wide variety of lubes from which to choose—some with warming and cooling sensations or even ejaculation-delaying lube. It is important for each couple to experiment to find the lubricants that work best for them.

One thing to note in selecting your lube, and/or other sexual tools, is to be aware that, in the United States, the Food and Drug Administration does not currently regulate lubricants or sex toys unless they make a medical claim (e.g., "This product vaginally retains a natural pH balance"). Thus, companies can put ingredients in their products that could actually hurt your body by causing allergic reactions or contributing to infections. Read the ingredient list, do your research, and make informed decisions.

Here, I provide some general information to help get you started on this journey. There are several different types of lubricant, as listed below, along with some advantages and disadvantages of each type:

Water-based

Advantages:

- Most commonly used lube
- Easy clean-up
- Compatible with all condoms and sexual accessories
- Does not stain fabric

Disadvantages:

- Not as long lasting; need to reapply more frequently
- Becomes sticky with friction

Plant oil-based (Stay away from petroleum-based products)

Advantages:

- Great for whole-body moisturizing
- Fun foreplay

Disadvantages:

- Can ruin surfaces of sex tools
- Stains fabrics
- Do not use with latex condoms
- More likely to promote yeast infections and/or UTIs

Silicone-based

Advantages:

- Feels silky smooth
- Long-lasting
- Hypoallergenic
- No smell or taste

- Can use with latex condoms
- Works well with water-play

Disadvantages:

- Do not use with silicone sexual tools; will break down material over time
- Often stains fabric

Hybrid (emulsified base solutions of silicone and water)

Advantages:

- Compatible with all high-grade sexual tools
- Unlikely to cause allergic reactions
- Compatible with condoms

Sexual Tools

In my work as a therapist, I have found that some couples may feel reluctant to talk about sex toys because the word "toy" feels inappropriate to the sanctity of their sexual relationship. If this is how you feel, please know that you're not alone, and that it's okay to feel uncomfortable with that term. For you, I invite you to use the reframe of "sex tool" in place of sex toy. A tool is an instrument, usually held in the hands, used to serve a particular function. There are a variety of tools that can be instrumental in accomplishing sexual pleasure and orgasm. As always, I encourage direct, reflective, educated, and open-hearted communication as you decide together if, when, how, and what you want to do with sexual tools or toys.

Talking to your partner about using sexual tools can sometimes feel a little awkward. Some women feel worried that this will be insulting, or that perhaps their partners will feel displaced if a sex tool is introduced in the bedroom. What I have found in my experience as a therapist, is that most husbands are happy for their wives to use vibrators, knowing that this can help them experience more sexual pleasure. If the conversation still feels uncomfortable, consider reading this chapter together before having this vulnerable conversation about sexual tools.

Vibrators

I believe that vibrators are the most underused tool in enhancing your sexual experience. Vibrators are not dirty or unnatural any more than a *KitchenAid* mixer is an unnatural, dirty way to make baked goods in your kitchen! Especially for women who have a slower pace at achieving orgasm, using a vibrator can help her experience pleasure faster, easier, and more often. Some women claim to have more intense orgasms with a vibrator.

There are so many different styles of vibrators that it can feel overwhelming to know what to choose. Vibrators can be used to stimulate the nipples, clitoral glans, vagina, perineum, and anus for women. For men they can also be used on the nipples, penis, scrotum, perineum, and anus. Vibrators can be classified in the following categories:

- **External:** These vibrators are designed for external stimulation and should be used with a lubricant. Most of these vibrators have options for a variety of movements, including pulsing, up and down, side to side, and circular. For most individuals, vibrators made of soft, plush material feel better than those that are made of hard material. When using an external vibrator, always start the stimulation on breasts, nipples, legs, inner thighs, and labia before going to the clitoral hood. Do not start touch directly on the clitoral glans as this will create an uncomfortable, even painful, experience. Remember, go slow, and warm up along the way.
- **Suction:** These are a relatively new style of external vibrator that provide a suction-type action that resembles the gentle sucking motion provided by oral sex. In my private practice, this type of vibrator has been the most helpful in assisting anorgasmic women to experience orgasm! It is exciting for these clients to finally experience the pleasure of a longed-for orgasm. The brain places an incredible importance on the processing of a first orgasm. The brain cells, or synapses, build a neurological pathway, a brain-to-genital connection that, once experienced, will function again more easily.
- **Internal:** These vibrators are meant to go inside the vagina and include more subtle movement options. Some of these vibrators have a heating option that provides nice vaginal warmth and pressure. Use

these vibrators with a lubricant. They vary in size, shape, and texture. These should be chosen based upon the amount of deep vaginal pressure a woman prefers. Curved internal vibrators can be used to stimulate the female prostate. These vibrators may not be the best choice for a woman who is looking to orgasm through external clitoral stimulation; however, if desired they can be used externally as well.

- **Dual:** The Rabbit is the most popular dual vibrator, where one end of this vibrator is used vaginally for stimulation while the other end is used to flutter on the clitoral glans, providing two different mechanisms to stimulate two different parts of the body. There are mixed opinions about dual vibrators; some women find them wonderful, while others feel there is too much stimulation going on at the same time. This relatively new style of vibrator provides a wide variety of pleasure options, including thrusting motion settings and even remote-powered Bluetooth synchronization to music playlists. The new We-Vibe® dual vibrator is a device that has, in some ways, revolutionized sexual tools by being incorporated into penile-vaginal intercourse.
- **Penis Vibrator/Penis Ring:** This is a band or ring that a man wears around the penis to restrict blood flow. It helps achieve firmer erections and assists in maintaining erections longer. It is often worn around the base of the penis but can also include the testicles. There are stretchy, jelly penis rings, and more rigid penis rings made from silicone, rubber, leather, metal, and rope. Vibrating rings can provide an exhilarating vibrating sensation for both partners. They are easy to use and may be used with condoms.

There are four primary components to consider when selecting a vibrator:

- **Strength**: If you know you need a lot of stimulation, look at vibrators that are both larger in size and rechargeable. Battery-powered vibrators will be less powerful and can run out of power at very inopportune times.
- **Size**: Smaller vibrators are easier to slide between partners during intercourse. These tend to have less power and provide less pressure if used internally.
- **Noise**: This is a concern for parents with children at home and for

couples who live in apartment complexes with thinner walls. Most vibrators that are rechargeable will not be loud enough to be heard. Battery-powered and electric vibrators, with a plug-in attachment to power, will be noisier.

- **Cost**: Costs range between $20-$350. Research has shown that price doesn't impact the quality of the orgasm! I suggest that you start with less-expensive vibrators.

Dildos

These are typically phallic-shaped devices that are used to simulate vaginal or anal penetration. While there are some remote-controlled vibrating dildos, most do not vibrate. Dildos are typically made with harder materials including metal, glass, silicone, and medical-grade plastic. Some jelly dildos are more flexible. Using dildos can increase the depth and breadth of deep vaginal pressure and penetration. They are also helpful in stimulating the female prostate. Dildos are less expensive than vibrators and come in a large assortment of sizes and shapes. If you are interested in trying a dildo, as with all sexual decision-making, I encourage both partners to be on board and agree with the ways you would like to incorporate this tool into your sexual play and pleasure.

Butt Plugs

A butt plug is a sex tool that goes in the anus. It is usually shaped like a cone, starting narrow and getting wider before narrowing again. They also have a wide base to prevent the toy from going in too far. The anus has nerve endings that can feel good when stimulated with lubrication. The pleasure, along with the pressure, provided by this toy can be exciting for both partners. Be certain to clean toys and hands thoroughly, and remember, never use a tool in the anus and the vagina in the same sexual encounter.

Sex Furniture

The market for various types of sex furniture continues to grow. These accessories include wedges, pillows, ramp cushions, rocking chairs, and swings all to make having sex in a variety of positions more comfortable. Popular brand names include *Liberator*, *NaEnson* and *MISSTU*. This furniture can assist a couple in achieving sexual positions with greater ease. In my experience working with couples where one or both partners experience chronic pain, having supportive sex furniture can contribute greatly to their ability to have sex more comfortably.

A few precautions

- Never initiate direct stimulation of the clitoral glans or female prostate with a vibrator. These areas are packed full of nerve endings. This type of direct touch at the beginning of a lovemaking experience can be painful.
- Avoid tools made from non-medical-grade plastics and jelly-like toys. These porous surfaces absorb bodily fluids, making them difficult to keep sanitary.
- Cleanliness is essential! Never use a sex tool in both the anus and the vagina.
- To avoid the risk of blood-borne infections, don't use a sex tool when there are any cuts or sores around the vagina, anus, or penis.
- It is not safe to share sexual tools. If you purchase something, keep it just between the two of you.
- Buy sexual tools that can be recharged rather than toys that require batteries. You often cannot fully clean a toy that uses batteries.
- Follow the instructions that come with the sex tool for appropriate cleaning measures.
- If you are allergic to latex, do not use condoms or sexual tools that contain latex.
- I encourage you to seek information for purchasing toys or tools from AASECT member recommendations. This organization specializes in training sexual educators, counselors, and therapists.

In concluding this chapter, I want to again emphasize the importance of gently introducing the idea of incorporating sexual tools into your lovemaking. In no way should this conversation become a critique of your sexual relationship. Be lovingly direct as you frame your request. Remember the hamburger approach to communication. Look for sexual tools together, and be willing to compromise. Anytime you try something for the first time, it will feel a little strange. Take plenty of time to learn together, communicate together and, most importantly, *play* together with your new sexual tools.

Finally, remember that the market of sexual tools is ever growing. With expanding technology, the variety of sexual tool functions will continually change. I encourage couples to occasionally add something you both want to try to your sexual toolbox, without making tools the main event. Remember your loving, orgasmic, emotionally-focused connection is much more important than orgasm-focused, try something new, Western-style sex. While sexual tools can add variety and ease to time-constrained lovemaking experiences, I believe it is important for couples to continue making love without vibrators and other tools as often as they can to keep strengthening their body-to-body connection and knowledge.

THINK. Journal your deeply held beliefs about sexual accessories. Can you recognize where these beliefs come from? Who taught you these ideas? Are they beliefs that are serving your marriage and sexual relationship well? Why or why not? Now create a list of accessories and your comfort with trying or using them on a 1-10 scale.

PAIR. This can be a vulnerable conversation for many couples. I suggest you share an activity that you both enjoy doing together. After the activity, settle in for this conversation by breathing deeply and looking into one another's eyes.

SHARE. Openly discuss your journaled ideas about sexual accessories. Listen to understand your spouse. Recognize that unless both of you are on the same page, it is not wise to move forward. For example, if one of you is hesitant to use a vibrator, don't get a vibrator. Compare your scaled lists of accessories. Where are you the same? Where are you vastly different? What do you both agree you would like to try next? Create a plan for beginning this practice.

Adding to your Sexual Playbook: Review what you've written previously about sexual accessories in your sexual playbook. What would you like to add? What would you like to modify?

Experiential Activities to Enjoy

Sensual Candles and Wax

Use a soft massage candle created for this purpose that doesn't burn too hot (do NOT use regular candles for this). Recognize these candles are not intended for full body massages; use a massage oil for full body massages. The candle will slowly melt wax that can be rubbed into the body. It works best when used on breasts and genitals. One person will be the giver, while the other receives. Once there is some wax melted, gently pour it directly on to the body part you are wanting to awaken and arouse. Spend time rubbing the wax into these body parts. The heat from the wax is tempered. It will not burn, but the warmth and arousal oils will feel exciting as you massage it into your lover's body.

Lingerie

Select a piece of lingerie that feels especially nice on your skin. After a relaxing shower followed by lotion, put this lingerie on. Observe yourself in the mirror. Love your beautiful body. Wear this lingerie while waiting to share yourself with your spouse. Once you are together, begin to make love with the lingerie on. Kissing and licking the body through the lingerie can be especially arousing as it slows down the direct stimulation, increasing and heightening the desire for more stimulation. Take your time before removing the lingerie.

Vibrator

Depending on the type of vibrator you purchased, read the instructions to know how to charge and use your product. Test out the different speeds and styles of pulsation that are available. Decide which setting you want to use to begin your exploration. Make sure to apply plenty of water-based lubricant, then start by touching areas that are erogenous but not full of too many nerve endings. Make certain your partner is ready before you move the vibrator to the vulva or penis. Make it fun as you learn together what each of you enjoys.

PART IV

Sexuality Across the Lifespan

CHAPTER 28

The First Time

I'm including a chapter on making love for the first time in this book for two reasons: first, it is for couples who are reading this in preparation for marriage and their first sexual experience with their spouse. Second, you may know a couple who will soon become sexually active. Please consider sharing this information with them. It could make a significant difference in the lifetime of their whole sexual relationship. In addition, as you read this, you may recognize unhealthy sexual dynamics in your own relationship that stem from early lovemaking experiences. If this is the case, reading and talking about concepts in this book will be a blessing as you navigate a more informed approach to your sexual relationship. It may help you to come to terms with your first sexual experiences.

Whether it's a first date, a job interview, or simply a new co-worker, first impressions often have an important impact on future interactions and opportunities. The fact of the matter is, you never get a second chance to make a first impression. You never get a second chance to make love for the first time either. As such, the first sexual experience(s) can become a pattern for future lovemaking experiences.

Years ago, I worked with a couple who had been married 27 years at the time of our first session. They came to therapy determined to make their marriage work. Their five children were raised, they both enjoyed fulfilling careers, and overall, they were pretty good friends. On my initial assessment, I discovered that she had never had an orgasm; despite medical examinations and pelvic floor therapy, she continued to experience pain with penetration. She completely believed that sex was created for men. I asked her to describe her honeymoon sexual experiences. As I suspected, their sexual debut was horrific, to say the least. The wedding night sex began with about three minutes of kissing, followed by a quick and painful penile-vaginal penetration, which ended less than three minutes later with a premature ejaculation. This was how sex was shared repeatedly throughout the honeymoon. They became pregnant within the first weeks of marriage, which created a new sexual challenge when she became violently nauseous whenever she smelled her husband. Ten years and five children later, without much changing in the bedroom, she had a tubal ligation and let her husband know that she would have sex with him once a week. He chose Sundays. Seventeen years later, their youngest child was leaving home for college, and they realized they profoundly needed sexual help as they both wanted to stay together for their children and grandchildren. Isn't this heartbreaking? Although this scenario may seem extreme, I frequently meet with people who share similar experiences. Sexual avoidance and distress in marriage is often informed by early sexual experiences. As in this couple's experience, the wife honestly believed that she (and women in general) was not intended to enjoy sex. Given her experience, how could she have thought otherwise?

Sex is intended to be enjoyed fully by both husband and wife, and part of the journey of sexual stewardship in marriage is learning what's sexually satisfying for both of you. This will take time and communication, as true lovemaking is so much more than just intercourse. When coming together equitably as partners, take time to explore and learn what feels pleasing; go ASAP—*as slow as possible*. There is absolutely nothing wrong with choosing not to have penetrative sex on your wedding night, or for several nights, while you adjust to being together naked and intimately touching. Choosing together to wait can remove a lot of unnecessary pressure and anxiety. Particularly if you've been highly conservative in the romantic touching you've shared before marriage, I encourage you to take your time before intercourse. The wife needs to be highly aroused for sexual penetration to feel good. Taking time to figure this out together sets your sexual relationship up for success.

Not learning, or not choosing, to go slow sexually in the beginning of your marriage relationship can create marriages that, over time, become heartbreakingly dysfunctional. You may be thinking I'm being dramatic here, but I'm not. Going slow, and waiting for penetration until she is ready, can make for a lifetime of happiness. Why? Because marriage is a sexual contract, and you don't want your first sexual encounters to be associated with pain. As mentioned in the beginning, as you start sharing a bed together, you are also creating another first impression. By slowing down and waiting for penetration, you are reducing the probability of discomfort and pain for her. When penetration occurs before her body is fully aroused and ready, the tension and anxiety felt will tighten the pelvic floor. This makes the body work against itself. A tightened, contracted pelvic floor reflexively creates a tightened, contracted vagina. Pushing an erect penis into a contracted vagina will generate sharp pain, thus her first penetrative sexual experience will become associated with pain and discomfort. This first experience shapes future sexual encounters, often marring them with negative emotions and sensations rather than the beautiful, connecting feelings that loving sexual relationships were designed to generate. Premature penetration is a horrible way to transition to the marital bed!

Unfortunately, in strict religious cultures where sexual pleasure is not openly discussed, women often grow up believing that sexual pleasure is either bad, dirty, or sinful. Subliminal, and sometimes very direct messages, that some women receive throughout childhood suggest that a good wife takes care of her husband's sexual needs. When first sexual experiences are associated with pain, it can reinforce the framework that sex is for men, and women just do it to accommodate them. Perhaps you are thinking that I speak here from a previous era of patriarchy, but unfortunately, in this very day and age (2022) I hear many experiences from female students and clients alike, who have been counseled by parents and leaders to make sure to have sex frequently in order to "keep her husband" from looking at pornography or straying. Women are *not*, nor have they ever been, in charge of monitoring or controlling men's sexual choices. When this type of information is taught or implied, it doesn't take long for this servicing model to create deep sexual and relational resentment between both husband and wife. Over time, as sexual desire differences become increasingly extreme, I see these couples in therapy where feelings of unhappiness, hopelessness, and lack of safety having become foundational pieces of their marriages.

For a woman in a situation like this, it becomes easy to not truly show up sexually in marriage. If this is you, I challenge you not to stay in this servicing model! Staying in the service or duty-sex model may feel safer and easier than working out the real issues. Choosing to stay stuck will prevent you from experiencing many joyful opportunities to mature and progress in your sexual development. You were designed to have so much more!

If any of this information is triggering for you due to your own experiences, please know that there is help available for you and your relationship. You don't need to stay in unhealthy sexual patterns. You can own your sexuality and claim fulfilling joy in your marriage. The first step to owning your sexuality is to vulnerably choose to talk together about this aspect of your relationship. Silence is *not* golden in the bedroom. It will be necessary for you to be honest with yourself and each other as you learn to become passionate lovers. Here are a few phrases that you could use to get a conversation started:

- "I'm reading a book called *Replenish*. I would like to share it with you."
- "Sex hasn't gone well for us, and I would like to change."
- "I've learned that beginning sexual experiences can shape a lifetime of sexual experiences. Can we try to start over?"
- "We were not prepared for sharing a healthy sex life. Let's learn how to do this better."
- "I've been in the dark sexually; I want to come into the light with you."
- "We have been commanded to multiply *and* replenish. I want to learn how to feel sexually replenished in our marriage."
- "I know our sexual history hasn't been the best. I am willing to learn together so that our future can be better than ever."
- "I want to talk about what we both really want sexually, not just what we think we should be doing."

I want to discuss a few sexual principles to help you as you begin creating a healthy sexual relationship. First, sex is part of our Heavenly Parents plan for Their children. It is designed to be a source of joy, pleasure, connection, and happiness in marriage. It's important for you to know that both men and women have been given bodies that are designed for pleasure.[77] According to the research of a dear colleague and friend of mine, Dr. Jennifer Finlayson-Fife, women who were raised understanding that sexual feelings are good and normal better integrate this part of themselves within a marriage partnership. They feel free to both give and receive sexual pleasure and love.[78] Sharing pleasure replenishes both individuals, the marriage relationship and, ultimately, the entire family system. Robust, passionate sex between equal partners helps create security within the family system, adds a healthy, loving dynamic to the home environment, and helps model happiness in marriage for children. A respectful, fulfilling sex life helps build strong families.

A second principle to help guide your adjustments to being sexual together in marriage is sexual agency. As two separate individuals with equal power, you each get a voice in determining when, where, how, and what you do sexually. Review *Chapter 2: The Gift of our Sexual Theology* as you make these decisions together. Make sure to remember that anytime a person feels they *must* do something, desire goes out the window! Begging, demanding, whining, manipulating, or coercing your partner to have more sex or to participate in particular sexual behaviors will damage your relationship. To be meaningful and delightful, sex needs to be freely given.

The third principle is that becoming familiar with your anatomy and your spouse's anatomy is essential to your success in becoming one another's lovers. Please read the chapters that discuss erogenous zones in this book. Doing the experiential activities together will give you important information as you learn about your bodies. The genitals, or the most sensitive organs, need to be stimulated to experience pleasure. Consecrate time in the first year(s) of marriage to explore and really look at *all* your body parts, especially the genitals. The brain is the body's largest sexual organ. Thinking self-consciously about the way your body looks and/or focusing on sexual performance will shortchange your ability to fully enjoy sexual pleasure. Focus on the beauty of this special opportunity to be naked and share love. Remember that you are both created in the image and function of Heavenly Father or Heavenly Mother. Reverence the knowledge that your body is housing the greater substance, your spirit. Communicating about your bodies with one another should be done with gratitude, respect, and charity.

Finally, accepting the goodness of the gift of sexual pleasure will strengthen your resolve to live wholeheartedly. Understanding where and how you like to be touched and communicating this to your spouse is essential as you become familiar with and create your shared sexual stewardship. Don't hesitate to ask questions about what feels good. Tell your spouse what you enjoy. Clear your mind and be present as you experience pleasure. You can do this more fully if you breathe deeply. I encourage you to find one another's pulse points and touch them, feeling the loving, beating heart of your spouse. Recognize that the heartbeats indicate life; your spouse is alive and there with you, body and spirit. While feeling your spouse's pulse, make eye contact. Maintain eye contact as you touch other body parts, especially as your spouse becomes increasingly aroused. Watch his/her eyes dilate with pleasure and know within your soul that all of this is very good—and all good things come from God.

While learning together how to give and receive sexual pleasure, move at the pace of the person with the slowest response. Take your time replenishing your love in this new and exciting way.

THINK. Reflect on your first sexual experiences together. How have those experiences shaped your sexual relationship? If you're reading this in preparation for marriage, what considerations are important to you? Why?

PAIR. Come together in a loving embrace. Hold one another for a few minutes. Then, in a quiet place, look into one another's eyes as you prepare to share.

SHARE. Communicate about your thoughts and feelings. Listen to understand. Decide together what actions you might take as a result of this experience. For couples who are no longer even remotely close to your first lovemaking experience, what information can you use to help prepare your children for their first sexual experiences?

Adding to your Sexual Playbook: Write down a plan for how you will "restart" your sexual experiences when you find your sexual relationship getting stuck in a rut, a servicing model, or other negative cycles.

Experiential Activities to Enjoy:

Preparing for The First Time

1. **Preparation is key for success!** Bring your own supplies. You want to have everything you need to make it wonderful. Lubrication increases pleasure for both partners. Find a good, high-quality lube, and don't use brands that are harmful to your body (see Chapter 27: Sexual Accessories for some information on selecting what lube is best for you!).
2. **Bring both sexy and comfy clothes.** *Mentionables* and *Adore me* are great places to find sexy, beautiful lingerie! *Mentionables* does not use live models in displaying their lingerie, which makes this a great site to visit together if desired. Along with the lingerie, pack your comfort clothes, including baggy t-shirts and your favorite pair of sweats.
3. **Stay clean.** Some women will bleed following penetrative intercourse for the first time. The natural exchange of bodily fluids that occurs during sex can also create a mess. You can prepare for this by placing towels in the bed before having sex or having a spare pair of sheets on hand to put on the bed following sex. Hand towels and unscented wipes by the bed make it quick and easy to clean yourselves off as well. Ladies, always urinate after having penetrative sex; this will help reduce the likelihood of urinary tract infections (UTI).
4. **Take it slow.** Remember, take it slow! There is no problem in

waiting a few days to move from exploring each other's naked bodies to penetrative sex.

Honeymoon Workshop

On my website (tammyhill.com) under the Events tab, you will find a wonderfully informative virtual course to help you prepare sexually for marriage, particularly the honeymoon and newlywed phase.

CHAPTER 29

Marriage and Menstrual Cycles

Periods. They're something that nobody wants to talk about. Women often feel frustrated and ashamed, while men may believe they have no place to comment on this uniquely female phenomenon. One thing I regularly see in my office are young couples struggling to manage difficult times and to repair damage done during hormonally-charged arguments. The conversation will often start with the husband saying, "I think my wife may be crazy!" The wife then becomes defensive or feels great embarrassment as I further assess the purpose for marriage counseling. Our conversations will generally follow these three phases:

- Female brains and menstruation
- Behavioral strategies for managing menstrual cycles
- Relational suggestions for unity and peace

Female Brains and Menstruation

I have heard it said that the female brain marches to the beat of estrogen's drum. There is a lot of truth to this statement, as estrogen affects most everything a teenage girl or middle-aged woman experiences. The estrogen receptors are activated in the hippocampus 24/7, creating monthly rhythms that impact both the brain and the body. Mood, body temperature, sleep, growth, and even breathing all are directly influenced by estrogen. The most obvious cycle controlled by estrogen is the menstrual cycle.

During the first two weeks of a woman's monthly cycle, estrogen acts almost like a fertilizer on cells. The brain is activated, making women feel more confident, social, and verbal. They experience sharper cognitive and memory abilities. Week 2 is particularly productive and energy filled as a woman's libido is turned on high while estrogen levels are peaking. Around day 14 of the cycle, estrogen is replaced with the hormone progesterone which acts more like a weed killer on the brain receptors, causing a woman to feel more sedated, slower paced, less focused, and to gradually increase in irritability. Most women experience mild to moderate degrees of premenstrual syndrome (PMS), with about 10% getting extremely edgy and angry. Other symptoms of Week 3 include mild depression, increased sadness, crying, cravings (particularly for high sugar, high fat foods), headaches, and body-dysmorphic episodes. It is not uncommon for women to want to end relationships during this time as they feel more aggressive irritation. In Week 4, menstruation begins, and progesterone production slows, allowing for emotional calm and lethargy. Once estrogen begins transmitting from the ovaries to the brain, energy increases, verbal capacity and memory are enhanced, and a woman is starting this four-week cycle all over again. She will repeat this cycle every month for roughly 40-years!

Ladies, start tracking your menstrual cycle now! A couple of apps that I am familiar with are *CLUE* and *FLO*. I'm sure there are other apps that are great, these are just the ones I have used or that have been used by my students and clients. I encourage you to take a moment and download the app now. Before you move on, get started on this important part of your menstrual-informed journey. Share the app or calendar with the man in your life. Diligent tracking will bless your life and your relationships as you begin to recognize patterns in your behavior.

Behavioral Strategies for Managing Menstrual Cycles

The process of Cognitive Behavioral Therapy (CBT) has been found to be highly effective as individuals begin to identify negative thought patterns and automatic assumptions about their character that are not based in reality. Cognitive distortions are exaggerated thought patterns or beliefs that are irrational and misrepresent reality; they can often promote continuous negative thinking. This automatic internal negative chatter that ruminates in the brain is believed to stem largely from traumatic and dysfunctional childhood experiences. These negative automatic thoughts often combine with negative emotional or physical symptoms to form maladaptive thinking patterns that can, over time, produce serious mental health issues.

It has been my experience, as a woman and as a therapist, that tracking menstrual cycles is key to recognizing irrational thinking patterns that contribute to unhealthy behaviors during a natural 28-day menstrual cycle. Do you spiral and say hateful, cruel things? Do you injure your body with negative self-talk, poor eating, pulling hair, or cutting? Do you curl up in a ball and want to die? Do you push away love and kindness? Are the people you love concerned about you? Have you felt sorrowful shame for your behavior once your period starts? If you truthfully answered, "Yes!" to any of these questions (which I suspect most women will), it is time to make changes.

The first step to healthy change is to recognize the truth! Track the menstrual cycle for several months, record emotions, distorted thinking patterns, and behavioral reactions. In a few months, you will be amazed to discover a cyclical trend where increases in harmful thought and behavior patterns are correlated closely with Week 3 of the menstrual cycle. This is a common problem for most menstruating women and a typical cause for conflict in relationships.

Another helpful tool in preventing harmful thoughts from leading to unhealthy behaviors is focusing your energy on things that you really value. For instance, if connected relationships are really important to you, focus on the relationship in your interactions. This might include creating a little distance or space during the most challenging days each month. Explain to the people you love when you need to withdraw and why you need the space. If cleanliness is really important to you, there may be certain times each month when you don't have the energy to keep up with your standards. Allow yourself to step back. Don't require yourself to function at a certain level when you lack the strength to meet those standards. As you assess your values, look over the information you have learned from tracking your cycle, and allow harmful, negative thoughts to pass, you will more easily figure out a plan of action that will preserve your relationships and things you value most.

Once you begin taking better care of yourself, by loving and accepting who you are, the more natural it will be for you to cognitively recognize your emotional and physical needs during the menstrual cycle. Men can encourage and support the women in their lives as they may need some extra care during Week 3. Husband, ask your wife how you can best support her as her body moves to estrogen's rhythm. Working together to create a plan of action will bless both of you.

Things to remember:

- Females did not ask for their brains and bodies to function this way. It is a learning and growth bonus awarded to them at conception when the XX chromosomes joined together. This menstrual system is simply part of being female.
- Women and men both deserve to claim joy in mortality. Learn what you love! Learn what your spouse loves. Support one another by participating in activities that create energy, happiness, and love.
- Men and women can learn and grow through understanding, acceptance, and planning. This "thorn in the flesh" can become a great relational gift with time and devoted work.
- Emotional intelligence and maturity are necessary as we choose to behave according to who we *want* to be, regardless of how we feel in the moment.
- Ladies, you need to know that even though your brain is signaling many negative emotions, you are still accountable for your behavior during Week 3! You cannot, I repeat, you cannot blame your period for your actions. We are here to act, not be acted upon.

Relational Suggestions for Unity and Peace

Couples want to feel like they're on the same page together. You got married to share life and love. You deserve to feel confident in your ability to behave in self-respecting ways towards yourself and your spouse. Here are some suggestions:

- When both husband and wife are in a good state of mind, talk honestly and compassionately about what is happening during Week 3. It is important that you talk clearly about how you are feeling, focusing on the problem and not making the person the problem. If this creates too much tension and conflict, I encourage you to seek help from a counselor or marriage therapist to work through the issues.
- There are excellent books to read that can help everyone better understand the female brain, hormones, and menstruation. Get a book and read it together, making time for open discussions. *The Female Brain* by Louann Brizendine is one of my favorite books. There is valuable information to help women understand their brains throughout the lifecycle. *Change Your Brain, Change Your* Life by Daniel Amen is a book that does just as the title predicts. This book is full of scientifically advised protocols for brain health. *The Body Keeps the Score: Brain, Mind, and Body in the Healing of Trauma* by Bessel van der Kolk is incredible—it's one of the best books for a comprehensive understanding of the brain and body connection.
- A husband can be helpful by listening to his wife's feelings (which are real), avoiding the temptation to fix symptoms rather than understanding root causes, and asking for suggestions as to what could help her the best in the moment.
- Make a plan together of how you can manage Week 3 more productively. Try the plan. Then adjust and try again and again. This is a process that will need continual attention and adjustments.
- Utilize the Savior's Atonement in forgiving yourself and one another. Invite God to be part of your conversations. Spiritually create your day with Him prior to going about your day.
- During Weeks 1-2, rejuvenate your loving connections. Make love frequently, do activities you enjoy, and recommit to your covenants and each other. Record your happy times together through pictures and journaling. This way, when you are deep into Week 3, you can look back and remind yourself of these good times.
- Create a personal mantra to recite when times are tough. For exam-

ple, during difficult times, I always say, "The sun will shine again" or "Just keep swimming."

- Know that you're not alone. Support and nurture one another within your home. Extend understanding to those outside of your home.

Our Heavenly Parents created men, women, and marriage. They want us to become more complete together through marriage. The beauty of a covenant marriage is knowing that the Savior is even more invested in your marriage than you are. We each can turn toward Him as we strive to be more like Him.

THINK. Take time to find 5 things that you enjoy and that help *create* energy for you. Write these five things down. If you haven't already, take the authentic happiness inventory (www.authentichappiness.org) to help you identify the things that bring you joy. Once you know what naturally brings joy to your soul, start including these activities in your daily routines. Schedule time for these activities, and make sure you are doing at least one of them each day.

PAIR. Connect with your spouse in whatever way you both choose.

SHARE. After connecting with your spouse, share the activities you wrote down with each other. Make plans for how you can support each other by engaging in activities that create energy in your lives on a daily basis.

Adding to your Sexual Playbook: Write down your plan for maintaining your loving relationship throughout the ups and downs of the wife's menstrual cycle. Focus on what you will do to prevent negative spirals during week three.

Experiential Activities to Enjoy

Period Sex

Yes, you can have sex while menstruating. Just make sure to prepare for more of a mess with towels, old sheets, or cheap shower curtains. Have wet wipes or a washcloth handy for clean-up. Having period sex while in the shower makes clean up easy. I personally don't recommend oral sex during period sex, but each couple can choose for themselves. Make sure to remove tampons or bloody cups prior to penetration; however, menstrual discs can be worn during sex.

Having sex while on your (or your wife's) period can have some great benefits[79]:

1. Orgasm can relieve menstrual cramping. Uterine contractions release the endometrium (the blood lining) from the uterine wall. When a woman orgasms, the muscles of the uterus contract and release repeatedly. This often brings pleasurable relief to menstrual cramping. Additionally, the uterine muscle contractions from orgasm may contribute to shorter periods by releasing and pushing out the endometrium faster.
2. Endorphins and other neurotransmitters released during sex can enhance feelings of happiness, hopefulness, and peace. This may help take the mind off menstrual discomfort.
3. With blood as a lubricant, and as blood flow to sexual organs is necessary for sexual arousal, menstruation can provide a double benefit of acting as a lubricant and of being naturally present in higher concentrations.
4. Many women feel more interested in sex during menstruation because the fear of becoming pregnant is not part of the experience.
5. There is some evidence that orgasm relieves headache pressure. Because nearly half of women experience headaches during their periods, having sex can partially or completely relieve headache pain.
6. Because the position of the cervix often shifts to a higher position

within the vagina during menstruation, deeper penetrative sex can feel more comfortable during menstruation. If "doggy-style" or other deep-penetrative positions are typically uncomfortable, gently try them during menstruation to determine comfort level.

Breasts may feel fuller and nipples may be more sensitive to touch during the menstrual cycle. Pay attention to the breasts to determine sensitivity. This could be a time when nursing and sucking action creates greater arousal.

Doggy-style

Though I don't particularly care for the name of this sexual position, it is what most people are familiar with, so I use it here.* Because this sexual position can feel more comfortable for women during menstruation, this might be a time to give it a try. This position is when the wife is on all fours receiving vaginal penetration from the husband who is either standing or kneeling behind her. You may need to make adjustments to make this position more comfortable. I highly recommend that the wife is very aroused and well-lubricated prior to penetration happening.

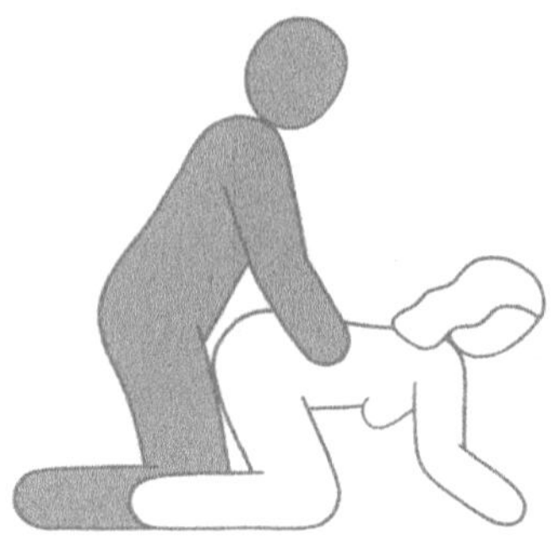

Doggy-style Position

Because this position prevents eye contact and kissing, it can feel less connecting than other positions. However, there are ways to make this position feel more connecting:

1. The husband can wrap his arms around the wife's body, giving a warm loving touch.
2. You can place a mirror in front of both of you so that you can

* At no time ever would I want to confuse human sexual activities with those of animals. Remember, humans are the only creation, out of all of God's creations, that have agency to choose to act rather than merely being acted upon. As sons and daughters created in the image and function of Heavenly Parents, I encourage you to always strive to choose to act with integrity, both in and out of the bedroom.

watch each other's faces and make eye contact through the mirror.

3. Making sure there is skin-to-skin contact both before and after can enhance the connection of this sexual position.

There are some pleasurable benefits to this position:

1. Because of the angle of the penis, there is more contact with the female G-zone or prostate gland.
2. The deep penetration can feel especially arousing for men. Women have some control over the depth of penetration by lowering herself to her elbows to increase depth or arching her back to decrease the depth of penetration.
3. The weight of the husband's body is not on the woman, which can make this position more comfortable in some ways for the wife.
4. The clitoral glans is in a perfect position to be stimulated by either the husband or the wife.
5. There is still plenty of room for breasts to be touched and enjoyed. As the hands are coming from behind, it can be a uniquely pleasurable experience.
6. Wives wiggling or bouncing her buttocks up against her husband's penis as he penetrates can be especially arousing for him.

CHAPTER 30

Multiplying as Equal Partners

Decisions regarding the number and spacing of children, should be made by husband and wife as equal partners, who empathetically communicate and seek divine inspiration and confirmation together. Too frequently, I see couples not actively working together in making critically important decisions, such as having a baby. In my professional life, both as a professor and a therapist, couples often visit me with problems that stemmed from decisions made by one spouse that critically impacted both spouses. I call this "unequally-yoked decision-making."

An extreme example of unequally-yoked decision-making in marriage is found in the experience of a couple I met several years ago where trust had been violated because of the wife's unilateral decision to become pregnant. Using false names to protect my clients, I will share this example. Kenzie had felt promptings to have a child for several months. She had turned to Jake, her husband, telling him about the sweet feelings and impressions she was receiving. She believed that it was time to start their family. Jake was afraid that having a child during school, with graduate school still to come, would be too difficult. It didn't make logical sense to him, and the idea of becoming a father was frightening. Kenzie pushed her opinion, and Jake pushed his. After nearly a year of this conflict between them, Kenzie took matters into her own hands and decided to stop taking her birth control pills without informing Jake. I saw this sweet couple when she was nearly five months pregnant. Jake was devastated that Kenzie had made this important decision without his knowledge.

How could he trust her?! Kenzie was frustrated too! She was listening to the Spirit, following what she felt God was directing her to do, while Jake's fears were holding him back from seeking his own spiritual revelation about starting their family. Both spouses made mistakes. Jake's fears kept him from seeking revelation, and he chose not to listen to his wife. Kenzie made a unilateral decision to bring Jake's child into the world without his knowledge or consent.

I could write about countless scenarios of couples making decisions while unequally-yoked. This pattern creates conflict and negatively impacts trust and validation. It is not the pattern of heaven. Making consequential decisions that deeply affect others, without their knowledge, is inherently wrong! In doing so, one is taking away the other's agency, which was the very cause for the war in heaven. President Gordon B. Hinkley said, "In the marriage companionship there is neither inferiority nor superiority. The woman does not walk ahead of the man; neither does the man walk ahead of the woman. They walk side by side as a son and daughter of God on an eternal journey."[80]

Because marriage and family decisions are a shared stewardship, both wife and husband will have access to revelation for their lives. Unless both spouses agree to seek outside counsel together, these decisions should be privately made with equal counsel and equal consent. In these conversations there needs to be full knowledge, full participation, and full partnership.[81] Once a united decision is made, the husband or father has the responsibility to provide guided leadership in helping the couple or family implement the mutually agreed-upon decision. *This is how husbands can preside in equal partnership.*

No one else, especially not your parents or parents-in-law, should be allowed in the decision-making process. Nor should you ask your parents to continue to receive revelation for your life as an adult. Cleaving together as a couple means that your family of creation begins with your marriage vows. Together, as teammates with equal voices, you seek revelation for your life. This is especially true when making the eternal decision of having a baby.

Members of The Church of Jesus Christ of Latter-day Saints understand that human beings, both male and female, are beloved spirit children of Heavenly Parents. According to the Church's essay entitled *Mother in Heaven*, Susa Young Gates, a prominent leader in the Church, wrote in 1920 that Joseph Smith's visions and teachings revealed the truth that "the divine Mother, (is) side by side with the divine Father." Prophets have taught that our Heavenly Parents work together for the salvation of the human family. The essay also includes the following teaching from M. Russell Ballard, "We are part of a divine plan designed by Heavenly Parents who love us." There is a family order in Heaven, a divine pattern. God the Father, along with our Mother in Heaven at His side, create the vast hierarchical system of the human family. The system is hierarchical because we, as Their children, are not equal partners with Them but are below Them in power. It is Their plan that was first introduced pre-mortally to us, Their spirit children. This is the family Order of Heaven.[82]

The Family: A Proclamation to the World clearly outlines this pattern to help us in organizing our families in mortality. Adam and Eve were commanded in the Garden of Eden to "multiply and replenish the earth," and so too, we, as members of The Church of Jesus Christ of Latter-day Saints, know that ". . . God's commandment to multiply and replenish the earth remains in force."[83] Providing mortal bodies for the spirit offspring of our Heavenly Parents is an essential part of the eternal plan of happiness. David A. Bednar said,

> Marriage between a man and a woman is the authorized channel through which premortal spirits enter mortality. Complete sexual abstinence before marriage and total fidelity within marriage protect the sanctity of this sacred channel. The power of procreation is spiritually significant. Misuse of this power subverts the purposes of the Father's plan and of our mortal existence. Our Heavenly Father and His Beloved Son are creators and have entrusted each of us with a portion of Their creative power. . . . How we feel about and use that supernal power will determine in large measure our happiness in mortality and our destiny in eternity.[84]

Husband and wife are responsible to decide together when and how many children to invite into the world. The Church Handbook states:

> Sexual relations within marriage are not only for the purpose of

> procreation, but also a means of expressing love and strengthening emotional and spiritual ties between husband and wife. Husband and wife are encouraged to pray and counsel together as they plan their families. Issues to consider include the physical and mental health of the mother and father and their capacity to provide the basic necessities of life for their children.
>
> Decisions about birth control and the consequences of those decisions rest solely with each married couple.[85]

A couple must also recognize that the decision to become parents involves much more than deciding together to start trying to conceive a baby. Parenthood is a forever calling and responsibility, but most intensive from conception to about age 25. For this length of time, a couple is commanded to help each other as equal partners to nurture, protect, and provide for their children. The Proclamation also outlines a family system wherein the wife and husband share equal power, while beloved children remain in a subordinate position of power. Allowing children into the parental hierarchy creates dysfunctional relationships within the family. As parents, it is essential to listen to and counsel with your children about family life decisions. Then, as wife and husband, take the suggestions and counsel together in private, make a united decision, and then in love explain the decision to your children. It is critical to let your children understand the reasons for the decision. Prayerfully ask for unity within the family as you move forward with change.

Learning to truly become equal partners is a process that requires trust, patience, and time. I firmly believe that this process is one of the most critical aspects of our journey toward exaltation. We must walk side-by-side, as our Heavenly Parents do, in navigating important decisions for family life.

THINK. Independent of one another, journal your thoughts about equal partnership in marriage. As you consider the order of heaven, how is your relationship similar? Different? How is your family system similar? Different? What specific changes do you need to make to function more fully as equal partners? How do you feel supported as a spouse by your spouse? How do you feel you could be better supported by your spouse? It is important to consider your responsibilities as parents to your children as you navigate this conversation. Spousal stewardship includes supporting one another as equal partners in your roles as mother and father.

PAIR. Create space to connect emotionally through eye gazing, praying together and cuddling.

SHARE. Share with your spouse the thoughts you journaled about equal partnership in your marriage. Listen and be vulnerable in sharing both what you personally could do better and changes you could make together as a couple. Decide together on one or two specific goals.

Adding to your Sexual Playbook: Based on your journaling and discussion, add to your sexual playbook specific ways you will act in equal partnership in making decisions about childbearing and childrearing, as well as in your romantic and sexual relationship.

Experiential Activities to Enjoy

Pulse Points

Find your spouse's pulse points with your finger. Each time you locate a pulse, rest your finger while contemplating the gratitude you feel for your spouse's life. Now lightly lick and then blow each of the pulse points. Because pulse points are found closer to the surface of the skin, a little wetness, followed by a quick breath of air, will immediately cool the skin. This sensation on top of a pulse point can be very sensitive and exciting. Now rotate, it's your turn!

Add Eye Contact and Gratitude

Each time you locate a pulse, rest your finger, feeling the pulse while contemplating the gratitude you feel for your spouse's life. Now make eye contact with your spouse. Look into one another's eyes for 15-20 seconds before telling him/her about the grateful thought you had. Think of and share a different thing you're grateful for with each pulse point.

CHAPTER 31

Pregnancy and Postpartum Sexuality

One of the greatest blessings given to mortals is the opportunity to create new life through a sexual relationship. However, the physical and emotional changes that accompany pregnancy and childbirth can become a challenge to a couple's sexual relationship. I wrote this chapter with the intention of helping you claim more sexual joy and replenishment during pregnancy and the period following childbirth.

I marvel continually at the trust our Heavenly Parents give us with this most sacred responsibility to clothe Their spirit children with physical bodies. Yet, even with this eternal knowledge and reverence for the significance of raising children, there really is nothing that changes life more than becoming a parent. According to Dr. John Gottman's research, most couples are dissatisfied with their relationship after a child is born. Gottman claims that the real secret to successfully managing the transition to parenthood is to keep the friendliness in your marriage relationship strong.[86] Isn't that interesting!? Couples are commanded to multiply and replenish together: multiply by bringing children to earth; replenish by strengthening the wholeness of their relationship, including their sexual friendship.

As you well know, both a man and a woman are needed for the perpetuation of human life; this is how the plan was designed. Although a woman's body is profoundly impacted with its life-supporting capacities, a man is also needed, despite the fact that his contributions are often societally viewed as lesser in importance. Ladies, I urge you not to follow the trend of man-hating and blaming your husband for your pregnancy conditions. Your hormones, mood swings, nausea, cravings, weight gain, and discomfort are really not his fault! Too often I have clients come in for therapy where real relational damage is founded in negative exchanges during pregnancy. Without negating the truth that a wife's divine role in parenthood requires an unmeasurable physical sacrifice, a loving husband also sacrifices for the greater whole of eternity. Recognize that each pregnancy will be a unique experience for every couple; the same couple can have a variety of experiences with different pregnancies, but in every fruitful pregnancy, the wife and husband manifest their unity in creating a new life.

Unless your medical doctor has prescribed otherwise, a robust sexual relationship throughout the pregnancy can be replenishing to both spouses. Having said that, it's imperative to understand that the constant changes taking place in a mother's body, including the way hormones are interacting, the sudden onset of queasiness, and extreme fatigue are impossible to predict. These types of situations happen frequently in pregnancy. Choosing to focus energy on the things you can control will help the mind/body connection much more than getting frustrated with the way things are in the moment. I have found that changing the way you talk about what is happening can lead to a much closer emotional connection.

I tell my female students and clients to expect to be a different type of animal during pregnancy! It has been said that a pregnant female is more different hormonally from a non-pregnant female than a non-pregnant female is different from a man. You're not going to feel the same during pregnancy as you did before pregnancy. You both need to recognize this truth and decide how you will respond to the unexpected circumstances that come up during the pregnancy. You can prepare for this, in part, by choosing how you will respond to circumstances that are less than desirable and by determining to focus energy on the emotional connections that can arise within these varied situations.

For example, smells were very much intensified for me during pregnancy. Multiple times I would begin kissing my husband, only to end up retching and vomiting because of my hyperosmia. One evening, I got sick while we were lying in bed together sharing an intimate kiss. The smell of my husband's cologne suddenly hit me, and before I could get up, I unfortunately vomited all over the bed and my husband. This situation was certainly less than desirable for both of us. I could have cried and felt like an utter failure as a wife. My husband could have become angry and frustrated. Instead, he quickly removed the bedding to wash up the mess, changed his clothes and came back to comfort me. I will always remember his arms warmly around me as he whispered in my ear, "Getting you in bed is always a surprise!" We both laughed. I laughed until I cried. Throughout it all, he held me close and together we replenished our marriage with touch, laughter, and emotional closeness. There is no doubt that we made love that night—without ever having intercourse.

In the following sections, I provide information on things to consider with each trimester, including typical physiological changes and sexual encounters that might be enjoyable during this stage of pregnancy.

The First Trimester

Physical Changes

The first sign of pregnancy might have been a missed period. You can expect several other physical changes in the first 3 months, including:

- Tender, swollen breasts
- Nausea with or without vomiting
- Increased urination
- Fatigue
- Food cravings and food aversions
- Heartburn
- Constipation

Emotional Changes

Even if you're thrilled about being pregnant, a new baby adds emotional stress to your life. It's very natural to worry about your baby's health as well as your adjustment to parenthood and the financial demands of raising a child. If you are working, you might worry about how to balance the demands of family and career. You might also experience mood swings. What you are feeling is normal. Take care of yourself. Look for support from loved ones, especially your husband. If your mood changes become severe or intense, consult your healthcare provider.

Sexual Considerations

During the first trimester, your body will look much the same as it looked prior to pregnancy, although nausea, fatigue, breast and nipple tenderness can all negatively impact libido during this stage of pregnancy. There are also some changes that can positively impact the ease of sexual arousal, such as the additional blood flow to the labia, clitoral glans, and vagina, which bring about feelings of tingly awareness and increased lubrication. This can lead to more frequent or more intense orgasms and increased comfort with penetration. There is also the factor that many women find pregnancy sexually freeing as they no longer have to worry about birth control. There is no reason to worry that you might hurt the baby by having sex unless your medical doctor has advised otherwise.

The Second Trimester

Physical Changes

During the second trimester, you might experience some of the following physical changes:

- Growing belly and breasts
- Skin changes
- Nasal stuffiness and nosebleeds
- Dental issues
- Dizziness

- Leg cramps
- Vaginal discharge
- Urinary tract infections

Emotional Changes

Typically, you will feel less tired and more up to the challenge of preparing for your baby during the second trimester. To ease your anxiety about labor and delivery, learn as much as you can by enrolling in childbirth classes or reading helpful books. Focus on making healthy lifestyle choices that will help both you and your baby have the best chances to thrive.

Sexual Considerations

Be mindful during sex by recognizing that what feels amazing one week, may feel a little awkward the next. With continued blood volume increase in the vulva, lubrication and arousal can occur much more quickly. Increases in breast volume and reduced tenderness is another important factor that can contribute to feelings of sexual awareness and desirability. Some position adjustments might need to be made in this stage of pregnancy to accommodate growth and comfort for the woman. Side-by-side lying (a great option because it keeps the weight off both the woman's back and belly), pregnant partner on top (it also doesn't put any pressure on the belly, and as an added bonus, it allows the woman to be in control of both penetration depth and clitoral stimulation) and rear-entry (it means your partner doesn't have to maneuver around your belly, which can make things a little easier for you both) are all great options.

Sexual tools can stay in your repertoire, as long as they're clean and feel comfortable. With oral sex, the husband should never blow air forcibly into the vagina. This can be life-threatening as, in rare cases, it could cause an air embolism. As your baby bump continues to grow, make sure you're not engaging in positions that put weight on your belly. If there are feelings of cramping after an orgasm, this is typically harmless discomfort that can last for about 30 minutes after intercourse. As in the first trimester, there is no reason to worry that you might hurt the baby by having sex unless your medical doctor has advised otherwise.

The Third Trimester

The third trimester will bring more movement from your baby and more growth for you. You can expect to experience many of the following changes:

- Weight gain
- Larger breasts and nipples
- Braxton Hicks contractions
- Backaches
- Shortness of breath
- Heartburn
- Spider veins, varicose veins, and hemorrhoids
- Frequent urination

Emotional Changes

Your emotions may fluctuate as fears about childbirth might become more persistent. The reality of parenthood may also begin to create more real-time anxiety, especially if this is your first baby. Stay calm by preparing yourself for the transition to parenthood. Continue to invest in the friendship of your marriage relationship as you prepare for birth.

Sexual Expectations

The cervix, the opening of the uterus, is soft and engorged during pregnancy. It's not uncommon to notice a little blood spotting after sex late in pregnancy, particularly with deep penetration. This bleeding is generally harmless, but it's never a bad idea to let your doctor know about it. Sexual positions should continue to keep weight off the wife's belly. As in the other trimesters, there is still no reason to worry that you might hurt the baby by having sex unless your medical doctor has advised otherwise.

Postpartum Sexual Expectations

After delivery, women will have a bloody vaginal discharge called lochia that typically continues for up to six weeks. A woman should not have penetrative sex prior to this discharge stopping to prevent infections. In addition, premature penetration may result in the tearing of episiotomy stitches in the perineum after childbirth. These concerns, along with the comfort and desire level of the mother, can also put sex on hold for longer. Typically, a woman will have a medical examination six weeks after delivery to ensure that her body is healing appropriately. Often couples view this as a "green light" for resuming sexual relations. The most critical decision for vaginal penetration to resume is a woman's desire for intercourse and the comfort in which she can experience penetration. I believe resuming intercourse after childbirth is never the husband's decision. External stimulation to orgasm is completely fine, if desired.

I highly recommend that if there is any sustained discomfort or pain involved with intercourse (*dyspareunia*) that a couple stops penetrative sex. Continue to take more time in the excitement phase of your sexual experiences, use plenty of lubrication (CBD or hemp infused is helpful), and go slowly with finger penetration first. Start with one finger, gently running the finger around the vaginal opening and into the vagina. Add another finger to the mix as you continue to prepare for more comfortable penetration. The *fourchette* (the crevice along the lower part of the vaginal opening where the labia majora connect) and the perineum are the areas that likely are the most sensitive. Scar tissue can also be uncomfortable to touch. Go at the pace, depth and breadth that is most comfortable for the woman. If there is continued discomfort, please seek help from a pelvic floor therapist. The exercises and treatment recommendations can significantly help a woman fully heal and strengthen her pelvic floor.

There are times when pregnancy and the birthing process can create a prolapsed uterus. This is particularly common when a woman has had several vaginal deliveries, given birth to a large baby, or has experienced birthing trauma. When this occurs, the pelvic floor muscles and ligaments are weakened to the point where they no longer support the uterus. In severe cases, the uterus can slip down or protrude from the vagina, which can require surgery. Both severe and mid-uterine prolapse makes sexual penetration uncomfortable. Seeking medical help, along with pelvic floor therapy, is essential to regain strength and sexual comfort.

Fatigue is another factor that negatively influences postpartum sexuality. Both mothers and fathers take a big hit to their sleeping routines as they adjust to a newborn. As a matter of fact, research shows that 57% of 6-month-olds were not sleeping for 8 hours, while at 12 months, 43% still woke up in the middle of the night.[87] This lack of sleep can cause new parents to lose sexual desire and sensation.

Once a mother has given birth, estrogen levels decrease significantly, which decreases the production of natural lubrication. This makes it more important to include good lubricants during lovemaking. These hormonal changes can also result in more sadness and even lead to postpartum depression that can persist for months. If this is a situation you are experiencing, I urge you to get professional help with medication and/or therapy.[88]

Breastfeeding

Breastfeeding is good for bonding. It is also a source of perfect nutrition for the newborn. However, considering all demanding variables in a mother's life, it ultimately needs to only be the mother's choice. Sexually speaking, breastfeeding can either get in the way of your sex life or it can enhance your lovemaking experience. Nursing or pumping milk can make breasts feel tender, leakage can cause embarrassment, and a new mom may not want her breasts to be touched. Some women feel like baby-feeding machines and prefer not having breast stimulation during sex while breastfeeding. Other women, due to increased blood volume, size of breasts and nipples, and slight uterine contractions that take place during nipple sucking, find sex more pleasurable and erotic during breastfeeding. I encourage women who choose to breastfeed to try breast play and nursing action in their sexual relationships. You never know if you are going to really like it until you try. That said, it is solely the choice of the couple, largely the woman, to decide how to incorporate breast play into lovemaking activities.

THINK. As you consider the information in this chapter, what new insights have you gained? Are there perspectives you have not seen? Have you experienced feelings of gratitude for women, particularly women in your life, and the life-giving process?

PAIR. This time I want you to get skin-to-skin, and both really observe the wife's body with reverence and gratitude. There's no need to talk yet, just look and see the beauty of a body that has given or may give life to a spirit son or daughter of Heavenly Parents. Try to mentally pray to see the divinity of the body, the sanctity of providing life to a new soul, and the godliness of it all.

SHARE. Listen to understand the thoughts and feelings of your partner. Take turns sharing. Perhaps this could be a bonding opportunity to pray together in gratitude for the miracle of creating life, of being refined through the process, and for the gift of your love.

Adding to your Sexual Playbook: Based on your specific stage in life, including whether you have experienced a pregnancy together before, are currently pregnant, or are hoping to become pregnant, carefully consider what you would like to add from this chapter into your sexual playbook.

Experiential Activities to Enjoy

Mirror Touching

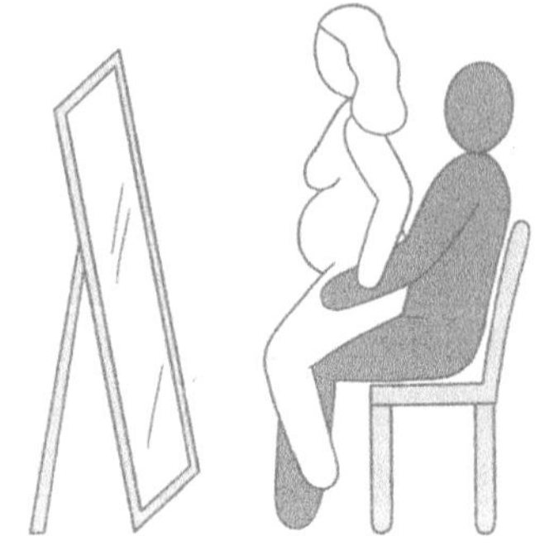

Mirror Touching While Pregnant

This experience can be highly arousing sexually and spiritually! Prior to starting, both of you clean up and get comfortable being naked together. Adjust the lighting to be soft and romantic; consider using a flickering candle or two. In front of a full-length mirror (or as full of a mirror as you can find), stand together with the husband's arms wrapped around his wife's body. Now, slowly touch your wife's body as you slightly sway against each other. Observe one another in the mirror as you touch. She can also guide his hands to touch her in ways that she enjoys. It is also very erotic for the husband to watch his wife touch her own body in pleasing ways. Go slow! There's no hurry as you watch one another enjoy touching this beautiful body that can hold life within it.

Sexual Positions During Pregnancy

When enjoying sex during pregnancy, it's best to find comfortable positions that help keep weight off the baby, especially during the last trimester of pregnancy. Below are three positions that are typically quite comfortable and enjoyable during the third trimester.

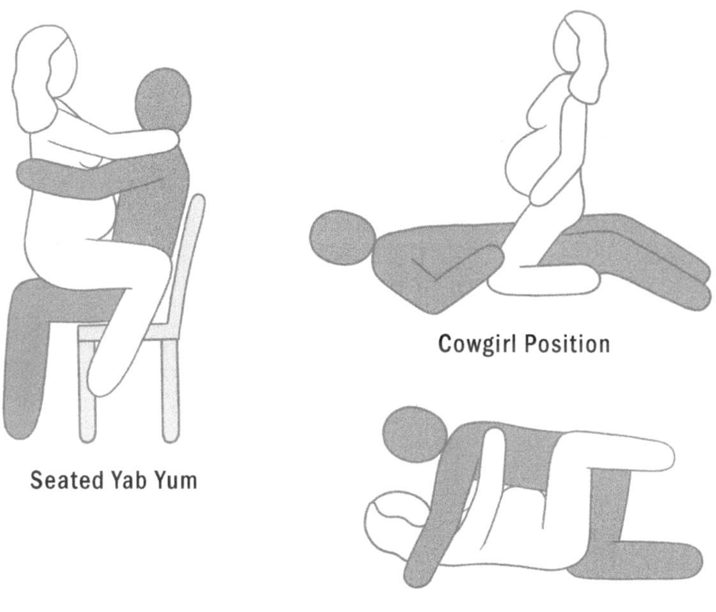

Seated Yab Yum

Cowgirl Position

Modified Missionary

Mutual Self-Touch

This type of lovemaking can occur anytime, but I think pregnancy, and especially postpartum sexual play, might be a time where self-touching can feel especially nice. This allows a woman to feel for herself what feels nice and what level of penetration (if any) she is ready to experience. This form of lovemaking might feel uncomfortable to some of you; if so, I would encourage you to process the discomfort together with your spouse. Remember, you two get to create the sexual environment in your relationship, no one else!

Get naked and comfortable together. Now find a good position where you can see one another's eyes. It's nice to start by sharing slow touch, kissing and emotional connection. Use plenty of lubrication as you apply it to your spouse's genitals, and hold your hands there in a genital-holding or cupping position. Share some time here with eye gazing and synchronized breathing. When you feel connected and ready, place your hand on your own genitals and touch yourselves while kissing. As you become increasingly aroused, pull back and watch each other enjoy this mutual self-touching time. You get to decide what happens next!

CHAPTER 32

Sex and Infertility

God's commandment is to "multiply and replenish" the earth. This book is about replenishing sexual relationships in marriage, and when sexual relationships lead to creating a new body for a child who will be part of your family for all eternity, it becomes particularly replenishing. Indeed, many couples report that sexual intercourse is especially satisfying when they are trying to have a baby. However, some couples struggle with infertility, which can feel devastating. Infertility can negatively affect the couple's sexual relationship as well as their marriage. This chapter will focus on coping with infertility.

Infertility is defined as the inability to conceive while having unprotected sex 2-3 times per week for a minimum of one year. My late husband, Mark Mulford, and I went through 13 years of infertility. I experienced Polycystic Ovary Disease (POD) and Mark had a low sperm count. During these long, seemingly-endless years, we were blessed to adopt a son, and I went through several rounds of various medications to promote ovulation. I really tried not to let myself get offended by all the thoughtless things that well-intentioned people said to me during those long years, such as:

- "It must be so fun not worrying about birth control."
- "Just have more faith."
- "At least you have Jordan." (He is my oldest son, born naturally before our infertility years.)

- "Oh, my husband would love not needing to use condoms all the time!"
- "You're too high strung. If you relaxed more, you could get pregnant."

These types of comments are not helpful. Check yourself if you tend to offer unsolicited advice or speak out about "silver-linings." I know that I have said things to others that, despite my intent, have caused pain. It is wise for each of us to learn how to just listen and love.

Infertility treatments often bring incredible amounts of sexual stress, both psychologically and physically. For many couples, making love is a way to connect emotionally, but when sex becomes associated with failure to conceive, it adds strain to the relationship. The pressure to perform on schedule, or to abstain from sex due to infertility treatment plans, can make sex less enjoyable. Once sex becomes focused on baby making, couples often stop making love for pleasure, connection, and expressions of love. Relational distress can worsen as fertility treatments extend over longer periods of time. Prolonged time spent trying to conceive may lead to an increased incidence of sexual dysfunction, decreased individual happiness and emotional well-being, as well as increased financial stress.

The typical sexual problems experienced by infertile couples include problems in any of the phases of sexual response (desire, arousal, orgasm, resolution) as well as pain disorders. Diminished libido, difficulty in having and/or maintaining erections, premature or retarded ejaculation, vaginal discomfort and tightness all negatively impact sexual functioning of couples undergoing medically-prescribed infertility interventions. Many couples begin to avoid sexual intimacy during non-fertile times and claim a loss in pleasure from sexual activity, which leads to a significant loss of affection overall, leaving couples feeling more tense and disconnected.[89]

Even as I write this chapter, my mind goes back in time to the years of infertility Mark and I experienced together. My heart aches with these memories. I remember how devastating it was each month when my period would start. Often, Mark would find me in tears on the bathroom floor, grieving for an intense loss of a righteous desire. I think back to how every lovemaking experience became a time of yearning in prayer that this time I would get pregnant. The years I spent believing that if I just could be more righteous as a woman, God would certainly bless me with more children, were depressing at best.

My sweet friends, any of you experiencing infertility, please know how much I understand your pain and suffering. I'm sorry for your monthly losses, for the sexual interference infertility plays with your pleasure, and especially if, in any way, you feel unworthy of the blessing of a baby. If my experience helps you, please read what I've learned from infertility and the power found in regular scripture study.

I know that the scriptures are the Word of God. I am rarely more invigorated than when I truly apply my mind to studying the scriptures. Many times, my understanding has increased, I have felt enlightenment come, and I know that my spirit was being fed pure manna from heaven. I still clearly remember such an occurrence that greatly blessed me in 1992. At this time in my life, I was desperate to have another baby. Jordan was six years old, Mark and I had been unsuccessful at several fertility treatments, and our adoption file was yet to be selected by a birthmother. I had convinced myself that my infertility was a result of my imperfections as a person. My realization that God was aware of my struggles occurred one morning while I was reading Luke 1:5-7 which says, "There was in the days of Herod . . . a certain priest named Zacharias, and his wife was, Elisabeth. And they were both righteous before God, walking in all the commandments and ordinances of the Lord blameless. And they had no child, because that Elisabeth was barren . . ." As I read those verses, a piercing feeling went through my heart. I began weeping as the Holy Ghost let me know *through the scriptures* that my inability to have children had nothing to do with my worthiness before God!

In counseling with couples experiencing infertility, here are some of the strategies that I suggest:

1. Normalize that when you experience infertility, your sex life will change while you're trying to conceive.
2. Stay focused on your relationship, not the infertility. Continue to do things you enjoy, and talk about things other than the infertility.
3. Talk about sexual experiences that you are enjoying, what creates desire and arousal, and have realistic expectations that some sex-

ual spontaneity will be lost as you undergo your infertility procedures.

4. While being sexual, focus on the sensual mindfulness you are experiencing. Take time to hold one another caressing, kissing, and communicating after you have sex.
5. Make sure to have sex at times other than when you are ovulating. During these times, try being spontaneous, affectionate, and flirty.
6. Keep the bedroom associated with love, passion, and romance. Keep your communication about infertility in other areas of the home, along with any fertility books, medications, injections, or thermometers.
7. It is okay to take a break from infertility treatments. The pressure to achieve pregnancy, along with the physical and emotional side effects of fertility treatments, can weigh heavily on both physical and mental health. It's okay to pause and focus on your relationship.
8. Self-care is a must. Eat nutritiously, get sunlight, exercise, and make time for plenty of sleep. Continue to participate in energy-producing activities.
9. It is okay to not answer probing questions from family or friends. Together, set boundaries on what you will discuss with others (review *Chapter 5: Sacred Sexual Boundaries* for more details on setting boundaries). You can decide a way that works best for you to deflect conversations from topics you don't want to discuss.
10. Always support one another in reaching out for relational therapy. As a relational therapist I might be biased, but I firmly believe that a systems approach to therapy works best most of the time. You are a team; get help as a team.[90]

Infertility, for couples who desperately want children, can be one of life's biggest challenges. If you and your spouse struggle with infertility, I hope you will realize that your marriage is bigger than this challenge. You can take action to strengthen your marital connection, especially by continuing with replenishing sex.

THINK. Journal about your experiences with infertility.

- How has it made you feel when you're alone? With your family? With your neighbors and friends?
- Is infertility bringing you closer as a couple? Is it tearing you apart?
- How is infertility impacting your ability to emotionally regulate? When do you feel the most volatile? Sad? Hopeless?
- What is this experience doing to your faith in God and His divine plan for you?
- Are there events you are avoiding because of your infertility experience?
- How frequently do you think about infertility?

Take the time to write about any other related thoughts or experiences.

PAIR. Make sure you have adequate time for this; you might want to block out a few hours as there can be a lot of things to unpack. If needed, one partner can share one time and the other partner can share the next time. Hold each other in a comfortable place where you have eye contact.

SHARE. Take turns sharing and listening to understand. As you better understand how this experience is impacting your spouse, offer empathy and love. Talk about specific things that you can do to make this experience less painful and traumatic. Listen to each other. My experience is that often a man's experiences are not valued as deeply as a woman's experience. Make sure that both of you have the space, time and understanding you need to make the experience one that you can draw strength from as a couple.

Adding to your Sexual Playbook: Integrate what you have learned and discussed from this chapter to make a plan for replenishing and prioritizing your relationship amidst infertility struggles.

Experiential Activities to Enjoy

"GET OUT" of the Bedroom

Find an object (or a picture of an object) that both of you really do not like. Maybe it's a can of spinach, old socks, or a picture of a snake. Whatever it is, both of you need to agree that you don't like this object. Now, journal everything that you would like to say to your infertility. If your experience with infertility could hear you, what would you like it to know?

Example:

- "I hate you! You can't destroy my life!"
- "You make me feel sad."
- "I question my worth as a person because of you!"
- "You are disrupting my marriage."

Write everything you want your infertility to hear. Don't leave anything out! Now, together take the object you both hate, and place it in front of you. Take turns telling this object (which is now named "infertility") what you want it to know. You can yell, swear, shake your fist, flip the bird, cry, etc. Do whatever feels purging or cleansing. You may feel like this is a crazy idea, you may even feel a little crazy doing it, but know that there is a therapeutic process in this madness. You are externalizing your painful emotions. The stuff you've bottled up inside is now able to come out. It can be channeled toward something you don't like to represent the infertility that you don't like.

Once you both feel liberated (and if done correctly, externalization should feel liberating), hold on to each other. Cry if you need to but hold on for at least five minutes and just feel what starts happening in your brains. It can be amazing.

I encourage you to do this exercise before you have sex. Do it outside of the bedroom. As you externalize your frustrations toward the object representing infertility, let it know that it can no longer have place in your bedroom. No more will you allow this thing you hate to come between your relationship and your lovemaking. It is not welcome in the bedroom. Close the bedroom door and make love. Anytime during your lovemaking that thoughts of conception or infertility come into your mind, pause. Acknowledge the thought, and then tell it to leave. It is not welcome in the bedroom anymore.

This will take practice. Depending on how long you have been experiencing infertility, it can be more challenging to rid yourself of the mental script involved with sex and infertility. This process does work. As you make concerted efforts at externalization, this experience will be more beneficial for you.

Blindfold Taste Testing

This experience can be shared at any time in the relationship. I added it here to clearly demonstrate ways to make sex more creative and fun, especially at times when focusing on conception is the norm. For this activity, you will need to make a platter of yummy treats, take it into your bedroom, and feed each other with your hands. You can make this really sensual or really playful! It's up to you. I personally believe that it can be a little bit of both. To make this feel special, put your snacks in pretty bowls or plates, then pile everything onto a nice tray. You may also want to have water or something to drink as you go along. Here are some items you could include:

- Fruit
- Cheese
- Nuts
- Olives
- Chocolate
- Whipped cream
- Ice cream
- Candy

Get comfortable on the bed, blindfold your spouse and, one-by-one, feed him/her the various treats with your fingers. Allow your fingers to seductively stay in his/her mouth. Have your partner guess what it is that you are feeding him/her. There's something really fun and sensual about eating with your hands and feeding each other, especially when blindfolded. Once you have fed your spouse, it is your turn to be fed!

CHAPTER 33

Aging Bodies

Thirty-eight years ago, as a 22-year-old new mother, I was asked to minister to (formerly called visit teach) an older woman in my ward. This lady was spunky and fun. Even after 60+ years of marriage, she openly flirted with her husband. I will never forget one afternoon, I was putting my 8-month-old son in his stroller, preparing to leave, when out of nowhere she said, "Tammy, never use Vaseline for lube! In a pinch we used it, and I have the worst yeast infection." I remember standing there speechless, blurting out my thanks, and walking home in a daze. I had no idea people in their eighties still had sex!

Living in a society that places so much emphasis on the beautiful energy found in youth, and being not-so-young myself anymore, I frequently find myself feeling totally out of place. Especially shopping for lingerie. From the sheer, lacy small-cup bralettes that I literally have to scoop my breasts off my belly in order to fill, to the thong-style underwear, finding beautiful nighties and underwear can feel so intimidating. The media has not done a helpful job at normalizing senior couples with vibrant sex lives. Not to mention the fact that as humans, our life expectancy has grown with improved healthcare and nutrition. Do we really want to live a lot longer without enjoying sex? Not me! So, I'm here to change the assumption that celibacy accompanies mid-to-later life adults. It does not have to. You have a choice to make; will your love life totally rock or basically suck in retirement?! I hope you will choose to invest in the erotic goodness that can be created in your marriage throughout your lifespan. When children leave the home and retirement comes, many couples have a lot more uninterrupted time alone and opportunities to create quality time together. In many ways, this season of life really can become golden years.

Regardless of age, we know that sexual satisfaction contributes to life satisfaction, overall happiness, relationship satisfaction, and improved mental and physical health. In short, a satisfying sex life significantly contributes to a higher quality of life. Older couples engage in sex less frequently than younger couples, but studies indicate that individuals over the age of 60, who are in committed relationships of 30 years or longer, often enjoy satisfying sex. How do these couples, despite challenges with sexual dysfunction, medication, and physical limitations, report having satisfying sex? Some of the common words and phrases used when describing their sexual encounters included "authenticity," "being fully present," "living in the moment," "sharing intimacy, exploration, and risk," and "having extraordinary communication and experiencing transcendency in sex." This research should provide hope in, and a determination to live for, mid-to-later life sex.[91] Personally, I believe that romance and commitment go hand-in-hand. Marriages thrive when couples choose to actively keep each other on the top of their "to do" lists (pun intended) throughout all life's difficulties.

According to the National Institute of Aging, some typical changes can be expected with age. Women's vaginal walls atrophy, becoming thin and dry and less natural vaginal lubrication is produced upon arousal. Men experience more erectile dysfunction (ED), which indicates a loss in the ability to have and maintain erections, as well as an increased length of time between erections. Illnesses, including mental health diagnoses, chronic pain, and side effects of necessary medications all contribute to sexual frustrations as people age. With these natural bodily changes, aging adults may not feel as comfortable in their own skin, even with a lifelong partner. Fear of no longer being attractive or sexy can also interfere with enjoying a fulfilling sexual relationship. With so many things working against positive sexuality in later life, I like to focus on things you can do to create more erotic energy with age.

First, talk with each other and with your doctor about the situations causing frustration. For example, ED can be managed, or even reversed, with medications and/or other treatments. It's also so important to understand that ED does not need to limit orgasm for men. While the experience will feel different and perhaps a little less intense, it can still be very enjoyable with more of the entire groin area involved, rather than just the penis. When penetrative sex is not possible, it is common for men to avoid a partner's sexual touch on a flaccid penis. There are so many underlying societal messages about masculinity and the penis that not having an erection can create sexual shame. But it doesn't have to! Don't stop having fun together because ED is part of your stage of life. Sexual fun can still be part of your experience. Many women prefer performing oral sex on a flaccid penis, as it is softer and there is less of a gag reflex. Also, using an external vibrator or body massager, with plenty of lubricant, can create ejaculatory experiences on a flaccid penis. I strongly encourage you not to let age, ED or sexual shame interfere with the pleasure you are still capable of experiencing.

Menopause is another challenge couples face as they age. Menopause is defined as a 12-month period of time where a woman does not have a menstrual period. For years prior to this date, women go through peri-menopausal bodily changes that include night sweats, insomnia, hot flashes, fatigue, memory loss, central weight gain, vaginal dryness, and low libido. Some women will experience these changes intensely, while others have much milder experiences. Even though menopause marks the end of reproductive years, it doesn't need to mark the end of a sexually fulfilling life. A woman's perspective on aging and sexuality is a key variant in her ability to transition through menopause. You are capable of what you believe you are capable of—the mind largely determines the sexual possibilities, especially as you age.

Vaginal dryness and insufficient sexual desire can be treated with bioidentical hormone replacement therapy. Research done by Dr. Joann Pinkerton, Director of the North American Menopause Society, largely answers questions about this process. Here is what we know:

- Hormone Replacement Therapy (HRT) is both safe and effective. It will prevent night sweats, hot flashes, and bone loss.

- Starting HRT when you first start experiencing peri-menopausal symptoms is very important to the degree of success or relief that you will achieve by undergoing HRT.
- The risk for breast cancer is significantly reduced by using bioidentical hormones. Since 2015, there has been vast improvements made in achieving bioidentical HRT.
- Women can use HRT for 5-10 years safely. When they need to wean off the treatment, doing so with a slow taper is most helpful.
- HRT strengthens a woman's libido, her ability to be aroused and the quality of her orgasms. When lack of hormones (testosterone in particular) is the fundamental cause for sexual dysfunction, HRT can make a significant contribution to sexual satisfaction by raising a woman's desire and interest in sex.
- Estrogen replacement is most safe when you are less than 10-years from reaching menopause.
- HRT can significantly increase your quality of life. For most women, utilizing this information with an informed and trusted medical provider can greatly benefit your overall vitality and cardiovascular health.

If you are looking for answers to sexual questions, I encourage you to seek professional help. Often what you're struggling with can be managed—or even fixed—with advice from a trained medical doctor, sexual therapist, or counselor. As you continue learning about your sexuality as you age, Dr. Batsheva Marcus is an excellent resource for up-to-date, practical medical sexual advice. She is the author of the book *Sex Points* and the former director of the Maze Women's Health Institute in NYC. Her website and Instagram accounts are full of helpful sexual information. I have found her research to be exceptional and especially helpful to couples advancing in years.

Adequate exercise and sunshine are very important to both happiness and sexual desire throughout the lifespan, but they are especially necessary in the mid-to-later years. Incorporating cardiovascular exercise, core training, pelvic floor therapy, and balancing exercises to your lifestyle are all ways to improve your sexual confidence.[92] When possible, make time to be outside, and get your heart rate up while enjoying the sunshine.

Wear sunscreen and hats to protect your skin while you soak in the goodness of 15-20 minutes of sunlight, which the latest research claims adds to passionate love by providing hormonal boosts.[93] Active aging involves keeping your body moving and your brain engaged in learning.

According to Masters and Johnson, two of the pioneers in understanding human sexuality, one of the best ways to stay sexually active throughout your sixties and seventies is to continue having sex. Yes, sex begets sex! The old adage to "use it or lose it" holds true with sexual activity in later life. Maintain your sexual fitness by being sexually active. Just as any exercise program, continued activity allows for better functioning and health. Especially in women, having sex at least once a week helps maintain the ability to lubricate efficiently. Having sex can, quite literally, keep the sexual juices flowing![94]

Expand your definition of sex by being open to finding other ways to intimately connect. Intercourse is just one way of having sex; you and your partner can create new ways of being together sexually. Both of you should openly share your wants and needs. Determine to actively do things that feel enlivening to your relationship. With age it typically takes more time for arousal to occur. Use this time to enhance the stage for romantic connection by sharing erotic fantasies or stories, incorporating new music and dancing, giving slow erotic body massages, playing games, learning more about tantric sex, or adding sexual accessories to your lovemaking. These activities can add some spice which truly benefits long-term, committed relationships. Indeed, there is plenty of evidence that sexual novelty releases dopamine in the brain, so changing things up in the bedroom will positively affect both your interest in and mood for sex.[95] I can't emphasize enough how helpful it can be to read aloud and discuss together information from good sex books (look in my references for dozens of excellent reading options). Since you're reading this book, I wonder if you know of an "older" couple who could benefit from the information you're learning? Don't hesitate to share!

Continue romancing each other. Get naked, and watch a movie skin-to-skin in bed. Hold each other while describing memories of special times you've shared, including your first kiss, wedding and honeymoon, steamy passionate times, and deeply connecting moments throughout the years. Remembering the life you've made together has a natural way of bringing meaning and getting the spark back in the present moment. Bask in the goodness you've created. Breathe with one another while gazing into your souls; savor the sweetness of your experiences. We never outgrow the need for emotional closeness and belonging.

Regardless of your age, I challenge you to commit the energy and effort that's required of a couple to become magnificent lovers. It requires willingness and courage to get naked and really show up for each other. Recognize that even great lovers have humdrum sex sometimes. The trick is to invest in creating a sex life that is worth wanting. As a therapist, I cannot count the number of times I've had couples say how much they wish they had invested in their sex lives earlier, including communicating about sex and overcoming sexual anxieties. These types of comments bring up two differing emotions for me. First, I feel sad for the couple. So much of their time together has been spent in poor-to-mediocre sexual experiences. Second, I feel excitement in knowing that their sexual future is bright as they apply therapeutic principles. Don't let your time together be wasted with poor-to-mediocre sex. Embrace the sexual capacities you were created to enjoy! Commit to courageously pursuing a lifetime of passionate living.

Remember, old doesn't mean inferior. It means you are well-seasoned! Use your wisdom, experience, and knowledge to bless your sexual experiences rather than comparing them to younger, firmer-bodied experiences. Focus on the benefits of your stage of life:

- Years of experience in truly knowing what this person loves sexually
- More control in your lovemaking, meaning that slower sex is more of an option
- More freedom from parenting demands
- More space and time in your schedules
- Often, more financial freedom to travel and explore sex in new places
- No more menstrual periods and fear of pregnancy or need for birth control

Developing a deeper peace with yourself and choosing to look for the sexual positives in this season of life can make all the difference in both attitude and connectedness. Look for the good—I promise you will find it!

THINK. Alone, ponder on the way that your body is changing as you age. What are the differences you are noticing with your sex drive and functioning? Assess if these changes are typical for your age and health. Determine if there is a need to seek for medical or therapeutic help.

PAIR. Both of you get comfortable and feel close. This conversation can be an emotional one as aging, chronic pain and bodily changes can create dissatisfaction with yourself. When we are not happy with ourselves, we typically project our unhappiness on to others, especially our spouses. So, in this pairing, simply hold one another, and perhaps take a little time to mourn the changes that are taking place in your bodies.

SHARE. Gently discuss the things you wrote in the thinking portion of this assignment. Encourage one another to be vulnerable about pain, changing bodies and aging. Discuss how these issues are affecting your sexual relationship. Make a plan of action for help or preventative measures you can work on together.

Adding to your Sexual Playbook: What would you like to integrate from this chapter and your discussion into your sexual playbook?

Experiential Activities to Enjoy

Soft Entry Penetration

This technique does not require an erection.[96]

1. Spend time with full-body caressing and pleasuring.
2. Kiss and speak lovingly with one another. There is no pressure to perform; the focus needs to be on connection.

3. Lubricate the vagina and penis generously.
4. The woman lies on her back, moving her pelvis close to the man's pelvis. He lies on his side, facing his wife.

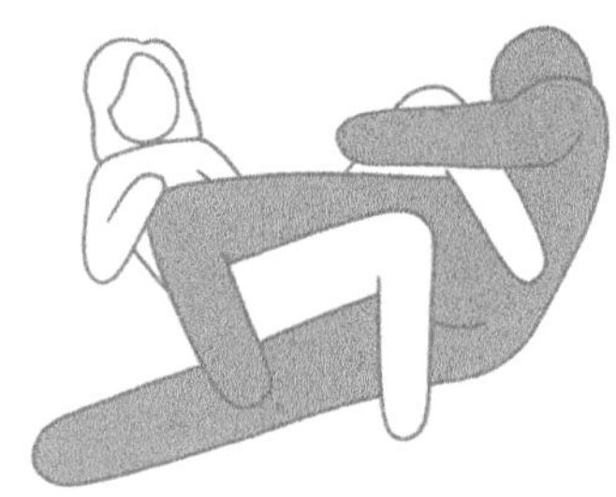

Soft Entry Penetration Position

5. Genitals come together with legs opened and intertwined. Experiment to decide what feels most comfortable. Use pillows or a Liberator for support.
6. The woman inserts the penis into her vagina, using the "finger feeding" method. She places her 2 largest fingers of one hand, scissor-style, under the penis glans and then does the same thing with the 2 largest fingers of the opposite hand placed behind the first fingers. Squeeze the fingers together and feed the penis into the vagina, repeating the finger movement until the penis is fully inserted into the vagina.

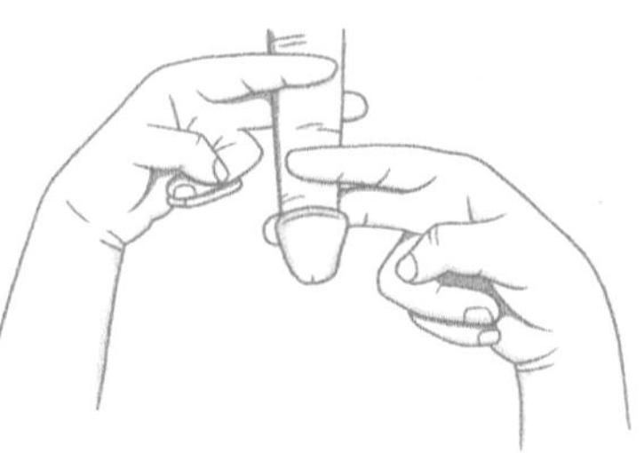

Finger Feeding Method

7. The woman then folds back her labia. This will allow for more direct clitoral stimulation. Bring pelvises closely together, holding your bodies still once you're comfortable and connected.
8. Eye contact during this time will enhance the feelings of emotional connection and love. Speaking loving words, reflecting on erotic times you've shared and communicating about what you're feeling can also increase feelings of love.
9. Change positions whenever you need to move for more comfort.
10. With the penis in the vagina, in time there may be subtle shifting in the penis as it begins to grow within the vagina. There may also be buzzing or humming sensations as the penis slowly and steadily becomes erect. The penis may also relax and return to a non-erect state, only to start growing again.

11. The more relaxed, present, and welcoming a woman can be to this type of penetration, the more she will recognize the receptive capacity of the vagina. The awareness of the vaginal and cervical sensations as the penis grows within her body can bring exhilarating satisfaction and fulfillment.
12. Maintaining eye-contact and gently communicating about the experience during this exercise will magnify the experience for both of you. It can become a timeless experience, as the sexual exchange is focused on genital connection through soft receptiveness.

Self-Pleasuring Together

1. Set the stage for your time together. Create a romantic environment with music, candles, and sensual massage oils. Get fluffy, comfortable pillows, and set them at the head and foot of the bed. Allow for at least 60 minutes of uninterrupted time.
2. As you come together, freely touch and kiss lightly. Talk lovingly with eye contact.
3. While watching one another, slowly strip, touching your body and moving with the music. Breathe deeply, relaxing into erotic playfulness. Touch yourself in ways that you find appealing and arousing. Remember, there is nothing more arousing to a husband than observing arousal in his wife.[97]
4. Once both of you are undressed, position yourselves on the bed so that you can see each other clearly. Continue to seductively touch your body while your spouse watches. Take turns watching one another.
5. Continually breathe for relaxation, especially if this type of activity is new for you. Return your eyes frequently to your spouse's eyes, watching the arousal grow between you through his/her eyes.
6. Apply sensual massage oil to your body while your spouse watches. Generously apply the oil or lube to your genitals, and stimulate yourself while your spouse watches.
7. Let this experience flow freely between you. You decide what

works best for both of you as you continue to pleasure yourself while your spouse watches.

8. Try to maintain eye-contact with one another as you bring yourself to orgasm, or as you shift to share an orgasm together. It is also totally okay not to orgasm; it's your decision.
9. Hold one another and talk about the experience you just shared. What did you learn? What do you want to try differently next time?

Conclusion

As I write this conclusion, it is six days before this book goes to print. I am very excited! I am also doing some second-guessing with questions like, "Is it good enough?" or, "What will people think of me as they read this?" As you know, talking about sex is very vulnerable. Doing so in a published book creates apprehension and feelings of being fully exposed. I know that my openness in educating people about sexual passion often helps others feel comfortable, particularly in my teaching and therapy. As I finish re-reading (for at least the tenth time) my written thoughts, feelings, and experiences, it somehow feels even more vulnerable. If you, the reader, find the contents of this book offensive or objectionable in anyway, please don't reach out to tell me! Believe me, after 10 years of teaching about sexuality at Brigham Young University, I have heard more complaints than you can imagine. I also have received, many times over, countless expressions of gratitude and appreciation for my courage to teach, write about, and promote on social media concepts centered around sexual wholeness. I hope that most of the readers of this book will feel likewise.

We're at the end of a book, but not the end of a journey. This is your sexual journey of continual learning and trying new things as a couple. As I mentioned in the introduction, my primary focus in writing this book is to help you embark on your marital sexual development with anticipation, patience, and gratitude, without regret. Choose to start somewhere! Risk being vulnerable while remembering that comfort does not promote development. If you are sexually comfortable in your marriage, shake it up, and grow a little! Find satisfaction in your capacity to feel desirable and fully beautiful. Embrace the possibilities you have in both giving and receiving sexual pleasure; you're worth the time and effort! As you embark on this journey together, recognize what transpires within your relationship. Are you better friends? Does your spouse have greater influence or significance in your life? Are you laughing more frequently? Is there tangible energy between the two of you? Are you making your marriage a higher priority? I hope so. I truly hope the THINK PAIR SHARE experiences have strengthened your relationship. Together you are the strong, invaluable oxen, equitably shouldering, while side-by-side, pulling your family to the Promised Land. Claim joy, find pleasure, and hold on to each other and your covenants. I pray you will both replenish yourselves as you enjoy together the choicest blessings available to us in mortality.

I want to leave you, dear reader, with a small portion of my most cherished possession, my personal witness of Jesus Christ and my testimony of His gospel. He lives! I understand that the order of marriage and family life is the foundation for eternity. I know that when I center my faith in Jesus Christ, when I testify of Him, and when I am obedient, I feel peace, light, and happiness. My choice to live personally-aligned includes standing as a witness for our Savior.

If you have found this book helpful, enlightening, and enjoyable, please take a moment to write a review on Amazon. You doing this would mean the world to me! Check me out at www.tammyhill.com or connect with me daily on Instagram @tammy_hill_lmft. Please, let's stay in touch as we encourage one another forward and heavenward. Let's keep on keeping on!

Endnotes

[1] Bagley, N. (2018, March 7). What the church's standard regarding oral sex? Mormon Marriages. https://www.mormonmarriages.com/blog/whats-the-churchs-standard-regarding-oral-sex

[2] Oaks, D. H. (2010). Two lines of communication. The Church of Jesus Christ of Latter-day Saints. https://www.churchofjesuschrist.org/study/general-conference/2010/10/two-lines-of-communication?lang=eng

[3] The Church of Jesus Christ of Latter-day Saints (n.d.). Mother in Heaven. The Church of Jesus Christ of Latter-day Saints. https://www.churchofjesuschrist.org/study/manual/gospel-topics-essays/mother-in-heaven?lang=eng

[4] Meyer, Y. Z. (2014, April 17). Parashat Song of Songs / A 'handle' for the Torah. Haaretz. https://www.haaretz.com/jewish/portion-of-the-week/.premium-parashat-song-of-songs-a-handle-for-the-torah-1.5245359

[5] Holland, J. R. (1988, January 12). Of souls, symbols, and sacraments. BYU Speeches. https://speeches.byu.edu/talks/jeffrey-r-holland/souls-symbols-sacraments/

[6] Ibid.

[7] Ibid.

[8] Snyder, S. (2018). Love Worth Making: How to have ridiculously great sex in a long-lasting relationship. St. Martin's Publishing Group.

[9] Holland, J. R. (1988, January 12). Of souls, symbols, and sacraments. BYU Speeches. https://speeches.byu.edu/talks/jeffrey-r-holland/souls-symbols-sacraments/

[10] Wade, J. (2004). Transcendent Sex: When Lovemaking Opens the Veil. Gallery Books.

[11] Gottman, J., Gottman, J. S., Abrams, D., & Abrams, R. C. (2016). The man's guide to women: Scientifically proven secrets from the "Love Lab" about what women really want. Rodale.

[12] Eldemire, A. (2020, November 3) How to set (and respect) boundaries with your spouse. Psychology Today. https://www.psychologytoday.com/us/blog/couples-thrive/202011/how-set-and-respect-boundaries-your-spouse

[13] Smyth, Sinead. (2021, March 11) *Accepting influence: Find ways to say "Yes".* The Gottman Institute. https://www.gottman.com/blog/accepting-influence-find-ways-to-say-yes/

[14] Hawkins, A. J., et al. (2000). Equal partnership and the sacred responsibilities of mothers and fathers. In D. C. Dollahite (Ed.), Strengthening our families: An in-depth look at the proclamation on the family (pp. 63-82). Salt Lake City, UT: Bookcraft.

[15] Gottman, J. (2015) The Seven Principles for Making Marriage Work. Hachette.

[16] Lawrance, K. & Byers, E. S. (1995). Sexual satisfaction in long-term heterosexual relationships: The interpersonal exchange model of sexual satisfaction. Personal Relationships, 2, 267-285.

[17] Brown, B. (2015). Daring greatly: How the courage to be vulnerable transforms the way we live, love, parent, and lead. Gotham Books.

[18] Loveless, A. S. & Holman, T. B. (2006). The family in the new millennium. Praeger Publishers.

[19] Day, L. C., Muise, A., Joel, S., & Impett, E. A. (2015). To do it or not to do it? How communally motivated people navigate sexual interdependence dilemmas. Personality and Social Psychology Bulletin, 41(6), 791-804. https://doi.org/10.1177%2F0146167215580129

[20] One Condoms. (2021, December 21). How does sex feel different to men and women? One Condoms. https://www.onecondoms.com/blogs/education/how-does-sex-feel-different-to-men-and-women

[21] Fowers, B. J., (2000). Beyond the Myth of Marital Happiness: How Embracing the Virtues of Loyalty, Generosity, Justice, and Courage Can Strengthen Your Relationship. Jossey-Bass.

[22] Gottman, J., Gottman, J. S., Abrams, D., & Abrams, R. C. (2016). The man's guide to women: Scientifically proven secrets from the "love Lab" about what women really want. Rodale.

[23] National Coalition Against Domestic Violence. (n.d.). How do domestic violence and sexual assault intersect? National Coalition Against Domestic Violence. https://assets.speakcdn.com/assets/2497/sexual_assault_dv.pdf

[24] Planned parenthood. (n.d.). Body image and sexuality: What's the Connection?. Planned Parenthood. https://www.plannedparenthood.org/files/1314/0042/3880/BodyImage_2008ENG.pdf

[25] Gottman, J., Gottman, J.S. (2016). The man's guide to women. Rodale.

[26] Abramovitz, B. A., & Birch, L. L. (2000). Five-year-old girls' ideas about dieting are predicted by their mothers' dieting. Journal of the American Dietetic Association, 100(10), 1157–1163. https://doi.org/10.1016/S0002-8223(00)00339-4

[27] Ackard, D. M., Kearney-Cooke, A., & Peterson, C. B. (2000). Effect of body image and self-image on women's sexual behaviors. The International journal of eating disorders, 28(4), 422–429. https://doi.org/10.1002/1098-108x(200012)28:4<422::aid-eat10>3.0.co;2-1

[28] Markey, C. H., (2022, April 14). I've studied body image for 25 years. Here's what boys don't know how to tell you. Huffpost. https://www.huffpost.com/entry/

body-image-boys-eating-disorders_n_624e231ce4b068157f800861?utm_source=-facebook&utm_medium=news_tab

[29] van den Brink, F., Vollmann, M., Sternheim, L. C., Berkhout, L. J., Zomerdijk, R. A., & Woertman, L. (2018). Negative body attitudes and sexual dissatisfaction in men: The mediating role of body self-consciousness during physical intimacy. Archives of Sexual Behavior, 47(3), 693-701. https://www.ncbi.nlm.nih.gov/pmc/articles/PMC5834587/

[30] Taylor, B. K., (2018, April). Am I a child of God? The Church of Jesus Christ of Latter-day Saints. https://www.churchofjesuschrist.org/study/general-conference/2018/04/am-i-a-child-of-god?lang=eng

[31] Greisler, M. (2013, November 14). Body image struggles. New Direction Counseling Services. https://newdirectionspgh.com/body-image/

[32] University of Pennsylvania, (2022). Questionnaire center. University of Pennsylvania. https://www.authentichappiness.sas.upenn.edu/testcenter

[33] Gottman, J. (2015) The Seven Principles for Making Marriage Work. Hachette.

[34] Westberg, G. (n.d.). Sex Expectations Lead to Sexual Problems. Dr. Westberg Sex Relationship Therapy. https://www.garciawestberg.com/the-role-of-sex-expectations-in-sexual-problems/

[35] Osho (2021, April 4). Saraha: Tantra Vision for Life. OSHO World. https://oshoworld.com/saraha-tantra-vision-for-life/

[36] Brown, B. (n.d.) Brené Brown: 3 ways to set boundaries. Oprah. https://www.oprah.com/spirit/how-to-set-boundaries-brene-browns-advice

[37] Ellwoood, B. (2021, November 18) Mindfulness during sex linked to improved sexual well-being and orgasm consistency in married couples, study finds. PsyPost. https://www.psypost.org/2021/11/mindfulness-during-sex-linked-to-improved-sexual-well-being-and-orgasm-consistency-in-married-couples-study-finds-62130

[38] Trudeau, M. (2010, September 20). Human connections start with a friendly touch. NPR. https://www.npr.org/templates/story/story.php?storyId=128795325

[39] Soo, M. (2020, July 31) Mindful sex. Sex Positive Psychology. http://sexpositivepsychology.com.au/blog/2020/7/31/mindful-sex

[40] Isador, P. (2016, November 4). How to make any kiss infinitely more sensual: A tantra expert explains. Mind Body Green. https://www.mindbodygreen.com/0-27403/how-to-make-any-kiss-infinitely-more-sensual-a-tantra-expert-explains.html

[41] Michaels, M. A. & Johnson, P. (2006) *The Essence of Tantric Sexuality*. Llewellyn Publication.

[42] Seltzer, L. F. (2017, May 10). What's so sexy about belly buttons? Psychology Today. https://www.psychologytoday.com/us/blog/evolution-the-self/201705/what-s-so-sexy-about-belly-buttons?amp

[43] Cleveland Clinic (2018, March 22). Surprising relief for your stuffy nose? Have sex. Cleveland Clinic. https://health.clevelandclinic.org/surprising-relief-for-your-stuffy-nose-have-sex/amp/

[44] Farnsworth, C. (2022, April). Are ear orgasms real, and how can people stimulate the ears? Medical News Today. https://www.medicalnewstoday.com/articles/ear-orgasm#summary. From Moaning To Heavy Breathing: These Sounds Turn People On During Sex, As Per A Study. Times of India (2018, August 28). *From moaning to heavy breathing: These sounds turn people on during sex, as per a study.* Times of India. https://m.timesofindia.com/from-moaning-to-heavy-breathing-these-sounds-that-turn-people-on-during-sex-as-per-a-study/amp_etphotostory/65578263.cms

[45] de Oliveira, P. S., Reis, J. P., de Oliveira, T. R., Martinho, D., e Silva, R. P., Marcelino, J., . . . & Lopes, T. (2018). The impact of sacral neuromodulation on sexual dysfunction. Current Urology, 12(4), 188-194. https://www.karger.com/Article/Fulltext/499307

[46] Williams, L. (2019, April 3). 6 erogenous zones you've probably never thought of. Balance. https://balance.media/erogenous-zones/
Cordeau, D., Bélanger, M., Beaulieu–Prévost, D., & Courtois, F. (2014). The assessment of sensory detection thresholds on the perineum and breast compared with control body sites. *The journal of sexual medicine,* 11(7), 1741-1748. https://onlinelibrary.wiley.com/doi/pdf/10.1111/jsm.12547
Krisher, H., (n.d.) *7 awesome erogenous zones.* WebMD. https://www.webmd.com/sex-relationships/features/7-awesome-erogenous-zones
Michaels, M. A. & Johnson, P. (2006) *The Essence of Tantric Sexuality*. Llewellyn Publication.

[47] Lloyd, R. (2009, February 13). Saliva: Secret ingredient in the best Kisses. Live Science. https://www.livescience.com/3328-saliva-secret-ingredient-kisses.html

[48] Rusnak, K. (2021, July 1). The six second kiss. The Gottman Institute. (https://www.gottman.com/blog/the-six-second-kiss/)

[49] Gottman, J. & Gottman, J. S. (2016). The man's guide to women: Scientifically proven secrets from the "Love Lab" about what women really want. Rodale Wellness.

[50] Finlayson-Fife, J. [@finlaysonfife](2021, November 19) Learning to love and be loved through the body is foundational to our spiritual and relational capacity. Instagram. https://www.instagram.com/p/CWexgSCMQDu/?utm_medium=copy_link

[51] Mintz, L. Becoming Cliterate: Why Orgasm Equality Matters--And How to Get It. HarperOne.

[52] Michaels, M. A. & Johnson, P. (2006). The Essence of Tantric Sexuality. Llewellyn Publications.

[53] Maister, L., Fotopoulou, A., Turnbull, O., Taskiris, M. (2020). The erogenous mirror: Intersubjective and multisensory maps of sexual arousal in men and women. Archives of Sexual Behavior, 49(8) 2919-2933. https://www.ncbi.nlm.nih.gov/pmc/articles/PMC7641941/

[54] Schnarch, D. (1991). Constructing the sexual crucible: An integration of sexual and marital therapy. W. W. Norton & Company.

[55] Kerner, I. (2004) She comes first: The thinking man's guide to pleasuring a woman. HarperCollins Publishers.

[56] Broster, A. (2020, July 31). What is the orgasm gap? Forbes. https://www.forbes.com/sites/alicebroster/2020/07/31/what-is-the-orgasm-gap/?sh=1511c71960f8

[57] Nuzzo, R. (2008, February 11). Female orgasms and a 'rule of thumb.' Los Angeles Times. https://www.latimes.com/health/la-hew-ordistance11feb11-story.html

[58] Earthly Parents. (2019). And It Was Very Good: A Latter-day Saint's Guide to Lovemaking. Earthly Parents Press.

[59] Fugere, M. A. (2017, January 26). Sexual 'afterglow,' and why It matters so much. Psychology Today. https://www.psychologytoday.com/us/blog/dating-and-mating/201701/sexual-afterglow-and-why-it-matters-so-much

[60] International Society for Sexual Medicine (n.d.). What are multiple orgasms? How common are they? International Society for Sexual Medicine. https://www.issm.info/sexual-health-qa/what-are-multiple-orgasms-how-common-are-they/

[61] Wibowo & Wassersug (2016). Multiple orgasms in men-What we know so far. Sexual Medicine Review. https://pubmed.ncbi.nlm.nih.gov/27872023/

[62] Keesling, B. (2007). How to Make Love All Night: And Drive a Woman Wild!. HarperCollins Publishers.

[63] Severson, A. (2022, July 5). How to have multiple orgasms for men. Get Your Marriage On. https://getyourmarriageon.com/multiple-male-orgasms/

[64] Progovac, A. (2015, August 16). Let's talk about sex and pelvic floor disorders. The American Journal of Managed Care. https://www.ajmc.com/view/lets-talk-about-sex-and-pelvic-floor-disorders

[65] Fyzical (2020, February 11). What is Pelvic Floor Physical Therapy. Fyzical Therapy & Balance Centers. https://www.fyzical.com/sarasota-downtown/blog/What-is-Pelvic-Floor-Physical-Therapy; The North American Menopause Society (2022). For better sex: 3 ways to strengthen your pelvic floor. The North American Menopause Society. https://www.menopause.org/for-women/menopauseflashes/sexual-health/for-better-sex-3-ways-to-strengthen-your-pelvic-floor

[66] National Institutes of Health (2008, September 17). Roughly one quarter of U.S. women affected by pelvic floor disorders. National Institutes of Health. https://www.nih.gov/news-events/news-releases/roughly-one-quarter-us-women-affected-pelvic-floor-disorders

[67] Morse, E. (2022, January 30). A guide to prostate massage. Very Well Health. https://www.verywellhealth.com/things-to-know-about-prostate-health-4066015

[68] Whipple, B. (2015). Female ejaculation, G spot, A spot, and should we be looking for spots? *Current Sexual Health Reports,* 7(2), 59-62. https://doi.org/10.1007/s11930-015-0041-2

[69] Goldstein, I., Goldstein, S. W., & Komisaruk, B. R. (2022). Should we call it (G-Spot) a G-Zone? *Sexual Medicine Reviews,* 10(2), 181-182. https://doi.org/10.1016/j.sxmr.2022.03.001

[70] Moalem, S., & Reidenberg, J. S. (2009). Does female ejaculation serve an antimi-

crobial purpose?. *Medical Hypotheses,* 73(6), 1069-1071. https://doi.org/10.1016/j.mehy.2009.07.024

[71] Schnarch, D. (2002). Resurrecting sex: Solving sexual problems & revolutionizing your relationship. Quill, An Imprint of HarperCollinsPublishers.

[72] Boteach, S., (2000). Kosher sex: A recipe for passion and intimacy. Harmony.

[73] Davis, M. (2018, December 9). How sexual fantasies affect your relationship. Big Think. https://bigthink.com/the-present/sexual-fantasy-marriage-relationship/

[74] RapierGroup (2018, August 23). How to make an event memorable: Engage the 5 human senses. RapierGroup. https://blog.rapiergroup.com/want-a-memorable-event-activate-the-5-senses?hs_amp=true

[75] Wies, P. P. & Herbert, C. (2017, August 22). Bodily reactions to emotional words referring to own versus other people's emotions. Frontiers in Psychology. https://www.frontiersin.org/articles/10.3389/fpsyg.2017.01277/full

[76] Product Resources - Sensual Massage Oils: https://mapleholistics.com/collections/pure-oils; https://thebloomi.com/collections/; Nipple Creams: https://exsens-usa.com/products/crazy-love-cherry-nipple-arousal-cream; https://www.systemjo.com/stimulants/jo-nipple-titillator-arousal-gel; Erotic Candles: https://simplipleasures.com/products/massage-candle/; https://www.truepheromones.com/amp/infused-candles/; https://skinnydipcandle.com/collections; https://kamasutra.com/products/ignite-massage-oil-candle; Arousal Oils: https://www.zestra.com; https://exploreforia.com/awaken-arousal-oil

[77] Assari, S. (2017, July 20). *Who's avoiding sex, and why.* The Conversation. https://theconversation.com/amp/whos-avoiding-sex-and-why-80788

[78] Finalyson-Fife, J. (Host). (2021, May 18th). Sprinkled with hope. [Audio podcast episode]. In Developing Intimacy. https://www.finlayson-fife.com/podcasts/conversations-with-dr-jennifer/post/developing-intimacy

[79] Levin R. J. (2002). The physiology of sexual arousal in the human female: a recreational and procreational synthesis. Archives of Sexual Behavior, 31(5), 405–411.

[80] Hinckley, G. B. (2002, April). Personal worthiness to exercise the priesthood. The Church of Jesus Christ of Latter-day Saints. https://www.churchofjesuschrist.org/study/general-conference/2002/04/personal-worthiness-to-exercise-the-priesthood?lang=eng

[81] Hunter, H. W. (1994, October). Being a Righteous Husband and Father. The Church of Jesus Christ of Latter-day Saints. https://abn.churchofjesuschrist.org/study/general-conference/1994/10/being-a-righteous-husband-and-father?lang=eng

[82] The Church of Jesus Christ of Latter-day Saints (n. d.) Mother in Heaven. The Church of Jesus Christ of Latter-day Saints. https://www.churchofjesuschrist.org/study/manual/gospel-topics-essays/mother-in-heaven?lang=eng

[83] The Church of Jesus Christ of Latter-day Saints (1995). The family: A proclamation to the world. The Church of Jesus Christ of Latter-day Saints. https://www.

churchofjesuschrist.org/study/scriptures/the-family-a-proclamation-to-the-world/the-family-a-proclamation-to-the-world?lang=eng

[84] Bednar, D. A. (2013, April). We believe in being chaste. Ensign or Liahona, The Church of Jesus Christ of Latter-day Saints. https://www.churchofjesuschrist.org/study/general-conference/2013/04/we-believe-in-being-chaste?lang=eng

[85] The Church of Jesus Christ of Latter-day Saints. (n.d.). Birth control. The Church of Jesus Christ of Latter-day Saints. https://www.churchofjesuschrist.org/study/manual/gospel-topics/birth-control?lang=eng

[86] Gottman, J. & Gottman, J. S. (2008), And Baby Makes Three, Crown Three Rivers Press.

[87] Pennestri, M. H., Laganière, C., Bouvette-Turcot, A. A., Pokhvisneva, I., Steiner, M., Meaney, M. J., & Gaudreau, H. (2018). Uninterrupted infant sleep, development, and maternal mood. Pediatrics, 142(6), 1-8. https://publications.aap.org/pediatrics/article/142/6/e20174330/37494/Uninterrupted-Infant-Sleep-Development-and?autologincheck=redirected

[88] Davis, C. P. (2021, April 16) Sex after birth: How your sex life changes. On Health. https://www.onhealth.com/content/1/sex_life_after_baby

[89] American Society for Reproductive Medicine (2015). Sexual dysfunction and infertility. American Society for Reproductive Medicine. https://www.reproductivefacts.org/news-and-publications/patient-fact-sheets-and-booklets/documents/fact-sheets-and-info-booklets/sexual-dysfunction-and-infertility/

[90] McBain, T., & Iqbal, A., (2022, May 11). Infertility's impact on your sex life & how to reconnect sexually. Choosing Therapy. https://www.choosingtherapy.com/infertilitys-impact-on-sex-life/

[91] Kukkonen, T., (2017, March 20). Still going strong: Sexuality in older adults. [Video]. YouTube. https://m.youtube.com/watch?v=pqLhPPOEJB4

[92] Schaefer, A., (2019, October 10). Better sex: Workouts to boost your performance. Healthline. https://www.healthline.com/health/better-sex-workouts-boost-performance

[93] Weiss, H., (2021, August 31). 15 minutes of sunlight for more passion and sex, says study. Fatherly. https://www.fatherly.com/health-science/study-sunlight-aphrodisiac-sex/amp/

[94] Leman, K., (2008). Sheet music: Uncovering the secrets of sexual intimacy in marriage. Tyndale House Publishers.

[95] Shaw, G., (2014, January 30).6 ways to get in the mood. WebMD. https://www.webmd.com/sex-relationships/guide/not-in-the-mood-get-in-the-mood

[96] Richardson, D. & McGeever, J. (2018). Tantric sex and menopause: Practices for spiritual and sexual renewal. Destiny Books.

[97] Penner, J. & Penner, C, (2017). Enjoy: The gift of sexual pleasure for women. Tyndale House Publishers.

Index

D

E

T

U

V

W

Y